DANCING WITH DISASTER

Under the Sign of Nature: Explorations in Ecocriticism

Editors
Michael P. Branch, SueEllen Campbell, John Tallmadge

Series Consultants
Lawrence Buell, John Elder, Scott Slovic

Series Advisory Board
Michael P. Cohen, Richard Kerridge, Gretchen Legler, Ian Marshall,
Dan Peck, Jennifer Price, Kent Ryden, Rebecca Solnit, Anne Whiston
Spirn, Hertha D. Sweet Wong

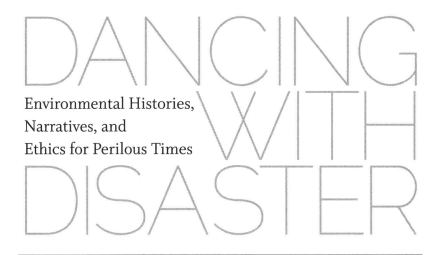

DANCING WITH DISASTER

Environmental Histories,
Narratives, and
Ethics for Perilous Times

KATE RIGBY

University of Virginia Press   Charlottesville and London

University of Virginia Press
© 2015 by the Rector and Visitors of the University of Virginia
All rights reserved
Printed in the United States of America on acid-free paper

First published 2015
9 8 7 6 5 4 3 2 1

LIBRARY OF CONGRESS CATALOGING-IN-PUBLICATION DATA

Rigby, Catherine E.
  Dancing with disaster : environmental histories, narratives, and ethics for perilous times / Kate Rigby.
        pages   cm. — (Under the sign of nature: explorations in ecocriticism)
        Includes bibliographical references and index.
  ISBN 978-0-8139-3688-8 (cloth : alk. paper) — ISBN 978-0-8139-3690-1 (pbk. : alk. paper) — ISBN 978-0-8139-3689-5 (e-book)
  1. Ecocriticism. 2. Natural disasters. 3. Ecology in literature. 4. Nature in literature. 5. Environmental literature. I. Title.
  PN98.E36R66 2015
  809'.93355—dc23

                                                              2014032062

For Sam

CONTENTS

ACKNOWLEDGMENTS

Many years in the making, the manuscript for this book was finalized with the assistance of a period of funded research leave from Monash University in 2013, for which I am immensely grateful. *Dancing with Disaster* takes its title from an article that first appeared in the "Ecological Humanities Corner" of the *Australian Humanities Review* in 2009 and was based on a paper that I had presented the year before at a symposium in honor of my friend and mentor Val Plumwood, held at the Australian National University's then Centre for Resource and Environmental Studies. I am indebted to Debbie Rose for the invitation to air the experimental thoughts that eventually got threaded into this book on that occasion, as well as for her friendship, support, and inspiration in so many ways before and since. I am also profoundly grateful for the ongoing conversations that Debbie facilitated in convening the Australian working group in the ecological humanities in 2000 and especially for the encouragement and advice that I have received over the years from fellow founding members Libby Robin, Tom Griffiths, Freya Mathews, and (ex officio, but crucially) Val Plumwood.

Among the innumerable others who have helped this work along the way in various valued capacities are Joni Adamson, Val Billingham, Tom Bristow, Verity Burgmann, Glenda Cloughley, Cath Connelly, Anne Elvey, Simon Estok, Bernd Fischer, Greta Gaard, Christine Hansen, Kevin Hart, James Hatley, Ursula Heise, Peter Huang, Serenella Iovino, Adeline Johns-Putra, Laurel Kearns, Catherine Keller, Seán Kerins, Richard Kerridge, Alexander Košenina, Alison Lewis, Yixu Lu, Mark Lussier, Amanda Lynch, Bernhard Malkmus, Iain McCalman, Andrew Milner, Grace Moore, Stephen Moore, Jan Morgan, Serpil Oppermann, Carolyn Rasmussen, Cate Sandilands, Caroline Smith, Will Steffen, Anthony Stevens, Heather Sullivan, Daryl Taylor, Jess Weir, Louise Westling, Wendy Wheeler, and Linda Williams. I would like to thank Boyd Zenner and the rest of the team at the University of Virginia Press, along with the series editors and anonymous readers, who provided enormously helpful and encouraging feedback on the manuscript. I am indebted to Carol Sickman-Garner for her patient and painstaking copy-editing, and to Caroline Colton for expert indexing. I am also very grateful to Claudia Terstappen for permission to incorporate one of her exquisite fire photographs in the cover design for this book. Claudia's *Fires* series explores the characteristics of large bush fires and aims to give a sense of place and situation, relating to important cultural, spiritual, and natural features of Australia.

To Robert Hartley I owe more than I can know, let alone enumerate. The book is dedicated to our son, Sam, with gratitude and admiration for the voluntary work that he has been doing with organizations such as the Australian Youth Climate Coalition and Amnesty International and in the hope that he and his fellow campaigners will succeed in helping to avert the worst, while learning to "dance" with the inevitable.

Earlier versions of parts of chapters 1, 2, and 5 appeared, respectively, in the following publications and are reproduced in revised form with the kind permission of the editors and publishers: "Discoursing on Disaster: The Hermeneutics of Environmental Catastrophe," *Tamkang Review* 39, no. 1 (2008); "'Das Erdbeben in Chili' and the Romantic Reframing of 'Natural Disaster,'" in *Wissensfiguren im Werk Heinrich von Kleist,* edited by Alison Lewis, Yixu Lu, and Anthony Stevens (Freiburg i.Br.: Rombach, 2012); "Confronting Catastrophe: Ecocriticism in a Warming World," in *The Cambridge Companion to Literature and Environment,* edited by Louise Westling (Cambridge: Cambridge University Press, 2014); "The Poetics of Decolonisation: Reading *Carpentaria* in a Feminist Ecocritical Frame," in *International Perspectives in Feminist Ecocriticism,* edited by Simon Estok, Greta Gaard, and Serpil Oppermann (London: Routledge [Taylor and Francis], 2013).

DANCING WITH DISASTER

INTRODUCTION

The idea that gave rise to this book was forged in the fires of a perilously warming planet. On January 18, 2003, after years of searing drought, with temperatures in the high thirties Celsius, humidity plummeting to 4 percent, and winds gusting up to eighty kilometers per hour, a hurricane of flame swept down upon Australia's federal capital from the forested mountains beyond the city, burning to within a few kilometers of Parliament House, destroying over five hundred homes, and badly damaging many more. The extent, speed, and violence of this firestorm, a conflagration of such intensity that it created and sustained its own fierce wind system, at one point even generating a tornado of flame,[1] meant that the toll on wildlife was horrendous. Within the city, many animal companions also perished, included those being cared for in the RSPCA veterinary hospital. Remarkably, only four human lives were lost, but hundreds of people required medical treatment, and thousands were left with no more than the clothes they were wearing when they fled the flames. In the course of the fires, two-thirds of the Australian Capital Territory were burned out, including 99 percent of Namadgi National Park and most of the Tidbinbilla Nature Reserve, wiping out some of the country's last remaining rock wallabies, which were being bred in captivity in a last-ditch effort to save the species from extinction. Twenty-seven thousand hectares of rural land were destroyed, along with the Mt. Stromlo Observatory and most of the territory's pine plantations (one of which had been planted virtually up to the door of several outlying suburbs of Weston Creek, which were particularly badly hit as a consequence). Many vital services were temporarily cut, and the city was in a state of emergency for ten anxious days.

Although I grew up in Canberra and returned regularly to visit family and friends, I would not normally have been in my old hometown at that time, but I was spending a few months there in order to begin work on a history of culture and environment in the Canberra area. And it was as I stood with others that day on a low rise known as Red Hill, not far from Parliament House and close to my childhood home, witnessing the wall of smoke surging toward us, turning day to night, with burned and smoldering leaves and twigs showering down around us, that I was struck, not only by the immediate need to hotfoot it to a safer spot, but also by the ill-preparedness of even so well heeled and well educated a city as this for the increasingly calamitous conditions that our anthropogenically altered climate was engendering. As well as giving direction and impetus to my work on Canberra specifically, this also got me wondering how research in the humanities might provide an enhanced understanding of the complex interplay between cultural factors and geophysical processes in the genesis, unfolding, and aftermath of calamities, such as the one that had recently befallen Australia's federal capital. From my interdisciplinary location within what some of us "down under" were then calling the "ecological humanities,"[2] I therefore set out to explore, first, what might be learned from the historical reconsideration of past disasters in the hermeneutic horizon of contemporary global ecological or, more precisely, ecosocial imperilment; and, second, whether narrative fiction might provide a vehicle for fostering deeper reflection on the ontological, epistemological, and ethical underpinnings and implications of different kinds of disaster narratives.

As Australian environmental historian Tom Griffiths has observed: "The story is the most powerful educational tool we possess; it is learning distilled in common language. It is also a privileged carrier of truth, a way of allowing for multiplicity and complexity at the same time as guaranteeing memorability."[3] Stories, however, can potentially obscure as much as they reveal. In a perilously warming world, the kinds of stories that we tell about ourselves and our relations with one another, as well as with nonhuman others and our volatile environment, will shape how we prepare for, respond to, and recover from increasingly frequent and, for the communities affected, frequently unfamiliar forms of eco-catastrophe: disasters, that is, that radically disrupt a collective more-than-human dwelling place, or *oikos*, be that a village, town, or region.[4] In particular, such narratives will crucially inform the ethos embodied in our responses to the risk, impact, and aftermath of eco-catastrophe—whether, for example, we adopt the bunker mentality that it's every man for himself; or whether we are prepared to lend a helping hand to total strangers, including those "strange strangers"[5] who are not of our kind. The stories that frame the meanings and moral imperatives that we discern in such disasters will also determine whether our responses are geared toward maintaining current systems, relations, and practices or whether they are transformative, enabling the emergence of new ways of being and dwelling that might prove not only more adaptive but also more just and compassionate, in the long run.[6]

Across all cultures throughout the world for most of human history, "natural disasters," as they became known in English only during the latter part of the nineteenth century, were interpreted very differently: namely, as a response to human wrongdoing on the part of God, or the gods, or an indwelling power inherent in the sacred order of things. In this hermeneutic horizon, morality and materiality, social relations and natural phenomena, were understood to be interrelated: how people comported themselves with one another, and with other others, had environmental consequences; and environmental disturbances, especially big ones, had moral, religious, and political reverberations. In socially differentiated and hierarchically ordered agrarian cultures, the high and mighty in particular were liable to be held to account if the harvest failed or was devoured by insects. The powerful for their part would seek to act swiftly to identify and bring to justice perceived wrongdoers in order to shore up their authority; rarely, if ever, would such rulers acknowledge that they themselves were at fault, as Sophocles's King Oedipus was tragically forced to do as a consequence of his own investigations (a fictional instance that should have a particular resonance for people of privilege, myself included, in our own disastrous times). Alternatively, the relatively powerless many, especially in urban settings, might set upon the marginalized few, scapegoating a distrusted minority as the source of the disorder by taking upon themselves the prerogative of punishment in the guise of a lynch mob.

This way of making sense of calamities induced by phenomena such as earthquakes, floods, droughts, wildfires, avalanches, tornadoes, hurricanes, and pandemic disease, long looked upon askance by some European philosophers and theologians, began to wane in earnest with the rise of a mechanistic and atomistic view of matter during the seventeenth and eighteenth centuries, at least among the intelligentsia and political elites. In the wider society, the shift was slow and uneven, with Christian versions of the punishment paradigm persisting well into the nineteenth century (and among biblical literalists, even beyond). Eventually, however, the modern understanding took hold, according to which the merely material realm of nature followed its own mechanistic principles that were entirely separate from human morality and social relations. Such calamities were now seen to have purely physical causes; formerly referred to by philosophers and theologians as *natural evils,* by the turn of the twentieth century they had become fully secularized and rationalized as *natural disasters.*

This interpretive schema has proven highly beneficial in certain respects. By letting those deemed deviant off the hook, it has favored an

ethos of humanitarian assistance to people afflicted by disasters, in preference to blaming the victims by speculating as to what they must have
done to earn such divine disfavor. By promoting the systematic scientific
investigation of the physical causes of such phenomena, the naturalization
of disaster has also enabled the development of practical measures, such
as early warning systems and improved building codes, that can help to
ameliorate their impacts, if not, in most cases, prevent their occurrence.
These undoubted advances have nonetheless come at a cost—a cost that is
evident in the fact that by the end of the very century in which the premise of "natural disaster" became commonplace, the toll that the calamities thus designated were taking on both human and nonhuman lives and
abodes had actually begun to escalate.[7] By the beginning of the twenty-first
century, the words with which Theodor Adorno and Max Horkheimer
summed up their thesis of the "dialectic of enlightenment," composed in
the catastrophic midst of the Second World War, appear all the more prescient: "The fully enlightened earth radiates disaster triumphant."[8]

In their critical analysis of the entwinement of certain forms of
gender-, class-, and race-based oppression with the project of the domination of nature in modern industrial societies, Adorno and Horkheimer
show how the myth-busting prowess of enlightened rationality is underpinned, paradoxically, by a mythic fear of nature as Other. Bringing
to completion the extirpation of animism initiated by monotheism, the
techno-scientific "disenchantment of the world," in their analysis, had engendered its own irrational notions and narratives.[9] It is the premise of
this book that the concept of "natural disaster" is one such modern myth,
which, in a new twist to the dialectic of enlightenment, has become implicated in the worldwide proliferation of calamity. That does not mean that
I am arguing for the restoration of the premodern punishment paradigm,
however. Rather, I am advocating what might be described as an ecological
enlightenment of the Enlightenment—one that nonetheless departs from
Adorno and Horkheimer's extremely gloomy diagnosis, which remains
committed to a modernist mindset even while despairing of its telos, by
undertaking an ecologically informed postcolonial reconsideration of
particular nonmodern onto-epistemologies in order to open up an alternative, countermodern way of framing, anticipating, and responding to
eco-catastrophe.[10] In particular, I propose to show how both historical reflection and narrative fiction might contribute to the material-discursive
praxis of learning more skillfully to "dance" with the increasingly unruly
elements of our disastrously anthropogenic environment.[11]

The concept of "natural disaster" owes its genesis to what Michel Serres has termed the "Modern Constitution," which became embedded in the institutionalization of knowledge production during the nineteenth century, severing the "natural" from the "human" sciences.[12] This epistemological divide arises from a longer-standing set of interlocking (and strongly gendered) metaphysical dualisms: notably, between culture and nature, man and beast, mind and body, spirit and matter. The German term for what English speakers call the humanities, namely the *Geisteswissenschaften*, the sciences of the mind or spirit, is particularly telling: under this ordering of the faculties, the "nature" to be examined by the scientists is evidently assumed to be mindless, while their own kind is assumed to only be of interest to humanists in their mental and spiritual aspect. Under the Modern Constitution, cultural-historical differences also got mapped onto this dualistic schema: to become "modern" implied transcending nature by means of the internalization of civilized constraints along with the ever more expansive techno-scientific domination of the material realm. "Primitive" peoples, it was thought, lived in, or close to, nature, while "modern" peoples, whether for better or for worse, were deemed to have left nature behind. As Bruno Latour has demonstrated, however, this is another of those modern myths: all people live in natural-cultural collectives, which is to say, in socially structured networks of interrelationship among diverse human and nonhuman agents and processes. The exact configuration of those collectives can nonetheless vary widely, with significant implications for the relative sustainability of the societies in question.

Ironically, the dualistic onto-epistemology of the Modern Constitution took shape and struck root at precisely the time when science and technology were enrolling ever more nonhuman entities into the complex networks that are constitutive of industrial (and, for that matter, so-called postindustrial) societies. Along with the things that most of us value, such as refrigerators and motorcars, this process has unintentionally generated sundry seriously undesirable natural-cultural hybrids, including such "hyperobjects," as Timothy Morton calls them, as ozone depletion and global warming.[13] Meanwhile, coming to terms with these hybrid phenomena, which can only be understood and redressed through a transdisciplinary lens, has been rendered all the more difficult because of the great divide between the sciences and the humanities, along with the marginalization of alternative knowledge systems (notably, those of colonized peoples). Similarly, the crucial task of recognizing and address-

ing the multiple human and nonhuman agencies and processes that go
into the making of eco-catastrophe has been severely hindered by the
modern myth of "natural disaster." Ironically, the very period when long-
term human impacts upon the planet have escalated to such an extent
that our era has been dubbed the Anthropocene[14] is also the era in which
the entanglement of morality and materiality, social relations and natural
phenomena, has become veiled.

As it happens, *Dancing with Disaster* began its final passage from pen to
print during Australia's "Angry Summer" of 2012–13, when temperature
records toppled like trees in a forest being clear-felled. Over a ninety-day
period from early December to late February, no fewer than 123 records
for a range of heat extremes, including hottest daily maximum, hottest
monthly average maximum, and hottest night on record, were broken at
weather stations around the country. For seven days running, from January 2 to January 8, the average daily maximum temperature for the whole
of Australia was over 39°C, easily breaking the previous record of four consecutive days, and on January 7, the national area averaged maximum hit
an all-time high of 40.30°C. The heat was so extreme in the "red center"
of the continent, so-called for the ruddy pigment of the desert sand, that
a new color had to be added to the temperature map. Since the middle of
2012, moreover, much of the country had been drying out, with the lowest
ever July-to-December rainfall recorded across central South Australia and
below-average rainfall across almost all of southeastern Australia. These
extremely hot and dry conditions brought bushfires to every state and territory in the course of the Angry Summer. On several days during this period, the fire-danger warning for many parts of southeastern Australia was
ramped up to "catastrophic"—a new rating introduced in the wake of the
Victorian firestorm of February 7, 2009. In Tasmania, around forty wildfires broke out on January 4, burning over twenty-five thousand hectares
and destroying close to two hundred properties on the Tasman Peninsula.
Four days later, New South Wales was hit with around 140 outbreaks, 17 of
which were still burning out of control over a week later, by which stage
Victoria too was beset with several major blazes.[15]

And then a different kind of disaster struck: between January 22 and
January 29, while fires were still burning in the southeast, Queensland and
far north New South Wales were deluged with record-breaking rainfall,
inducing severe flooding in many areas. Elsewhere too there were heavy
downpours, toppling twenty-six daily rainfall records around the country,
along with five river-height records. This was a summer of wild winds, as

well: the floods in Queensland and New South Wales were brought by former tropical cyclone Oswald as it moved inland and south from the Gulf of Carpentaria, causing high waves and storm surges along the coast and contributing to several tornadoes—not a particularly common phenomenon in Australia, by comparison with parts of the United States—which struck Bundaberg and other central Queensland townships on January 26, interrupting Australia Day celebrations and causing widespread damage. At the end of February, the Pilbara region in northwestern Australia was also hit by a hurricane that had intensified into a category 4 cyclone on Australia's five-point scale, with 230-kilometer-per-hour winds at its center, before weakening to category 3 prior to making landfall on a thankfully sparsely inhabited part of coast.[16]

Meanwhile, in southeastern Australia, another heat wave was in the making: for nine consecutive days in early March, officially the first month of autumn in this part of the world, Melbourne sweltered with a run of days above 30°C, six of them above 35°, easily breaking the record previously set in February 1961.[17] There had been three other years prior to that with a run of eight consecutive days above 30°C since records began in 1856; but they all occurred in summer. This year, though, it was mid-April before autumnal weather at last arrived in southeastern Australia, and even then, the rain remained troublingly meager for many weeks.

According to Australia's chief climate scientist, Will Steffen, "Australia's Angry Summer shows that climate change is already adversely affecting Australians," and in the report that he authored in late February for the Climate Commission, he explains clearly and simply how global warming is contributing to the kinds of extreme weather events that the country was then experiencing.[18] Quoting from "My Country," a well-known patriotic poem by Dorothea Mackellar (1885–1968), Steffen acknowledges that Australia has long been a "land of droughts and flooding rain." Crossing a number of climate zones, Australia is characterized by its unruly weather patterns, including nonannual cycles, associated in particular with the El Niño Southern Oscillation (ENSO) and the Indian Ocean Dipole, along with low rainfall predictability and frequent extremes.[19] But as a consequence of the rising air and sea-surface temperatures, caused largely by a globalizing system of production and consumption that continues to increase the combustion of fossil fuels while reducing forest cover, these weather surprises are getting bigger and more frequent, placing Australia on the front line of climate change impacts.

Meanwhile, the wild weather with which Australians have always had to reckon (at least for as long as cultural memory reaches, which in the case of Aboriginal Australians is very long indeed) is beginning to go global, with potentially dire consequences for people around the world, including many who have contributed least to causing the problem. Whole ecosystems, too, are under threat in some regions, bringing untold suffering to countless animals and propelling many species toward extinction. For humans and nonhumans alike, the impacts of global warming will be particularly severe where they occur in conjunction with other environmental stressors, such as pollution, resource depletion, and habitat destruction.[20] "Climate has always changed," as Australian poet and essayist Mark Tredinnick reminds us, "but it's changing around us now like it may never have changed before. . . . The weather we have known—the weather that gave rise to the vivid and teeming, immaculate world in which the human species evolved, all that it has dreamed and learned and lost and made—is passing away. The weather of the Holocene is dying out; the weather of the Anthropocene is turning ugly."[21]

Just how ugly it turns is still up to those humans who are in the privileged position of being able to personally reduce or constrain their carbon dioxide emissions, while putting pressure on governments, institutions, and corporations to take concerted action to mitigate global warming through such measures as greenhouse gas reduction schemes, support for renewable energy production, biosequestration, and the protection of old growth forests. Whether or not the necessary action will have been taken to avert a global temperature rise much above the agreed guardrail of two degrees Celsius by the time this book is published is uncertain, however. Carbon emissions continue to rise and forests to fall; oceans are becoming more acidic and have probably reached the limit of their capacity to absorb more carbon dioxide; and, most troubling of all, greenhouse gases are beginning to bubble up from Artic seas and thawing permafrost, a process that is expected to be unstoppable once it really gets under way, releasing massive quantities of carbon dioxide and, worse still, methane, which have been trapped there for tens and in some cases hundreds of thousands of years.

There are some positive signs, however. Although a post-Kyoto global agreement on climate change mitigation continues to elude negotiators, some progress has been made regionally (notably in Europe). Renewable energy technologies and industries are advancing apace, and the grassroots planetary movement for climate justice is growing and becoming more vocal. Those changes to Earth's climate systems that are already under way as a consequence of historical and current greenhouse gas emissions mean that many of the planet's diverse life forms, including humans, are in for a seriously rough ride, one that will be, unjustly, considerably rougher for some than for others. But there is still room for hope that we might avert the worst: that is to say, the production of a planet that can no longer, or at least not for an unimaginably long time, support more than a tiny fraction of today's diverse biological species and human lives. The hope that I am invoking here, though, is more like an ethical commitment than the outcome of a rational assessment of the situation. In Rebecca Solnit's words, this "is not about what we expect. It is an embrace of the essential unknowability of the world, of the breaks with the present, the surprises." Far from feeding complacency, such "hope in the dark" has the capacity to inspire "those acts necessary to bring about some of what we hope for and to live by principle in the meantime."[22]

One of the widely recognized impediments to acting on climate change hitherto has been the negative equation between the (real or feared) immediate costs of mitigation and people's capacity to imagine the (actual or potential) future impacts of runaway global warming. This appears to have been particularly the case in those affluent countries, such as Australia, Canada, and the United States, where the national economy is closely bound to the fossil fuel industry. Not coincidentally, it is also in these countries that the denial or obfuscation of the inconvenient findings of climate change science has gained the most traction, leaving a large segment of the population either uncertain about or actively hostile toward genuine mitigation policies. In this context works of the creative imagination that depict a dystopian vision of a climate-changed future could play a valuable role in helping to motivate mitigation efforts—at least among those who have not been persuaded that the projections of climate science are themselves fictional, and in conjunction with improved measures to help people bridge the gap between what they know and how they act.[23] However, as indicated by Australia's Angry Summer—and as those who live in the Arctic Circle and on the islands of the South Pacific have known for many years—we no longer have to imagine the impacts of global warming: many are experiencing them right now.[24]

The increasing frequency and intensity of extreme weather events, one might have thought, would finally bring home the critical urgency of climate change mitigation, as well as adaptation, to those affected. The secretary general of the United Nations' Framework Convention on Climate Change, Christiana Figueras, is reported to have commented that such extremes as the catastrophic flooding in England, in conjunction with the polar vortex that plunged parts of the United States into Arctic conditions during the winter of 2013–14, could have a silver lining by boosting climate change action to the top of the political agenda.[25] It all depends, however, on how such calamities are framed. And, in my analysis, part of the reason for many peoples' evident reluctance to "connect the dots," as the activist organization 350.org puts it, lies in the continuing designation of these events as "natural disasters." Veiling the anthropogenic component of today's weather-borne eco-catastrophes, the use of this term also conjures a cultural narrative that is liable to foster a hostile attitude toward the natural world at the very time when we most need to appreciate the connectivities, both material and moral, linking human well-being with that of other living beings and with those volatile bio-physical systems that both enable and, at times, endanger our collective flourishing.

The maladaptive implications of the narrative of "natural disaster" are evident in many of the statements made both by those affected by recent extreme weather events and by politicians keen to demonstrate their empathy with the victims. Here, too, the case of Australia's Angry Summer is instructive. Former prime minister Julia Gillard, for instance, in expressing her condolences to the families of those who had died in the unfolding Queensland flood disaster while visiting others who were afflicted by bushfires in Victoria, declared that the whole country was being "challenged by nature," but that "we are a strong and smart nation and we'll get through this, as we always do, by pulling together."[26] In attributing these disasters to an implicitly violent and hostile Other—something called "nature" that is assumed to lie "over yonder"[27]—this comment both presupposes and reinforces the hierarchical dualism of "nature" and "culture" that many scholars in the environmental humanities have identified as contributing to our socioecological woes and impeding measures to redress them.[28] Moreover, in reassuring the country that "we'll get through this, as we always do," Gillard taps into a specifically Australian variant of nature-culture dualism, one that is currently acting as a further barrier to the recognition of the link between extreme weather events and climate change in this country. This is the settler stereotype of the matey "Aussie battler," struggling to make a life for himself in a land of promise but beset by droughts, fires, floods, poor soils, foot rot, and sundry plant and animal pests.[29] Gillard's reassurance suggests that it is once more us Aussie battlers holding out against the unruly elements; and it is our (exclusively human) "mateship," in conjunction with our superior intelligence, that will get us through it. As well as fostering that underlying contempt, fear, and even hatred toward the natural environment that Simon Estok has termed "ecophobia,"[30] this response militates against the acknowledgment of these extremes as something other than what settler Australians have experienced in the past: namely, as at least partially anthropogenic.

To give Gillard her due, while visiting a fire-ravaged town in Tasmania in early January, she acknowledged that "while you would not put any one event down to climate change . . . we do know that over time as a result of climate change we are going to see more extreme weather events."[31] Yet, when even this cautious reference to climate change led the acting leader of the opposition, Warren Truss, to accuse of her being "too simplistic,"[32] she was evidently cowed into retreating to the more populist Aussie-battler narrative in which "nature" is the adversary and we humans the innocent victims, whose only moral responsibility is to help our mates (which might include strangers, but only of the human variety). Unsurprisingly, this is the narrative that Gillard's right-wing successor, Tony Abbott, reiterated in response to the unseasonable bushfires that broke out in New South Wales in September 2013, ridiculing those, including no less a figure than Christiane Figueras, who linked them to global warming.[33]

While Abbott's rejection of this link, together with his dismantling of the entire scientific, administrative, and financial infrastructure that the former government had created to mitigate carbon pollution, could be seen to border on the criminal, Gillard's timorousness, if regrettable, was understandable. By the beginning of 2013, the climate change debate in Australia had become so politicized and vitriolic that climate scientists at Australia's National University, including Will Steffen, had been subjected to a barrage of abusive emails and even death threats over the past few years.[34] Those nonscientists who draw upon their expertise in commenting on extreme events have come under fire as well. One of Australia's preeminent environmental philosophers, Freya Mathews, for example, was also subject to abuse and threats in response to a courageous opinion piece in Melbourne's *Age* newspaper in the wake of the catastrophic Victorian firestorm of 2009. On February 7, toward the climactic end of a thirteen-year drought and in the midst of an unprecedented heat wave, several of the four hundred fires burning across Victoria converged, obliterating six small towns and badly damaging many more, taking 173 human lives and displacing over 7,500 survivors, burning out over 450,000 hectares of land and killing or injuring countless wild and domestic animals.[35] In her article, Mathews argued that the "fires we saw on Saturday were not 'once in a thousand years' or even 'once in a hundred years' events, as our political leaders keep repeating. They were the face of climate change in our part of the world."[36] Mathews's eagerness to interpret this eco-catastrophe through the lens of climate change might have obscured another of its key lessons: namely, the continuing failure of most Australians to reckon with the "holocaust fires," as Tom Griffiths terms them, that are endemic to some Victorian forests.[37] The one-sidedness of the environmental philosopher's evaluation was nonetheless exceeded by the counterposed narrative propagated by Australia's only national paper, the Murdoch-owned *Australian,* which led a veritable campaign to undermine any association between global warming and the extended drought and unprecedented heat wave that culminated in the so-called Black Saturday tragedy. In this account, responsibility lay exclusively with those environmentalists who had allegedly prevented the widespread prescribed burning, which, it was claimed, would have stopped the fires from becoming so ferocious. Miranda Devine took this fight against "eco-terrorism" to the *Sydney Morning Herald,* insisting that "it is not arsonists who should be hanging from lamp-posts but greenies."[38] It may well be that this particular campaign was being prosecuted, at least in part, by those with a vested interest in obfuscating climate science and derailing mitigation efforts. But this narrative was only able to gain traction with the public, in my view, because the traumatic experience of the fires had stirred up an underlying, culturally conditioned ecophobia, which could then be directed toward those traitorous "greenies" whose "love of nature" was construed as a betrayal of their own kind.

This example demonstrates the very real potential for eco-catastrophe to deepen nature-culture dualism and escalate ecophobia to a potentially lethal level. Short of homicide, though, it is clear that the categorization of such events as "natural disasters" is encouraging some worryingly counterproductive responses to the early impacts of climate change. During Melbourne's heat wave in March 2013, for example, water consumption and power usage surged, putting further pressure on dwindling fresh water supplies and—since almost all of Australia's electricity is still coal-fired—increasing carbon emissions. People's efforts to cool off with extra showers, fans, and air-conditioners are perfectly understandable; but if such actions are not to compound the problem to which they are a response, concerted measures will need to be taken to ensure that shower water is recycled and that far more electricity is supplied by renewable power generators. But if, as the "skeptics" insist, this period of hot and dry weather is just a matter of natural variability, why bother undertaking such costly innovations, especially at a time of economic downturn? Equally troubling are responses such as that of the survivors of the firestorm that destroyed the particularly picturesque Victorian township of Marysville on Black Saturday. According to a *Sydney Morning Herald* report, at a meeting to plan their first trip back to their burned-out township, where police were still sifting through the ash for human remains, the displaced residents declared their intention to "stand together and 'loudly reclaim' Marysville from nature."[39] This defiant stance not only exemplifies once more the eco-phobic conclusion that has been drawn from the experience of a disaster tagged as "natural"; it also indicates that such defiance could lead survivors to put themselves in harm's way again by seeking to restore what has been lost, rather than finding new ways, and potentially new places, to live more safely and sustainably as we move ineluctably into a climatically changed future. Alternative ways of speaking about, and responding to, the calamitous impacts of climate change are therefore urgently required, both as a spur to mitigation and in the interests of what is optimistically termed "adaptation."

Not unlike the increased UV radiation that now blasts parts of the planet at particular times of the year as a consequence of the ozone-depleting chemicals that industrialized nations once shunted into the environment, today's wild weather, then, is an increasingly hybrid phenomenon. But there is a sense in which the term *natural disaster* has always been a mis-nomer. This is not to deny the occurrence of genuinely nonanthropogenic phenomena that can prove seriously troublesome for affected communities. Earthquakes and volcanoes, hurricanes and tornadoes, droughts and floods, heat waves and cold snaps, landslides and blizzards: such things have always been a part of life on this volatile planet. While there is no longer any place on Earth that does not bear the trace of industrial civilization, as Bill McKibben argues in *The End of Nature,* other-than-human agencies and processes remain powerfully in play. As Nigel Clark observes in his study of "sociable life on a dynamic planet," new research in the biological and earth sciences reveals a story in which "instability and up-heaval, rhythmical movement and dramatic changes of states are ordinary aspects of earth's own history."[40] Indeed, there are certain global geophys-ical events, or "gee-gees," as they have wryly been dubbed,[41] such as large asteroid or comet strikes and volcanic super-eruptions, which have blitzed Earth in the past and are bound to do so again in the future, putting all our worst efforts thus far in the shade. But it takes two to tango and more than a violent geophysical phenomenon to give rise to a disaster: it also takes a vulnerable population. And vulnerability, as Hurricane Katrina revealed so starkly, is always, to a greater or lesser extent, socially produced and inequitably distributed.[42] Anthropologist of disaster Anthony Oliver-Smith puts it this way: "Social systems generate the conditions that place people, often differentiated along axes of class, race, ethnicity, gender, or age [and, I would add, dis/ability], at different levels of risk from the same hazard."[43]

For example, the movement of one of Earth's tectonic plates deep beneath the sea does not in itself constitute a disaster. Like the ensuing tsunami, though, it is a potential hazard, and one that is liable to have disastrous consequences for humans (among others) if it produces seismic and marine waves that impact a heavily populated coastline. Even then, the extent and nature of the damage will be determined not only by the magnitude of the quake and tsunami but also by anthropogenic alterations to the coastal environment, such as the absence of mangroves that might have slowed the sea's advance and the presence of built structures, such as cars and bridges, which can be become lethal debris, or nuclear facilities, which can release pathogenic radiation if damaged. Other critical factors include the ability of those threatened to perceive, or be warned, of its approach in time to take refuge; their familiarity with such places of refuge; and their physical capacity to get there. While forewarning might be enhanced by national, regional, and transnational scientific monitoring and communication technologies, in the midst of an extreme event such as this, local knowledge and local networks can mean the difference between life and death. On the other hand, as Bonnie Roos and Alex Hunt emphasize with respect to the catastrophic tsunami of December 26, 2004, locals too can be at risk for other reasons, especially if they are poor, such as the children who raced onto the sand exposed by the receding water to collect fish, only to be swept up in the oncoming wave.[44] In the medium to long term, moreover, the impact of a disaster is strongly influenced by what happens afterward: by the capacity of those affected to regroup and recover; the extent and quality of the assistance they receive; and their ability to make sense of what has happened to them in ways that could reduce their vulnerability to such hazards in the future.

The entanglement of human and nonhuman actors and factors in the genesis, unfolding, and aftermath of a "natural disaster" is now well recognized in the research field of disaster studies. Over the past thirty years or so, such disasters have been redefined, not as departures from the norm, but as endemic to the dynamic interactivity of society, technology, and

environment. As the editors of a major volume on the anthropology of disaster from 1999 observe in their introduction, "Disasters spring from the
nexus where environment, society, and technology come together—the
point where place, people, and human construction of both the material
and nonmaterial meet. It is from the interplay of these three planes that
disasters emanate, and in their unfolding, they reimplicate every vector of
their causal interface."[45] Occurring "at the interface of vulnerable people
and physical hazards,"[46] no disaster is ever purely "natural." Such calamities do nonetheless reveal much about how a given society relates to its
physical environment, something that is as much a question of culture,
values, and beliefs as it is of economics, politics, and technology. For this
reason, disaster research and policy development demand the expertise
not only of the natural and social sciences but also of the environmental
humanities, including environmental literary and cultural studies, along
with environmental history, philosophy, anthropology, cultural geography,
and religious studies.[47]

Generally framed as dramatic events, disasters are better understood
as material-discursive processes, in which the varying needs and interests
of the individuals, groups, and organizations affected are "articulated and
negotiated over the often extended duration of the entire phenomenon."[48]
Occurring in the context of longer-term processes of socioecological
development—or maldevelopment—even those eco-catastrophes that are
triggered by nonanthropogenic phenomena frequently participate in the
inequitable distribution of environmental harms that has been described
by Rob Nixon as a form of "slow violence." Indeed, Nixon himself questions the conventional division between human disasters (like Bhopal and
Chernobyl) and natural ones (like Katrina), while nonetheless focusing
on the former.[49] It is important to recognize, however, that privilege no
less than poverty can be a potent source of vulnerability. For example, in
their study of social vulnerability to flooding in Germany during the Elbe
flood disaster of 2002, Christian Kuhlicke and Annette Steinführer found
that those who were most at risk were not necessarily the less well heeled
but those who placed too much confidence, first, in the efficacy of human
control over the natural environment and, second, in the ability of the
authorities to forewarn and protect those likely to be affected by any environmental surprises that might nonetheless arise.[50] This case study points
to what Oliver-Smith terms the "hazards of domination."[51] Among such
hazards is the perilous condition of "human self-enclosure," as Val Plumwood calls it, to which those who enjoy the benefits of air-conditioning,

heating, ample food, fresh water on tap, and well-plumbed toilets are particularly prone.[52] The hazardous underestimation of vulnerability among the privileged is compounded by the "plasticity myth," according to which nature is infinitely malleable and can always be remolded to suit human amenity.[53] Closely allied with this myth is what I have called the "premise of predictability"—that is, the overestimation of the capacity of science to provide sufficient certainty to rule out unintended consequences from a given technological intervention. Such dangerously delusional thinking, I believe, underwrites those Faustian geo-engineering schemes that have been put forward to counter the impacts of global warming, such as the use of mirrors or aerosols to deflect some of the sun's rays.[54]

With or without reference to climate change, disaster is a hot topic at present across a wide range of disciplines and interdisciplines.[55] Those who approach it from a humanities perspective, like myself, generally have a weakness for words and are wont to inquire into the lexicon that is used to discuss such matters of concern. Let me begin with *disaster* itself. Entering English from the French noun *désastre* in the sixteenth century, this word is commonly thought to have referred originally to the malign influence of an unfavorable planetary aspect or conjunction: "ill-starred," in other words, or subject to "an obnoxious planet."[56] As such, disaster figures as a matter of astrologically determined misfortune. Whether or not it is paired with *natural*, then, the use of this term bears the trace of a premodern cultural narrative in which "nature over yonder" is, once again, made to cop the blame for human suffering. In modernity, the astrological referent might have become discredited and forgotten, but the connotation of bad luck lingers. The complex, multifactoral, and unpredictable nexus of nonlinear causality that appears to us as chance does of course play a part in the occurrence and unfolding of calamity. Too often, though, the interpretive frame of misfortune, which continues to resonate in the discourse of "natural disaster," masks the realities of human (ir)responsibility.

As I recalled at the outset, however, there is another historically and cross-culturally very powerful narrative about those calamities now designated "natural disasters," according to which they are not so much written in the stars as ordained by God, the gods, or an indwelling power. Here, far from being interpreted as a mere misfortune, calamity is decoded as punishment for transgression, whether personal or, more commonly, collective. Within the Western tradition, the best-known variant of this punishment paradigm is the biblical narrative of the Flood in Genesis 6–8, in which human wickedness is said to have provoked the Creator into bringing about a global deluge. Significantly, though, this collective calamity is cast as ultimately cleansing: the divinely ordained disaster turns out to be a blessing in disguise, paving the way for a new beginning, in which Noah and his descendants, along with those of all the other creatures he famously saved in the ark, are vouchsafed the opportunity to continue their earthly existence under a new covenant, secure in the knowledge that God will never again "destroy every creature" (Gen. 8:21) (which is not to say that errant humans might not do so).[57]

These days, the punishment paradigm is generally only invoked in Western countries by biblical literalists and cultural conservatives, who are occasionally reported in the press as shrilly attributing calamitous events involving elemental forces to such alleged human evils as legalized abortion and gay marriage. It is, I suspect, not only out of ecophobia but also out of an enlightened objection, perhaps even moral revulsion, to this mythico-religious construction of collective calamities, which smacks unpleasantly of blaming the victim, that politicians and the wider society cling so ardently to the modern discourse of "natural disaster." What is thereby occluded, though, is the recognition of the interrelationship between human sociocultural practices and the more-than-human physical environment that is inscribed into mythico-religious narratives such as that of the Flood, however dubious their account of causality might appear from a secular rationalist perspective. It is in the interests of recovering that recognition, albeit in a postmodern, socioecological, bio-inclusive and scientifically informed guise, that I prefer the term eco-catastrophe.

What, then, of catastrophe? This term comes to us, originally, from Aristotle's Poetics. Literally denoting a sudden turn or overturning (kata, down, against; strophē, turn), this word is used by Aristotle to refer to the change that produces the final outcome in a work of tragic drama (also known as the denouément). Entering English with the classical theory of drama in the sixteenth century, catastrophe was subsequently adopted by geologists to describe those dramatic alterations in Earth's history that some (the "Plutonists" of the eighteenth century and the "Catastrophists" of the nineteenth) attributed to violent geophysical events, such as volcanoes, earthquakes, and major floods. These geological turning points were also called "revolutions"—a term that was appropriated for political purposes in the late eighteenth century, thereby contributing to the disfavor with which catastrophism was viewed by those whose preference for gradual change in the sociopolitical arena found support in their insistence that Earth's alterations too had been incremental. By the early nineteenth century, *catastrophe* had found its way into ordinary parlance, as a synonym for disaster or calamity, whether personal or collective, but with the lingering connotation of a terrible event that is not only of great magnitude but brings about a change of direction or perception. A true catastrophe, then, is not only a *terminus* but a turning point. In the *Poetics*, the *katastrophē* is intimately associated with *anagnorisis*: the moment of realization, when the tragic hero or heroine is faced with the collapse of their underlying assumptions about themselves and/or others and is brought, painfully and sometimes fatally, to the recognition of the damage that has been wrought by their ignorance. Interestingly, in German, it is *Katastrophe* that got tied to *Natur* to form the compound noun that came into common usage only in the twentieth century to refer to what English-speakers had begun to term "natural disasters." From the perspective of this study, it is a shame that more disasters are not recognized as true catastrophes: that is to say, opportunities for deeper understanding and, potentially, new directions.

A catastrophe, one might say (turning from classical to biblical Greek), is a calamity with an "apocalyptic" dimension. Apocalypticism has come in for quite a bit of bad press in recent years, primarily, I think, because it tends to get confused with millenarianism: that is, the belief in the total destruction of the current, corrupt order of things as inevitable and indeed necessary to inaugurate a new and better one.[58] Within Christian eschatology, this millenialist expectation assumes the guise of the thousand-year reign of the "kingdom of God" to be ushered in by the Second Coming of Christ, as prophesied by a mysterious character known as "John" in the seriously scary last book of the Bible. Here, the catastrophic end is assumed to be not only inevitable but ardently to be desired as opening the way for a glorious new beginning. This is, indeed, one variant of apocalyptic writing. But it is important to recall that *apokályptein* simply means to uncover something that had been concealed (hence, Saint John's millenialist prophecy is termed "Revelation" in the English translation). The earlier prophetic books of the Hebrew Bible embody a form of revelation that differs significantly from later Jewish and Christian apocalyptic tradition in the stance it takes toward the historical hour and in the space that this allows for human agency: this prophetic vision might be seen as "counterapocalyptic" to the extent that it seeks to disclose the potentially catastrophic consequences of the track that society has taken, in the hope that a different path might yet be chosen and the worst averted.[59] The role of the prophet in this Hebraic tradition, as Terry Eagleton puts it, "is not to predict the future, but to remind the people that if they carry on as they are doing, the future will be exceedingly bleak."[60] Apocalypse, then, is not necessarily synonymous with the real or imagined end of *the* world; it can imply, rather, the end of *a* world, which is to say the end of a particular practice, or set of practices, of *world-making*. As an unveiling, moreover, "the apocalyptic event," as James Berger defines it, "must in its destructive moment clarify and illuminate the true nature of what has been brought to an end."[61] Potentially, this unveiling can become a trigger for transformation.

The biblical prophetic voice that castigates the high and mighty for their hubris, and calls upon the people to change their ways, is summoned forth in response to the cry of the oppressed; and in some biblical texts, that also includes the ravaged land and its more-than-human creatures.[62] Jeremiah, for example, echoing a trope from the earlier prophetic books of Isaiah (24:4, 33:7–9) and Hosea (4:1–3), in which the drying out of the land or earth (*erets*) is referred to with a verbal expression that also means to grieve or mourn, laments: "How long will the land [earth] mourn [dry up], / and the grass of every field wither? / For the wickedness of those who live in it / the animals and the birds are swept away" (12:4); to which Yahweh, speaking through the prophet, responds: "They made it a desolation; / desolate it mourns to me. / The whole land is made desolate, / but no one lays it to heart" (Jer. 12:11).[63] For Jeremiah, arguably the first in a long line of Jewish eco-prophets, the callous disregard for the plight of animals, birds, and the drought-stricken land is interlinked with the neglect of justice for the poor and marginalized: eco-catastrophe, in his reading, is symptomatic of a nation in breach of the covenant in its godless pursuit of power and profit.[64] The urgency that inspires such prophetic voices lies in their diagnosis of the historical hour as approaching a turning point. Referred to in Hebrew as *Et Ketz*, the "time of the end," this idea is echoed in the Greek of the Christian tradition in the concept of *kairos*, generally understood as an opportune moment for the kind of necessary action that breaks with existing trends and tendencies. *Kairos* is crunch time: a moment of grave danger that also harbors liberating potentials.[65]

This book is motivated, in large part, by the conviction that today's increasingly globalized world has entered into such an "end time" and that climate change in particular presents us all with a *kairos* moment. However, to the extent that certain kinds of eco-catastrophe are "already underway all around," such that a "future without their impact has become impossible to envision," this book is also crucially concerned with what Ursula Heise has termed "risk scenarios."[66] Indeed, the notion of "risk" is implicit in my framing of our own historical hour as "perilous." Also entering English from the French, *peril* comes originally from the Latin *periculum,* meaning "experiment" or "risk," and was used in particular with respect to the financial risks associated with investing in sea voyages. *Risk* itself, from the Latin *resecum,* denoting that which cuts, is related both to the Italian *richiare,* meaning to run into danger, and the Spanish *riesgo,* referring to that into which a ship, for example, might literally run: namely, a reef. As Marie-Hélène Huet observes, the concept of peril therefore carries a double connotation, alluding both to risk-taking speculation and treacherous natural phenomena;[67] alternatively, in my reading, it conjures their potentially catastrophic interaction.

At the present time, such perilous conjunctions are not only generating an escalation of some kinds of risk; they are also rendering the risks that many more-than-human communities face increasingly difficult to calculate. Under these circumstances, it is well to recall the alternative etymology for *disaster* assumed by Huet. In company with one of her key interlocutors, Maurice Blanchot in *L'écriture de la désastre* (1980), Huet traces this word to the French verbal expression *désastré,* dis-astered, which derives from the Italian *dis-astrato,* designating "the state of having been disowned by the stars that ensure a safe passage through life."[68] This derivation is helpful for my purposes in pointing toward one dimension of what it might mean to "dance with disaster": that is, to develop modes of personal and collective comportment that are no longer premised on certitude—the confidence of possessing a sure guiding star—but that instead presuppose the unforeseeable. The kind of dance I have in mind here would therefore have to be largely improvisational.[69] That does not mean that planning, preparation, and practice are not vitally important. Clearly, they are, from the personal and familial rehearsal of evacuation plans, for example, to the collective habits of mutual aid and self-organization fostered within local voluntary associations.[70] In a planetary context in which nobody's security is guaranteed, though, we will need to improve our skills of contingency planning and "adaptive governance," recognizing that we might need to change tack at any moment in response to unanticipated eventualities and ensuring a voice for all those potentially affected, especially local populations who might well have collective memories, situated knowledges, and social networks, which could prove critical in a crisis.[71]

There is no doubt that more scientific research and better technologies will be required to limit climate change and prepare for its impacts. But so, too, as environmental philosophers have long argued with respect to other kinds of environmental ills, is a more ecological ethos. As I see it, this would be an ethos that reckons with nonhuman agency and is prepared for surprises. It would also be one that is alert to more-than-human voices and concerned with more-than-human flourishing. And it would entail an explicit avowal both of the limits of human knowledge and of the infinite indebtedness of human existence to other-than-human entities and process. Rich conceptual resources for the formulation of such an ethos can be found among contemporary "new materialist" and "material feminist" philosophies, and I will be drawing on several of these throughout this book, itself an adventure in "material ecocriticism."[72] At the same time, I have also found myself in conversation with some thinkers whose affiliations lie with a rather different philosophical tradition, centered around notions of radical alterity and ethical asymmetry. Among these is Nigel Clark, whose *Inhuman Nature* foregrounds human "susceptibility to the earth's eventfulness" and "exposure to forces that exceed our capacity to control or even make full sense of them."[73] Regaining an appreciation of this dimension of vulnerability is central to countering the plasticity myth and the associated hazards of domination. However, my analysis draws away from Clark's in stressing the extent to which human attitudes and actions can either mitigate or exacerbate the risks, not only to fellow humans but also to other earthlings, inherent in our perennially unstable terrestrial conditions. "Dancing with disaster," then, points toward the multispecies performance, at once rehearsed and responsive, of an interactive and even "intra-active"[74] (which is to say, mutually constitutive) material-discursive *modus vivendi* in the midst of uncertainty—one that is oriented toward averting eco-catastrophe where possible; enhancing resilience should one such nonetheless eventuate; and enabling transformation should that prove necessary.

If such disasters are "sentinel events" of socioecological processes that are intensifying on a planetary scale,[75] then the investigation of the hermeneutics of eco-catastrophe constitutes a key area for research in the environmental humanities. In the chapters that follow, I trace the historical emergence of the modern concept of "natural disaster," which, as I have already intimated, veils the *kairos* moment that we are now facing in the interests of the maintenance of business-as-usual. In addition, I show how this concept has been put under pressure in a series of literary texts from the Romantic period to the present—during the very era, in other words, that the calamitous Anthropocene was in the making. In this analysis, the particular value of literature, and especially of narrative fiction, within the "cultural ecology"[76] of eco-catastrophe is shown to lie in its ability to hold up to scrutiny the kinds of often contradictory stories that people tell about collective calamities involving the dynamic inter-action of diverse human and nonhuman agencies and processes. In addi-tion, these literary narratives are helpful in revealing how the interpretive frames embedded in such stories inform the ways in which their charac-ters respond to the disasters in which they become embroiled. Each of these texts (re-)imagines a particular kind of calamity, and all are contex-tualized in relation to relevant historical disasters, from the Black Death of the Middle Ages through to the mega-cyclones of the early twenty-first century. Both the histories that I trace and the literature that I interpret open an ethical space of reflection upon the socioecological contours of eco-catastrophe, a space within which nonhuman as well as human inter-ests and interactions, lives and death, are seen to be salient.

While the first three chapters of this book, focusing respectively on earthquake, pandemic disease, and flood, have a predominantly European geohistorical locus, the last two return to the Australian socioecological contingencies that I touch upon earlier in this introduction. In part, this reflects my own formation, not only as an Australian of Anglo-Celtic ex-traction but also, and more significantly, as a member of the Australian ecological humanities community that was convened by Deborah Bird Rose and Libby Robin in the early years of the new millennium. As I have already intimated, though, there are also more impersonal grounds for highlighting these antipodean instances of the history and literature of eco-catastrophe. To begin with, the profound disjunction between the landscape memories, environmental attitudes, and conventional life-ways of the predominantly European (and mainly British) colonists who arrived in the late eighteenth and nineteenth centuries and the Indige-nous cultures and environmental conditions that they encountered here has disclosed the connectivities between the social and the ecological in a particularly stark, and frequently calamitous, fashion. This geohistorical experience, which provides the focus for my fourth chapter, on fire, prob-ably contributed to the early emergence and particular "edge" of environ-mentally oriented research in the humanities in Australia, especially in the fields of ecophilosophy and environmental history. As Tom Griffiths observed in an address to the Commonwealth Department of Education, Science and Training in 2003, "On such a continent, we can never blithely assume the domination of culture over nature, nor can we believe in the infinite resilience of the land. We are committed by history and circumstance to an intellectually innovative environmental enquiry."[77] These enquiries, moreover, have become increasingly transdisciplinary, enriched by the voices and perspectives of Aboriginal people, such as the Mak Mak women with whom Debbie Rose coauthored *Country of the Heart*, whose cultural inheritance reaches back some fifty thousand years. Indigenous Australian cultures are unique, not only in having weathered several massive climate changes in the distant past but also in the ingenuity and resilience with which the first Australians negotiated the challenge of creating sustainable lifeways on a continent that never settled into the reasonably regular annual seasonal cycles that emerged elsewhere on the planet in the wake of the last glacial maximum. Since the kinds of tricky climatic conditions with which Aboriginal people have learned so skillfully to dance are now going global, Australian socioecological histories and Indigenous narratives, such as those that I explore in relation to cyclones in the final chapter, have acquired a transnational significance.

1

MOVING EARTH

On the morning of November 1, 1755, the Portuguese capital, then one of
the world's largest and wealthiest cities, was rent by a massive earthquake,
followed in quick succession by two aftershocks. Large fissures appeared
in its busy town center, roofs collapsed, and several grand buildings were
reduced to rubble. Lisbon's famous port, the point from which numerous
voyages of exploration and colonization had set forth in previous centuries and still a bustling hub of international trade, was particularly badly
affected: underlain by unconsolidated sediments, which amplify seismic
waves, several stone quays subsided into the Tagus River and were swal-
lowed up by its swirling waters, taking with them all those who had rushed
out of the city center to congregate at the harbor.

The Great Lisbon Earthquake, as it became known, remains the largest
seismic event ever recorded in European history. Subsequently estimated
to have measured around 8.5 on the Richter scale, its force was felt on land
over an area of more than fifteen million square kilometers, from North
Africa to Scandinavia. From its epicenter deep below the ocean around two
hundred kilometers west-southwest of Cape St. Vincent, it sent a series of
tidal waves coursing across the Atlantic in all directions, cresting up to fifteen meters in southern Portugal, where they surged over the seawalls of
Cadiz. Damaging waves also lashed the coastlines of Algiers and Tangier,
while an elevated swell was noted as far away as North America's eastern
seaboard. Although the waters only topped at around six meters in Lisbon, the largest concentration of casualties was found there. Estimates of
fatalities lie between thirty and seventy thousand people, who were either
crushed by falling masonry, many of them in the crowded stone churches
where All Saints' Day celebrations were in process; drowned in the ensuing tsunami; or immolated in the fires that continued to burn for five days,
consuming most of what remained of the Portuguese capital.[1] Along with
the shattered buildings and lost lives, considerable economic and cultural
wealth was also destroyed, including immense quantities of gold and silver; hundreds of pictures, including works by Titian, Correggio, and Reu-
bens; thousands of books and manuscripts; and countless valuable pieces
of furniture, tapestries, and ornaments from churches and homes.[2] The

Portuguese were no strangers to earth tremors, but they had never experienced anything like this in living memory. The shockwaves that were felt across much of Europe in consequence of this catastrophe, moreover, were ideational as well as physical. In a striking instance of the entanglement of natural and cultural history, the Lisbon earthquake is frequently cast as a "turning point" or "watershed" dividing Europe's past from its future.[3] As I will show in this chapter, however, its force was felt all the more powerfully because the grounds of belief were themselves already shifting.

Quite apart from their powerfully destructive potential, earthquakes must surely count among the most unsettling of natural hazards, especially for those who live in seismically quiescent climes. Occurring without any discernible warning, even a small tremor shatters our everyday assurance that, however uncertain the rest of our existence might seem, one thing we can rely upon is the solidity of the ground beneath our feet. As Charles Darwin observed in his *Journal and Remarks* (1839), a "bad earthquake at once destroys our oldest associations: the earth, the very emblem of solidity, has moved beneath our feet like a thin crust over a fluid."[4] By the mid-eighteenth century, most Europeans had probably accommodated themselves on some level to the counterintuitive knowledge that the earth was neither flat nor the center of the universe but one of several spherical planets circling the sun. But their primary experience of the earth, like that of most people the world over, now and then, was "as a supportive and sustaining ground—as the resting point from which we register the movement and thingness of all other things."[5] It is the phenomenality of Earth as a solid foundation that gives rise to the figurative use of *ground* to signify a sure basis for truth. When the earth moves, therefore, more stands to be lost than the roof above our heads: our very confidence in the intelligibility of the world is potentially placed at risk.

In his graphic description of the experience of a large earthquake in his seminal book on seismology of 1904, the American geologist Clarence E. Dutton provides a glimpse of both the terror occasioned by a strong tremblor and the cognitive strategies that humans have commonly adopted to frame and, in some measure, tame this fearful phenomenon:

> The first sensation is a confused murmuring sound of a strange and even weird character. Almost simultaneously loose objects begin to tremble and chatter. Sometimes, almost in an instant, sometimes more gradually, but always quickly, the sound becomes a roar, the chattering becomes a crashing. . . . The shaking increases in vio-

lence. . . . Through its din are heard loud, deep, solemn booms that seem like the voice of the Eternal One, speaking out of the depths of the universe.[6]

As Dutton's reference to "the voice of the Eternal One" recalls, making sense of earthquakes, along with other geophysical extremes, has long been the business of myth and religion. In animistic cultures, they are most likely to be attributed to the stirring of the great creatures that dwell within or support the earth: in Japan, for example, it was a catfish; in China, a frog; in the Philippines, a snake; and in North America, a turtle.[7] There is a pale echo of animism in Dutton's description of the auditory aspect of the quake as beginning with "murmuring" and "chattering"; for Dutton, however, as the inheritor of a deanimated, reductively materialist worldview, this only adds to the "weirdness" of the phenomenon, in which objects that Dutton assumes to be inanimate acquire the uncanny semblance of vitality and voice. This glimpse of a disturbingly lively and communicative materiality is then swiftly subsumed into a monotheistic interpretive frame, in which the booming of the earth directs attention to the heavens, reminding the faithful of the sovereignty that the Creator continues to wield over His creation and raising discomforting questions regarding human obedience to divine law.

In the Christian West, numerous biblical passages from both the Old and New Testaments could readily be called upon to construe earthquakes as the consequence of human sinfulness. In some instances, divine anger appears to engender a kind of generalized quaking. In Jeremiah 10:10, for example, Earth is apparently accorded its own agency in response to the Lord's disfavor toward His fallen people:

> But the Lord is the true God;
> he is the living God and the
>   everlasting King;
> At his wrath the earth quakes,
> and the nations cannot endure his
>   indignation.

Elsewhere, though, the elements are apparently enlisted by the Almighty to prosecute more narrowly targeted acts of divine vengeance, such as that which befalls the wealthy and decadent towns of Sodom and Gomorrah in Genesis 24–28:

> Then the LORD rained on Sodom and Gomorrah sulphur and fire
> from the LORD out of heaven; and he overthrew those cities, and all
> the Plain, and all the inhabitants of the cities, and what grew on the
> ground. . . . And Abraham went early in the morning to the place
> where he had stood before the LORD; and he looked down toward
> Sodom and Gomorrah and toward all the land of the Plain and saw
> the smoke of the land going up like the smoke of a furnace.

In Revelation, moreover, in response to the oppression and corruption of
what was the closest thing to a global empire the world had yet seen—that
of the Romans (referred to here under the code name of "Babylon")—
God's targeted vengeance is anticipated to assume planetary proportions:

> And there came flashes of lightning, rumblings, peals of thunder,
> and a violent earthquake, such as had not occurred since people
> were upon the earth, so violent was that earthquake. The great city
> was split into three parts, and the cities of the nations fell. (Rev.
> 16:18–19)

At least one biblical text, namely the book of Job, nonetheless throws doubt
on the idea that those who are afflicted by what theologians subsequently
came to call "natural evils" should be assumed to have deserved their misfortune. Contrary to his friends, who are convinced that the upright Job
must be guilty of some secret sin for which he is being punished by the series of terrible calamities that have befallen him, the deity who addresses
him from the whirlwind (Job 38–41) simply bids Job to lift his gaze to the
infinitely more-than-human dimensions of creation; from the mountains
where the wild "goats give birth" (39:1) through the deserts, "empty of
human life," where the Lord's rain brings verdure to "the waste and desolate land" (38:26, 27), to the mighty Bethemoth and Leviathan, this is a
world that is shown to far exceed human comprehension and control. This
is, to be sure, far from providing a direct answer to the question of how an
allegedly just and all-powerful deity could allow bad things to befall good
people, and the book of Job has been interpreted in widely differing ways.
But it does suggest that destructive earthquakes and other such calamities
should not necessarily be construed by the faithful as direct manifestations of divine wrath toward anyone in particular, or humanity in general.

Since the time of the early church fathers, various arguments have
been put forward within Christian thought to explain the existence of such
"natural evils": that is, those forms of pain and suffering that arise from the

vulnerability of human beings, along with other living creatures, to the violence of the elements, disease, disability, and, ineluctably, death. For some, the existence of troublesome terrestrial phenomena such as earthquakes was a sure indication that the whole of creation was tainted by the Fall and either prey to satanic forces or subject to occasional blockages of divine beneficence. Others argued, sometimes with reference to Job, that these calamities were actually blessings in disguise, designed to develop human souls through the experience of undeserved adversity, bringing them closer to God and making them more sympathetic to the travails of others. While the judgmental took the part of Job's friends in maintaining that the individuals and communities so afflicted must be guilty of some wrong that had drawn divine vengeance, the less assuming reasoned that disruptive physical phenomena, which appeared to us as evil, perhaps served some greater purpose that was inscrutable to mortal minds.

Among the intelligentsia of the mid-eighteenth century, the notion that the earth itself was "fallen" (as distinct from merely afflicted by the consequences of humanity's sinfulness) had lost ground to the more optimistic view that the evidence for order in the natural world, as disclosed by those empirical inquiries launched by Sir Francis Bacon (1587–1657), the so-called father of modern science, testified to the fundamental goodness of creation and that all was ultimately for the best in this "best of all possible worlds," as the German philosopher G. W. Leibniz (1646–1716) put it in his *Theodicy* (1610). This *entente cordiale* between theology and science rested on the long-standing Aristotelian distinction between primary and secondary causes: while God was the primary author of creation, the physical world that He had summoned into being had its own operative principles, which were the worthy object of systematic human study. It was above all this enlightened faith in an ultimately beneficent divinely created natural order, otherwise known as "physico-theology," that was shaken by the Lisbon earthquake; and it was around this calamity that the modern concept of "natural disaster" began to crystallize.

Coinciding with, and contributing to, the rapid expansion of the publishing industry in the mid-eighteenth century, this terrestrial upheaval was also the first eco-catastrophe in history to become a transnational media sensation. Hundreds of tracts in almost every European language were published and republished for several years following the quake. Among these publications were eyewitness accounts, sermons, philosophical reflections, scientific disquisitions, fanciful tales, and a great deal of largely pretty awful poetry.[8] Within the widening public sphere that was

constitutive of the European Enlightenment, responses varied significantly. For more orthodox Christians, the Lisbon disaster offered a welcome opportunity to reassert the association between moral and natural
evils, which had been losing favor, at least among the intelligentsia, in the
previous decades.

Johann Gottlob Krüger, for example, a Prussian academician and professor of medicine and philosophy at Helmstedt University, asserted in
his moral observations on the "causes of the earthquake" of 1756 that "all
reasonable people consider the fall of Lisbon to be a story in which God
played the leading role."[9] The very fact that Krüger felt called upon to re-
affirm his faith in an interventionist and punitive deity in this context indicates, however, that this structure of belief could no longer be taken for
granted. Among those who shared this older interpretive schema, moreover, Catholics and Protestants were divided as to the intended target of
the Almighty's wrath. Protestants generally pointed the finger at the power
of the clergy, the superstitious beliefs and practices that they encouraged
in their benighted flock, and, above all, the cruelty and injustice of the
Lisbon-based Inquisition. Catholics, by contrast, were more likely to pin
the blame on the general immorality and faithlessness that had prolifer-
ated along with the worldly wealth of this bustling trading port, in which
largely Protestant Dutch and British merchants did lucrative business.
However, not all Catholics and Protestants even agreed among themselves
as to the precise moral evils that had called down God's wrath upon this
particular city.[10] While the French Catholic Jansenists joined Protestants
in targeting the Inquisition, Portuguese Jesuits, who were responsible for
overseeing its operations, countered that the problem was rather that the
Inquisition had grown too lax.[11]

As had perhaps always been the case, the punishment paradigm also
afforded the opportunity for forms of social criticism that challenged oppressive practices. On the Protestant side, for example, one English pastor
was inspired to highlight the crimes of colonialism, proclaiming, "Think,
O Spain, O Portugal, of the millions of poor Indians that your forefathers
butchered for the sake of gold."[12] Krüger himself took the more conventional Protestant view that it was the "more than satanic misanthropy"
of the Inquisition that really set Lisbon apart.[13] Not unlike the founder of
English Methodism, John Wesley, in his widely circulated sermon "The Late
Earthquake at Lisbon,"[14] Krüger nonetheless cautions that other big cities
were also at risk as a consequence of the vices that they bred, among which
he numbers greed, gambling, deceit, carousing, debauchery, and atheism.

At pains to reconcile this catastrophe with his earlier treatise on the revelation of God in the beauty and magnificence of Nature (*Naturlehre*, 1750), he also gives consideration to the physical causes of earthquakes and argues that God's strategic deployment of the subterranean gases that the science of the day held responsible for both earthquakes and volcanoes, which, as he put it, "stood ready for attack," awaiting "their orders" from on high, actually displayed His infinite mercy, along with His might: the ruination of Lisbon was but a tiny foretaste of what was to come and afforded survivors and witnesses the opportunity to repent and reform their ways before they met their Maker on the great Judgment Day.[15]

This mythico-religious interpretive schema, which, as in the case of Krüger, was often conjoined with scientific explanations, appears to have retained widespread popular appeal for at least another century.[16] It was given a considerable boost by the Protestant revivalist movements of the latter part of the eighteenth century and continues to inform some strands of US-style Evangelical Christianity to this day. The fate of the Italian Jesuit priest Gabriel Malagrida, however, is indicative of the increasing intolerance toward the punishment paradigm that developed among European elites in the wake of the Lisbon earthquake. The purportedly miracle-working Malagrida was among the most persuasive of those divines who questioned the reconstruction of Lisbon, urging instead prayer and penitence, scourging and fasting, in pious preparation for the Millennium. In particular, he attacked the Marquis de Pombal, the Portuguese chief minister, whose response to the catastrophe is considered an early model of successful state-directed reconstruction.[17] Having swiftly organized the disposal of corpses at sea to prevent an outbreak of the plague, established camps for the homeless and centers for the distribution of food and clean water, and ordered militia to prevent looting, the pragmatic Pombal had now turned his attention to rebuilding the city along modern lines. In the immediate aftermath of the earthquake, Pombal had worked closely and cooperatively with the Cardinal Patriarch, and it was the Catholic clergy, acting under his direction, who ensured the speedy disposal of the dead. In his pioneering historical account of the Lisbon earthquake and its aftermath from 1956, T. D. Kendrick praises the "magnificent work of the religious orders," citing evidence that many ordinary parish priests acted with "bravery and devotion," continuing as best they could to minister to their parishioners "in conditions of great danger and terrifying confusion."[18] By 1758, however, an ideational fissure had opened between Pombal and some of the Jesuits in particular, regarding both the interpretation of the disaster and how best to respond. As Susan Neiman succinctly characterizes this division: "Pombal wished to save citizens from sickness and famine; Malagrida wished to save souls from hell. Each worked under the shadow of a ticking clock."[19] In September 1758, an assassination attempt on King José gave Pombal the opportunity he had been waiting for, and Malagrida and other leading Jesuits were arrested on trumped-up charges. Several clerics were executed outright, Malagrida was strangled and his body burned following his trial in 1760, and the whole order was subsequently sent into exile and their property confiscated by the crown. Meanwhile, in 1758, Pombal had given permission for a daylong auto-da-fé in the center of Lisbon, thereby satisfying popular pressure for a cleansing sacrifice of sinners at the same time that he moved decisively to marginalize the influence of the church in public life.[20]

Neiman's conclusion that this signaled "the end of a form of explanation" is overstated, but the historical tendency that she discerns is incontrovertible: "After Lisbon, even relatively conservative Western cultures were no longer willing to tolerate God's hand in their daily affairs."[21] In today's liberal democracies, those Christian fundamentalists who attribute earthquakes and other geophysical extremes to divine wrath against such alleged vices as legalized abortion and gay marriage are allowed to speak their mind; but they are not given much of a hearing. On both counts, I believe, we can be profoundly grateful. However, the fact that since Lisbon, as Neiman puts it, "natural evils no longer have any seemly relation to moral evils"[22] has its own disastrous consequences, which now need to be confronted in turn.

The advancing interpretative schema, against which Malagrida and company were fighting a losing battle, was that articulated by the young Immanuel Kant (1724–1804), then a little-known private scholar, in a series of letters to the Königsberg press in 1756.[23] Foreshadowing his later insistence on the inevitable limits of human knowledge in his *Critique of Pure Reason* (1787), Kant argued that it was profoundly hubristic for any mere mortal to claim to have divined God's intentions by identifying the target of His presumed disfavor. In an early instance of the way that modern media renders us susceptible to the ethical call of far distant others, he maintained that, as Christians, our duty was to act with compassion toward the victims of such calamities, not to add insult to injury by speculating on how they might have incurred God's wrath.[24] As rational beings, Kant argued, we should nonetheless endeavor to comprehend the physical

causes and effects of earthquakes as natural phenomena. Having brack-
eted the possibility of divine intervention, Kant homes in on the quest for
rational understanding as the primary focus of his considerations.

In this, the Königsberg scholar was by no means alone. Reflection upon
the physical causes of extreme events in nature dates back to Greco-Roman
antiquity in Western culture, and following the Scientific Revolution of
the seventeenth century, such reflections were increasingly underpinned
by systematic empirical research. Scientific interest in the material causes
of earthquakes was spurred on by the tremors that were felt in London in
1750 and elsewhere in Europe the following year.[25] But it was the Lisbon
disaster that really catalyzed the development of seismology, beginning
with John Michell's *Conjectures concerning the Cause, and Observations upon
the Phaenomena of Earthquakes* of 1760. A professor of geology at Cambridge University, Michell developed a method for determining where
earthquakes originated that enabled him to correctly identify the source
of the Lisbon quake in the eastern Atlantic, leading him to be regarded as
one of the "fathers" of seismology.[26]

With this quest for greater knowledge of causation came the desire
for enhanced control. For many inheritors of Francis Bacon's "new organ
of knowledge," as ecofeminist historian Carolyn Merchant has demonstrated, the primary purpose of scientific investigation was assumed to be
the expansion of the empire of man, ultimately to the far reaches of the
universe.[27] On this point, however, Kant issues a noteworthy word of caution. Assuming that earthquakes, like volcanoes, were caused by a buildup
of flammable gases in the earth's interior, some adventurous naturalists,
including Benjamin Franklin, whom Kant refers to as the "Prometheus
of modern times," recommended boring through the earth's crust to release the pressure in a controlled manner. In Kant's view, such fantasies
of geo-engineering were testimony to the disproportion between human
ambitions and abilities, which time and again engender unintended consequences and the humbling recollection that we are, after all, merely
human.[28]

Kant's highly nuanced take on the Lisbon earthquake in these essays
bears a distinct trace of the metaphysical optimism in which he had been
schooled. His recently published astronomical treatise (*Allgemeine Natur-
geschichte und Theorie des Himmels*, 1750) includes quotes from Alexander Pope's influential *Essay on Man* (1733) as mottos for each of its three
sections. Despite its homocentric title, Pope's famous work of physico-

theology in verse is actually a celebration of divine Providence as manifest in the physical world of Nature, not all of which was yet, nor perhaps ever could be, fully comprehended by human reason. In Pope's words:

> Who finds not Providence all good and wise,
> Alike in what it gives, and what denies?
> . . . .
> All Nature is but Art, unknown to thee;
> All Chance, Direction which thou canst not see;
> All Discord, Harmony, not understood;
> All partial Evil, universal Good:
> And, in spite of Pride, in erring Reason's spite,
> One truth is clear, "WHATEVER IS, IS RIGHT."[29]

In accordance with this physico-theological faith, Kant ponders whether the processes that cause earthquakes might not also assist in the formation of valuable ores in the earth's crust and minerals in the soil, which, perhaps in conjunction with sources of subterranean warmth, fosters the growth of plants. Even when its manifestations are sometimes troublesome to us, we should be thankful for the God-given "economy of natural riches," Kant reasons, recalling that we are merely a part of Nature, not its whole purpose. Instead of trying to bend Nature to our will, he insists, we should endeavor to conform ourselves to its ways. Preempting current research on disaster mitigation, Kant therefore recommends such adaptive measures as not building cities in quake-prone areas or, if that is unavoidable, doing so in such as way as to minimize injuries. As an example of such a practice, Kant refers to the Peruvians, who, he says, restrict their houses to two stories at most and use reeds for roofing, which are likely to cause less damage to those below should they fall than did the heavy timber and stone ceilings in the center of Lisbon.[30]

Whereas Kant's essays testify to his continued confidence in creation as "a worthy matter [or object: *Gegenstand*] of divine wisdom and ordinance,"[31] the far more famous ode published by the older French philosopher Voltaire (1694–1778) in the same year totally repudiates the metaphysical optimism that he too had formerly shared. In his "Poème sur le désastre de Lisbonne," subtitled "Examen de cet axiome: 'Tout est bien'" (An examination of the axiom: "All is well"), Voltaire focuses on the unwarranted human suffering caused by the earthquake, which, in his view, obliges us to acknowledge the persistent prevalence of evil in the natural world: "Il le faut avouer, le mal est sur la terre" ("We must acknowledge that evil is in the world/on the earth"). In dismissing physico-theology, Voltaire drives a rationalist wedge between God and Nature and between Nature and Man: since "Nature is mute," meaning and morality must be confined to the exclusively human realm. While in its revised form the ode ends with the hopeful affirmation, "One day all will be well," the implication is that this will only come about if and when the earth is thoroughly humanized.[32] Stripped of any lingering traces of the divine, denied both communicative capability and ethical considerability, other-than-human nature would henceforth be handed over to scientific knowledge, technological control, and economic exploitation, while the emergent "humanities" were to confine themselves to the exclusively human domain of culture: the epistemological and ontological divide structuring what Michel Serres terms the Modern Constitution was framed amid the rubble of Lisbon.

Voltaire's aggressively anthropocentric take on the quake did not go unchallenged, however. Among its most renowned critics was the Swiss-born philosophe Jean-Jacques Rousseau (1712–1778). In a lengthy letter to Voltaire of August 18, 1756, which was published in 1759, Rousseau foregrounds the role of sociocultural factors in exacerbating the Lisbon catastrophe. At the same time, he endeavors to defend the inherent rationality and ultimate goodness of the laws of nature, not all of which, he stressed, were understood. In his analysis, the optimist's assertion "all is well" or "good" (*bien*) should be taken to mean, not that everything (*tout*) is wholly good, but that the whole (*le tout*) is good. Thus, for example, while my own death might well be experienced by me and those who love me as an evil, Rousseau reasons, this is a necessary evil that ultimately serves the good: for in becoming food for other creatures, my body in death fertilizes the earth and thereby contributes to the continuation of life. Death, from this perspective, is in truth a gift. The counterpart of Rousseau's materialist reconceptualization of the afterlife is a sociopolitical corrective to the assumption that nature was entirely to blame for the Lisbon disaster. In his analysis, the earthquake only had such a catastrophic impact because it occurred so close to a city where around twenty thousand houses of six to seven stories were packed tightly together and from whence, moreover, many occupants were reportedly initially reluctant to flee, evidently valuing their material possessions more highly than their lives. This was, moreover, a wealthy European city: earthquakes also occur in deserts, Rousseau observes, but these are not viewed as newsworthy because they do not affect an urban elite. In addition, he joins Kant in opining that the inhabitants of such climes were generally less vulnerable to earthquakes in that they were less encumbered by possessions in their flight, and their habitations tended to cause less damage when they fell.[33]

Rousseau's rebuttal of Voltaire's refutation of metaphysical optimism has been described as the first social scientific view of what would later be termed a "natural disaster" and an early attempt to conceptualize vulnerability.[34] Voltaire might also have supported the endeavor to reduce human vulnerability in the face of natural hazards, but he was unimpressed by Rousseau's defense of the underlying goodness of the natural world overall. In his later work *Candide* (1759), it is in Lisbon in the wake of the quake, while being flogged at the hands of the church on the grounds of having "listened with an air of approval" to his Leibnizian tutor Pangloss's disquisition on the necessity of "the fall of Man" to this "best of all possible worlds," that Voltaire's long-suffering protagonist finally rebels. While Pangloss is being executed, and he himself is "weltering in blood and trembling with fear and confusion," Candide wonders ruefully, "If this is the best of all possible worlds . . . what can the rest be like?"[35] Voltaire's construction of the relationship between humans and their earthly environs, which is no longer triangulated, as it was for the youthful Kant, by reference to God, is not wholly adversarial: the final words of this satirical novella, at any rate, imply an ethos of "cultivation" (*il faut cultiver notre jardin*) rather than all-out conquest. As Nigel Clark observes, the expulsion of moral significance from nature, which defines Voltaire's influential response to the Lisbon earthquake, nonetheless leaves humanity "unmoored and prone to being blown all over the place by vast, brutal and untameable forces." Herein lies the "wider 'dis-aster' of Lisbon: not only the falling away of firm ground under foot, but the loss of a divine guiding star."[36]

This double disaster also came back to haunt Kant in his later work, surfacing in his "Analytic of the Sublime" in the *Critique of Judgement* (*Kritik der Urteilskraft*, 1790). Here, earthquakes are referred to along with other awesome natural phenomena as prompting the human subject to realize his moral freedom as something that transcends, and is opposed to, the violence of the elements. For the older Kant, then, it is the recognition of human moral superiority in the face of those merely mechanistic material forces that could destroy our physical existence, not nature itself, which qualifies as "sublime." As Gene Ray observes, Kant neutralizes the "threat posed to a myth of progress grounded in natural law and a purported human nature" by "re-describing the feeling of the sublime as the subordination of sensible nature *in toto* to the suprasensible power or capacity of human nature. Through the power of reason and its moral law, the great evil of natural catastrophe is elevated, transfigured and 'sublimed' into a foil for human dignity."[37] Whereas he had previously recommended human accommodation to natural contingencies, the implication of Kant's mature philosophy appears to endorse the acquisition of scientific knowledge and the technologies that it enables to remake nature, with a view to preserving human freedom, without which, he proclaims, "all of creation would be mere wasteland, gratuitous, and without final purpose."[38]

While the historical transition that I have been tracing here was rather messier, more gradual, and less total than talk of "turning points" tends to suggest,[39] the rationalistic conviction that "nonhuman nature should have no direct bearing on the ethical, political or cultural strivings of human agents"[40] certainly gained ground after Lisbon, at least among the educated elite. The withdrawal of moral significance from the physical world that was entailed in this epochal shift did not go uncontested, however. In particular, it was resisted by those philosophers and writers of the Romantic period who were inspired in various ways and to different degrees by the counter- or alter-modern impulses of the radical enlightenment. Among the most salient of these were Baruch Spinoza's scandalously unorthodox alignment of God and Nature and his ethics of relational self-realization; Lord Shaftesbury's "System of all things" and advocacy of the wild order of natural places, unspoiled by human conceit and caprice; Rousseau's vision of human emancipation in consort with, rather than in opposition to, our contingent creatureliness; and Johann Gottfried Herder's repositioning of human history and cultural development within the wider history of the earth and its geographically diverse regions.

The cultural phenomenon that has become known as Romanticism was far from homogenous, so any summary statements of the Romantics' "view of nature" are liable to be refuted in particular cases.[41] In general, however, the European Romantics no longer perceived the natural world, as did Pope and Leibniz, as a hierarchically ordered, stable, and harmonious whole, even though some still held to the view that it was in some way divinely authored. Emerging evidence from various fields of natural history, including the study of rock strata and the fossilized bones of extinct animals, in conjunction with the shock of the Lisbon earthquake, contributed to a new appreciation of the earth as both inconceivably ancient and unsettlingly volatile. The examination of weird phenomena such as chemical reactions, magnetism, and electricity pointed to the liveliness of matter and raised questions about the hard and fast distinction between the animate and inanimate. Rather than constituting a fixed set of entities, Nature began to be reconceived as a dynamic process of temporal unfolding, in and through which all manner of things, including human lives and cultures, have been and are being variously interwoven and unstitched. Moreover, for these early "vital materialists" the nonhuman beings and processes with which humans inevitably find themselves interacting, and, in some cases, interdependent, were no longer assumed to be merely mechanical and devoid of moral significance.[42] Running counter to the hierarchical dualisms of mind and body, spirit and matter, culture and nature that frame the Modern Constitution, this kind of relational thinking also informs the treatment of eco-catastrophe in much Romantic literature. In the remainder of this chapter, I want to consider one such work: Heinrich von Kleist's novella "The Earthquake in Chile" ("Das Erdbeben in Chile," 1806). Although written some fifty years after the event and set in Santiago in May 1647 rather than Lisbon in November 1755, this is without doubt the most important Romantic-era literary narrative to have been generated by the theological, epistemological, ontological, and ethical aftershock of the disaster in Portugal.

Kleist's stature as one of Germany's greatest writers is evidenced not only in the voluminous secondary literature on his work but also in the prestigious literary prize named in his honor, first awarded in 1912, the centenary of his death. During his short lifetime, however, Kleist's success was decidedly limited, and he gained notoriety primarily for his suicide pact with the terminally ill Henriette Vogel, whom he shot dead before killing himself on the shores of the popular Kleiner Wannsee near Berlin in November 1812. Born in 1777 into a Prussian military family that had produced no fewer than eighteen generals, he was inducted into the new thinking of the French Enlightenment by his tutor of French Huguenot extraction, Samuel Henri Catel. After a compulsory stint in the army, he set out at age twenty-two to compose his own life's story, unshackled (at least in theory) from hereditary expectations. Having studied law and philosophy at the university in his hometown of Frankfurt an der Oder, he secured a post in the Prussian civil service and became engaged to the eminently suitable Wilhelmine von Zenge, a Prussian general's daughter. No wedding ensued, however, and he never settled into his official role, embarking instead on what might be described as a series of lifestyle experiments, involving a considerable degree of itinerancy and frequently interrupted by mishap. These experiments included a short-lived attempt at Rousseauian renaturalization on the Swiss island of Thun (where he wrote his first play, a Shakespearean tragedy called *Die Familie Schroffen-stein*) in 1801; a bizarre bid to join Napoleon's forces as they embarked for battle with Britain on the French coast in 1803; and a spell in a French prison, following his arrest in 1807, under suspicion of espionage, outside Dresden, then occupied by Napoleon's triumphant troops (which inspired one of his most famous short stories, "Die Marquise von O."). On his release from Fort Joux the following year, Kleist launched a literary journal, *Phöbus,* in Dresden with his friend Adam Müller, which flourished only briefly. After further travels to Austria and Prague, he then founded Berlin's first daily newspaper, *Die Berliner Abendblätter,* in 1810, which ran into so much trouble with the censors that it was forced to fold the following year. Along the way, he nonetheless produced a highly significant literary oeuvre, first published as a whole by the younger Romantic Ludwig Tieck in 1826 and including letters, essays, aphorisms, anecdotes, novellas, and plays, only one of which was staged during his lifetime (by no less a director than Goethe in the court theater in Weimar), but that are now considered the most important dramatic works of German Romanticism (excluding those of Goethe himself, whose relationship to the German Romantics, including Kleist, was extremely vexed).

The defeat of the Prussian army in the battle of Jena in 1806, which led to the dismantling of the Holy Roman Empire of the German Nation, was one of the two great traumas of Kleist's life, precipitating him into a fit of patriotism, during which he wrote the bloodthirsty drama *Die Hermann-schlacht* (*The Battle of the Teutoburg Forest,* 1808), beloved (if ill understood) by the Nazis. The other, intellectually and artistically far more productive trauma was his so-called Kant crisis of 1801. This was prompted by his assumption that the inevitable limits of human knowledge, as disclosed by Kantian criticism—that is to say, the withdrawal of "things in themselves," including our own abyssal subjectivity, from our cognitive grasp—put paid to his earlier plan of leading a wholly self-determined existence, based on a true understanding of reality and a firm moral foundation. The elusiveness of the truth, our own strangeness to ourselves, and the unpredictability of the consequences of our actions in a world of myriad interconnected contingences and interactive agencies: such are the concerns that haunt all of Kleist's mature writing and that evidently motivated his interest in the Lisbon disaster in particular.

When Kleist first offered this story for publication, together with a number of others, he subtitled his collection "moralische Erzählungen" (moral tales). With this designation (which was subsequently dropped),

Kleist placed his work in the French tradition of *contes moreaux* and per-haps specifically the subgenre of *contes philosophique,* of which *Candide* is the most famous exemplar.[43] However, whereas Voltaire uses narrative to mount a philosophical argument by literary means, Kleist's writing is insis-tently interrogative, using narrative to explore the very process of meaning making. This is a story about storytelling: about the use of narrative to make sense of an occurrence in ways that have critical implications for action. For what "The Earthquake in Chile" makes abundantly clear is that the ways in which human beings are likely to respond in the face of a cata-strophic event are conditioned, among other things, by the meanings that they attribute to it on the basis of inherited cultural narratives. In so doing, Kleist's novella clearly queries earlier notions of divine intervention. What has not been adequately remarked, however, is how this text also prob-lematizes the emergent concept of natural disaster.

In crafting this complex text, Kleist evidently drew upon a short story attributed to a certain Friedrich Theodor Neverman and entitled "Alonzo und Elvira; oder, Das Erdbeben von Lissabon." Published in Hamburg in 1795, Neverman's narrative is itself based on an allegedly true story that was separately recounted in two German weekly magazines, *Der Freund* and *Der Bienenstock,* in 1756.[44] This tale was one among several hundred sensationalized "event reports" sold cheaply in pamphlet form on streets throughout Europe following the Lisbon quake, centered on bizarre oc-currences involving one or more individuals.[45] It is with just such a strange contingency, albeit related in an exaggeratedly dispassionate style, that Kleist's disaster narrative begins: "In Santiago, the capital of the kingdom of Chile, at the moment of the great earthquake of 1647 in which so many thousands lost their lives, a young Spaniard called Jerónimo Rugera was standing beside one of the pillars in the prison in which he had been com-mitted on a criminal charge, and was about to hang himself."[46] Teasingly leaving the reader hanging with regard to what happened next, the narra-tor proceeds to recount, in a highly economical if significantly less dispas-sionate manner, how Jerónimo had been brought to this sorry pass. The story is the familiar one of forbidden love between a low-ranking tutor and his high-ranking pupil, which had become a touchstone for Kleist's gener-ation, following Rousseau's retelling of the medieval epic in the guise of a proto-Romantic manifesto of free love in *Julie, ou la nouvelle Éloise* (1764). Not only the plot but also the narrative perspective is emphatically Rous-seauian: in referring to the "malicious vigilance" of the heroine's "proud brother," who alerted their "old father" to this unseemly liaison (*EiC,* 51), the narrator seeks to engage the reader's sympathy for the lovers in opposition the prevailing social order that disallows their union.

In characteristically Kleistian manner, though, the conventionalized storyline is radicalized, as the secret tryst between the romantic hero and his beloved, Josefa, in the garden of the convent to which she had been banished by her indignant father, results not merely in an illegitimate pregnancy but in the scandalous spectacle of a nun collapsing in birth pangs on the cathedral steps in the midst of a Corpus Christi day procession. Both the guilty parties were consequently imprisoned, and, in accordance with convent law, Josefa was condemned to death at the stake. At the moment when the earthquake struck, then, Josefa was being led to her execution—albeit by beheading rather than burning, thanks to the viceroy's accession to the entreaties of her family and the abbess, "a decision," we are told, "which greatly outraged the matrons and virgins of Santiago" (*EiC*, 52).

The collective calamity of the quake is thus preceded by, and becomes entangled with, the personal, if nonetheless very public, disaster of the young nun's doubly illegitimate pregnancy. From the perspective of the pious townsfolk, this disaster too is sourced primarily in nature, to the extent that the lovers are deemed to have been unable to resist the evil promptings of their fallen flesh. From the lovers' more Rousseauian perspective, by contrast, this calamity is wholly social in origin, arising from the evils of a nature-denying, life-defeating civilization that prohibits love marriage across class lines. This view is apparently endorsed by the narrator. But by pitching these perspectives against one another, the text implicitly opens up a third possibility, according to which the problem lies neither in "nature" nor in "culture" per se, but in a contingent failure of mediation between bodily urges and social norms, feelings and morals. At the same time, we are alerted to the possibility of an instinctual element manifesting itself in a particularly malign manner among those most eager to uphold the social order: for, at the time that the quake struck, the bloody "spectacle about to be offered to divine vengeance" was eagerly being awaited by "the pious daughters of the city," as the narrator puts it with psychologically astute and socially critical irony, who were planning to watch it "in sisterly companionship" from the rooftops that had been rented out for occasion (*EiC*, 52).

Josefa's execution and Jerónimo's suicide are both interrupted by the earthquake, which not only saves the lovers' lives but also effects their reunion, in company with their baby boy, Felipe, in the countryside, which has survived unscathed the jolt that laid low the town. Jerónimo's escape is initially framed by the narrator as a matter of "chance": the complete destruction of the prison in which he was confined was fortuitously prevented by the "slow fall" of the building opposite, while a gap was torn in the front wall, through which the hero "slid" to his freedom, propelled willy-nilly back into life by an upheaval emanating from the very womb of the earth. His life is thus restored to him by means of a symbolic rebirth that releases him from subjection to a death-dealing society and transforms him, as it were, into a free child of *terra mater*. In the "midst of this general doom" all thoughts of suicide are driven from his mind, and he is propelled, "panic-stricken," by what looks very much like an unconscious survival instinct, the promptings of his own "inner nature," to the relative safety of the open land beyond the city gates (*EiC*, 53). Finding himself alive and unscathed in the "fertile surroundings of Santiago," he "thanked God" for what is now termed his "miraculous escape," weeping "with rapture to find that the blessing of life, in all its wealth and variety, was still his to enjoy" (54). This newly discovered delight in corporeal existence is nonetheless quickly dampened when he recalls Josefa, and, having received a false eyewitness report from a woman who claims she saw her hang before the quake struck, Jerónimo "wished that the destructive fury of nature might unleash itself on him once more" (54).

Two things are important to note here. First, much of the narrative discourse is focalized through the protagonists. Because this is rarely made explicit, though, it is unclear whether particular statements or descriptions reflect their perspective or that of the narrator, which, as already observed, is at times strongly biased and at others markedly dispassionate, leading one eminent Kleist scholar to conclude that there are actually two distinct narrative voices in play in this tricksterish text.[47] Second, the effects of the earthquake are attributed to God when they are felt to have favored Jerónimo, but to "nature" when they are assumed to have failed to save Josefa. Accordingly, when Jerónimo subsequently stumbles upon Josefa bathing Felipe beside a stream, God rather than nature is once again invoked as the perceived agent of the earthquake: "With what ecstasy they embraced, the unhappy pair, saved by a divine miracle!" (*EiC*, 55).

The following account of Josefa's escape with Felipe seems to lend weight to the idea that this was something other than simply fortuitous. Having dashed back to the convent to rescue her son, she is at first said to have emerged from the burning building with Felipe "as if protected by all the angels in heaven" (*EiC*, 55). But when mother and child also narrowly escape being hit by the falling gable that ignominiously kills the abbess, "together with nearly all her nuns," the subjunctive "as if" modulates into the confident assertion that it was indeed "heaven" that had restored to Josefa her "beloved son" (56). By contrast, all those representatives of the social order that had condemned the lovers seem to have been singled out for special punishment. As she flees the city, Josefa encounters "the mangled body of the Archbishop, which had just been dragged from the wreckage of the cathedral." In addition, the "Viceroy's palace had collapsed, the law court in which sentence had been passed on her was in flames, and in the place where her father's house had stood there was now a seething lake from which reddish vapours were rising" (56).

Assuming that the earthquake was divinely ordained, then, it appears that God's vengeance was directed against the social order that claimed to be acting in His name in its repressive regimentation of desire, rather than against the lovers who had flouted its conventions. However, when it is hinted that this whole description of the ruination of Santiago's ancien régime, narrated in the third person, follows Josefa's first-person account ("All this, in a voice filled with emotion, she now told Jerónimo" [EiC, 57]), the reader is subtly alerted to the possibility that this description of the impact of the earthquake might be no less skewed than that of the anonymous eyewitness who reported Josefa definitively dead. And if this is Josefa's account, it could be seen to betray an unacknowledged desire to see her enemies laid low that is uncomfortably reminiscent of the vengefulness and Blutlust previously attributed to Santiago's pious womenfolk.

This ever-so-subtle distancing of the implied authorial stance from that of the protagonists is taken to the brink of outright parody when the narrator subsequently observes that "it moved them greatly to think how much misery had to afflict the world in order to bring about their happiness" (EiC, 57). The intertextual referent here is twofold. Most obviously, this passage echoes the ever more absurd efforts of Voltaire's fictional philosopher Pangloss to demonstrate to his ill-fated pupil Candide that everything is "for the best" in this "best of all possible worlds." At the same time, the lovers' outrageously self-aggrandizing interpretation of the catastrophe as orchestrated to serve their interests alone necessarily also invokes the discourse of metaphysical optimism that is the target of Voltaire's popular satire of 1759.

Kleist's narrative does not unequivocally endorse Voltaire's moral humanism, however. On the contrary, at this point in the plot, the text appears to draw closer to Rousseau's counterposition. In keeping with the physico-theological orientation of the Rousseauian view, the middle section of Kleist's narrative shows how the destruction of Santiago, interrupting the workings of what is portrayed as a patently corrupt and oppressive social system, has facilitated the recovery of a beneficent naturality, both inner and outer, individual and collective, with the valley in which the lovers are reunited being cast as a veritable paradise regained. Whereas at first we are told that Josefa's joy is such that, for her, this "might have been the Garden of Eden," the following description seamlessly assimilates the physical environment to this mythical paradigm, once again turning an "as if" statement into an actuality: "In the meantime the loveliest of nights had fallen, wonderfully mild and fragrant, silvery and still, a night such as only a poet might dream of" (*EiC*, 57). While other survivors are said to be "preparing their beds of moss and foliage" and lamenting their loss, Jerónimo and Josefa slip away to revel in their joy in a "denser part of the wood," beneath a "pomegranate tree, its outspread branches heavy with scented fruit, and high on its crest the nightingale piped its voluptuous song" (57). The cloyingly sensuous language of this description serves to link the collapse, or at least suspension, of the old social order with the liberation of eros, as implicit in the symbolic association of the pomegranate with Aphrodite. Moreover, the following passage implies that on a collective level the "return to nature" is conducive also to a recovery of compassion, or (in the language of the New Testament) agape: that radically self-giving kindness to strangers that is proclaimed by all the world's major religions and exemplified in the Bible in the troublesome Jew Jesus's parable of the Good Samaritan (Luke 10:25–37).

The materiality of this model of neighbor-love is rendered emblematically in Kleist's narrative by the bodily gift of her lactating breasts that Josefa makes to another couple's child in response to a request from a young man whom she initially assumes to be a stranger. Discovering that he is in fact a family acquaintance, the formerly persecuted lovers find themselves readmitted to society, or at any rate, accepted without question into the midst of Don Fernando's noble party. Considering themselves doubly blessed, Josefa "had a feeling, which she could not suppress, that the preceding day, despite all the misery it had brought upon the world, had been a mercy such as heaven had never yet bestowed on her" (*EiC*, 59–60). There is once again a distinct hint of parody in this hubristic reading of events. But it is followed by a description that reveals how the earthquake had apparently been not only liberating for the lovers but salutary for the society as a whole:

And indeed, in the midst of this horrifying time in which all the earthly possessions of men were perishing and all nature was in danger of being engulfed, the human spirit itself seemed to unfold like the fairest of flowers. In the fields, as far as the eye could see, men and women of every social station could be seen lying side by side, princes and beggars, ladies and peasant women, government officials and day labourers, friars and nuns: pitying one another, helping one another, gladly sharing anything they had saved to keep themselves alive, as if the general disaster had united all its survivors into a single family. (60)

The watery connotations of the verbal construction, "being engulfed,"[48] recall not only the historical flood that accompanied both the Lisbon and Santiago earthquakes but also the biblical deluge: that mythic archetype of redemptive violence that had recently returned in secularized guise in the utopian imaginary of the French Revolution. For Kleist's generation, however, this political earthquake, as it was sometimes termed, had not culminated in the enduring triumph of the kind of *liberté, egalité,* and *fraternité* imaged here as the fruit of a literal earthquake, but in the bloodbath of the Terror and the dictatorship of the imperialistic Napoleon Bonaparte (toward whom the Prussian patriot Kleist harbored a particular hatred). Nor is this the end of Kleist's narrative. As it turns out, the plot structure of the stories that are being told around the scattered fireplaces of the survivors in the valley—tales of "extraordinary heroic deeds . . . of fearlessness, of magnanimous contempt for danger, of self-denial and super-human self-sacrifice, of life unhesitatingly cast away as if it were the most trifling of possessions and could be recovered a moment later"—is replicated at the end of "The Earthquake in Chile." However, the "sum of general well-being" (60) that Josefa is, once again, weighing up at this point is ultimately recalibrated at the lovers' expense.

Ironically, the tragic denouement of this twisted tale is precipitated precisely by the lovers' overly optimistic interpretation of the catastrophe, in terms of both the "spirit of reconciliation" (*EiC,* 59) that they perceive it to have engendered and the divine intention that they discern in it. On being reunited, they initially planned to take advantage of the general chaos in order to escape to Spain. Now, though, "the old order of things having undergone such an upheaval," in Jéronimo's assessment, they determine to petition the viceroy for a pardon—albeit, at Josefa's prudent suggestion, from the port of La Conception, thereby enabling them to make a hasty getaway should the appeal fail. First, though, Josefa insists on joining the throng of survivors returning to the one church left standing in the city in order to "cast herself down before her Maker . . . at this time, when His incomprehensible and sublime power was being made so evident" (61). Don Fernando's sister-in-law Donna Elisabeth, who had previously declined a friend's invitation to join her in witnessing Josefa's execution and was clearly concerned that the lovers' reprieve would be short-lived, prudently advises against this pious action; but Josefa is not to be dissuaded. Donna Elisabeth's fears turn out to be well founded. In departing from the "valley of the blessed," the errant couple fall victim to the murderous reconstitution of the old social order, facilitated by a reactionary interpretation of catastrophe. Grotesquely, Josefa's desire to "lay her face in the dust" is realized, but in a way that she did not anticipate.

Not insignificantly, the church in which this occurs is identified as Dominican, the Dominican order having historically been most avid in the persecution of witches in the German region. Subtle allusions to the fiery death to which Josefa too had originally been condemned are encoded in the opening descriptions of the church, where "all the candelabra were blazing with light"; the stained-glass window "burned like the very evening sun"; and a "flame of zeal" rose "to heaven" (*EiC*, 63). In this ominous setting, a sermon is preached likening Santiago to the biblical Sodom and Gomorrah, while the earthquake is construed as an act of divine vengeance against the city, not only for its "moral depravity" (63) in general, but specifically for the "impious" "indulgence" shown to the sinners who had perpetrated such an "outrage" in the convent garden. This rabble-rousing sermon is diametrically opposed to the pacific one preached by the bishop of Santiago, Gaspar de Villaroel, in the service that is documented to have taken place following the historical earthquake in Chile, in which the disaster was construed as a moral test of the community, but not as a punishment.[49] There is, however, a strong echo of Malagrida's take on the Lisbon disaster in Kleist's fictitious sermon, which is delivered by an old canon, or *Chorherr* (choirmaster) in German, a conventional title that is concretized as the preacher leads the choir of voices that call once more for the death of the lovers: "And the whole assembly of Christians in that temple of Jesus raised a cry of 'Stone them! Stone them!'" (65).

Implicitly recalling the biblical narrative in which Jesus intervenes precisely to prevent the stoning of an adulteress (John 8:3–11), the ironic tone of the narrative voice implies an emphatically critical view of the crowd, which becomes ever more pronounced in the course of this climactic scene. Addressed by Jerónimo as "monsters" (*EiC*, 65) and by Josefa as "bloodthirsty tigers" (66), and referred to by Don Fernando as "murderous villains" (65), the crowd is described by the narrator successively as a "furious mob," a "frenzied mob," and "butchers" (65, 66). Among them is Jerónimo's father, who, mimicking the punitive patriarchal violence attributed by the canon to God, surprisingly produces a cudgel—a distinctly odd implement to take to church, one might have thought—with which he slays his own son, along with Don Fernando's other sister-in-law, Donna Constanza, who had been standing beside him and was therefore mistaken for Josefa. The latter now declares her identity, as Jerónimo had done previously, in the hope of ending the fighting, and is murdered by the cobbler, Master Pedrillo, who had formerly worked for her. His "lust for slaughter not yet unsated" (66), this "prince of the satanic rabble" (67), as the congregation are now dubbed by the narrator, proceeds to dash out the brains of Don Fernando's baby boy, Juan, whom Josefa had been nursing and who was therefore mistaken for "her bastard" (66), against one of the pillars of the church. Again, the irony is pointed: the architectural feature that supports a building that is meant to be dedicated to the agapic teaching of Christ, whose crucifixion is considered the sacrifice to end all sacrifice, becomes the means of enacting a reversion to the primitive logic of the scapegoat in what René Girard interprets as a classic instantiation of mimetic violence.[50] In response to this, the bereaved father speechlessly "raised his eyes to heaven in inexpressible anguish" (67).

This gesture of bewilderment and dismay, which both echoes and contrasts with the description of an unknown man whom Jerónimo had previously witnessed during his flight from the city, "speechlessly extending his trembling hands to heaven" (*EiC*, 53), points to the inability of words to encompass so horrific an experience. On the one hand, this very failure of language might be seen to compound the trauma that, in the specific sociocultural context in which it occurred, the earthquake had brought in its wake. On the other hand, Don Fernando's abandonment of speech could also be seen as signaling a suspension of the hermeneutic violence implicit in the attribution of divine intentionality to the earthquake (an attribution that is evidently still in play in the other man's imploring hand gesture). As we have seen, a suspension of just this kind was urged by Kant in his recommendation that instead of hubristically speculating about who might have incurred God's wrath and why, the true Christian calling was to show compassion toward the victims of such calamities and, wherever possible, go to their aid.

In a final narrative twist, it is with precisely such an act of self-giving love that Kleist's narrative concludes. After a period of estrangement, Don Fernando's wife, Donna Elvira, is reconciled with her husband, whose reckless heroism had caused the death of their child, and together they adopt "the little stranger as their own son." The final words of the novella affirm that "when Don Fernando compared Felipe with Juan and the ways in which he had acquired the two of them, it almost seemed to him that he had reason to be glad" (*EiC*, 67). This seemingly redemptive ending nonetheless harbors a number of further ironies and uncertainties. For one thing, having championed the cause of eros throughout, the narrative suddenly seems to be emphatically privileging agape. Or is it? Don Fernando is described as "filled with superhuman heroism" when, with two babies tucked under one arm, he selflessly—and singularly unsuccessfully—seeks to fight off the lynch mob single-handed with the other. However, his earlier eagerness for Josefa to breastfeed his son and subsequent insistence on taking her arm on the way to church, against the protestations of the prudent Donna Elisabeth and his wife, could be read as betraying a certain erotic interest in this scandalously fallen woman. However that might be, and the narrator keeps us guessing, his attempt to put a positive spin on events is so qualified ("almost," "seemed," "as if he ought") as to indicate that his feelings remain profoundly mixed. Nobody's motivations and morals emerge unalloyed from this catastrophe. But, by giving love the last word—a very human kind of love, moreover, in which eros and agape are inextricably entangled—Kleist does allow the reader to discern in the dark and uncertain place to which his twisted tale has taken us a glimmer of hope in the possibility of a less violent future.

In its narrative exploration of a series of sociocultural responses to eco-catastrophe, "The Earthquake in Chile" conforms remarkably closely to the findings of recent disaster studies in the fields of anthropology and sociology. Susanna M. Hoffman, for example, has found that after a short period of "extreme individuation" in which people are "propelled by extreme states of anxiety into self-determined, self-saving actions," such disasters typically engender a sense of "shared humanity," temporarily dissolving social divisions based on religion, class, ethnicity, or race and fostering mutual aid.[51] While the first phase is most powerfully exemplified in "The Earthquake in Chile" in the description of Jerónimo's flight, Kleist also discloses some individual differences of response. Jerónimo is said to apprehend somebody groaning in the rubble, several others screaming from the rooftops of burning buildings, and many people as well as animals struggling in the rising waters of Mapocho River; but he does not stop to join the man whom he witnesses trying to rescue them (*EiC*, 53). Among the stories of bravery, kindness, and heroism told by the survivors, moreover, there are also reports of impromptu executions of suspected looters (59). Nonetheless, the middle section of the narrative could be seen to model the kind of egalitarian community, founded on an ecstatic form of hospitality (the hospitality, that is, of the unhoused), discussed by Rebecca Solnit in *A Paradise Built in Hell*. Michel Serres has speculated that it is precisely the disorder engendered by the periodic violence of the elements that has catalyzed human sociality. Commenting on Serres's notion of a "natural contract," Nigel Clark stresses that this "is not a call to re-embed the social in a stable substrate, but a stipulation that social and communal life always was and always will be responsive to the rumbling of the earth, to the periodic ungrounding of its ground."[52] Serres, however, is by no means the first to make this call: in his "Essay on the Origin of Language" of 1755, Rousseau too speculates about the emergence of human sociality out of the shared experience of earth-induced calamity.[53] Here, too, then, Kleist appears to be treading an optimistically Rousseauian trail, only to diverge from it all the more decisively at the end of his tragic tale.

The triadic structure of the novella both invokes and reverses Rousseau's triadic philosophy of history: whereas the latter traces a trajectory from nature through civilization to nature regained, Kleist's narrative moves from civilization through nature to the reassertion of civilization.[54] As the bloody culmination indicates, the breakdown of social order attending an interruptive event such as this provides a space not only for compassionate actions but also for hysterical reactions, in which kindness toward strangers is displaced by fear and anger, and the rhetoric of divine justice is deployed to legitimate a lynching. This also resonates with contemporary research on the aftermath of disasters, which indicates that the euphoric phase of mutual aid, or "falling together," as Solnit puts it,[55] is often followed by a period of estrangement not only from those who have not experienced the disaster but also among the survivors themselves as prior rules of inequality, alliance, and allegiance resurface, and earlier codes, roles, and expectations overwhelm newfound forms of solidarity. As Hoffman also observes, "Scuffles over 'framing'—whose definition of disaster, victimization, need, and other matters—trail every juncture of disunion."[56] Similarly, in "The Earthquake in Chile," human behavior in the face and aftermath of eco-catastrophe is shown to be variable and volatile and crucially informed by the social relations and cultural frameworks through which the event is experienced.

In thematizing what I have termed elsewhere the "hermeneutics of catastrophe,"[57] Kleist's narrative constitutes an exemplary work of Romantic fiction, conforming to Friedrich Schlegel's definition of "romantic poesy" as containing within itself its own theory of interpretation.[58] In the Romantic era, that which is proclaimed as proper to literature emerges out of the demolition of dogmatism. In my reading, "The Earthquake in Chile" represents a primal scene of the collapse of certainty out of which modern literature as self-reflexive art is born; and it was the earthquake in Lisbon, no less than Kant's *Critique of Pure Reason,* that arguably conditioned this epistemological rupture. Within the space of that rupture, moreover, a literature emerges within which it becomes possible to "think catastrophe," as something that arises from the complex and sometimes chaotic interaction of a diversity of human and nonhuman factors and actants, rather than as something that is either divinely orchestrated, purely natural, or exclusively social in its etiology. The ecocritical implication of my reading of "The Earthquake in Chile" is that we will need to find ways of dismantling the ontological and epistemological divide that has for too long structured the official knowledge systems of industrial modernity—a divide that is subtly subverted in Kleist's skillful work of narrative fiction— if we are to have a chance of negotiating more life-sustaining relations with natural phenomena, both inner and outer, that are never fully knowable and rarely entirely controllable. As I indicate in the final segment of this chapter, some of these phenomena are also capable of responding to our more reckless techno-scientific interventions in ways that are liable to make this lively planet yet more, rather than less, perilous for vulnerable populations, both human and otherwise.

I have taken the title for this chapter from Jonathan Watts's detailed account of the environmental impacts of China's rapid industrialization, *When a Billion Chinese Jump,* where the phrase "moving earth" is used both transitively and intransitively. In the former case, it refers to the monumental feats of earth-moving, along with river damming, entailed in China's enthusiastic embrace of hydro-electricity. In the latter case, it refers to the moving of the earth itself in the massive quake that shook Sichuan on May 12, 2008. As it turns out, however, the two might well be connected. According to some seismologists, the weight of the 320 million tons of water held back by the huge concrete wall of the Zipingpu megadam could have reactivated the Yingxiu-Beichuan fault line above which it had been constructed: "By stilling the water . . . the engineers might have moved the land."[59] Meanwhile, there is now strong evidence that the common practice of pumping wastewater into deep disposal wells drilled into porous rock in the process of coal-seam gas extraction can trigger seismic activity as well.[60] Concerns are also being raised about a potential increase in volcanos, earthquakes, and tsunamis in association with melting ice caps: in warming the atmosphere, we might be triggering changes that will shake the earth.[61] As the inheritors of Michell's quest to comprehend earthquakes have discovered in their research into continental plate tectonics, our planet's crust is constantly on the move. In addition to calling for adjustments in the ways and places in which we build, then, the liveliness of the lithosphere surely enjoins a responsibility to interact with the shifting ground beneath our feet with a considerably higher degree of caution than is manifest in such Promethean feats of geo-engineering as were first contemplated in the wake of the Lisbon earthquake.

2

SPREADING PESTILENCE

One of the primary ways in which different kinds of disaster can be distinguished is in terms of their spatiotemporal coordinates. While all disasters are embedded in longer-term socioecological processes and patterns of vulnerability extending beyond the locality in which they occur, geophysical occurrences such as earthquakes, tsunamis, and tornadoes occur abruptly over a matter of seconds, minutes, or hours, and their immediate impacts are confined to the region affected. The outbreak of a contagious disease with a high morbidity rate, by contrast, constitutes a slow-onset or "creeping" catastrophe, with the potential to afflict human (and in many cases some other-than-human) populations globally.[1] Disease epidemics and, in the worst-case scenario, pandemics also differ from those calamities induced by the liveliness of the lithosphere in the complexity of their etiology. Until very recently, and in most cases presumably still today, earthquakes and volcanoes are not anthropogenic in origin, even though, as we saw in the previous chapter, the eco-catastrophes that they trigger have a strongly sociocultural dimension. Epidemics, by contrast, are hybrid through and through: pestilence spreads, to be sure, and over the past 150 years our understanding of the multiple other-than-human agencies responsible for the proliferation of infectious diseases has grown enormously; but so too have those sociocultural practices through which humans themselves inadvertently spread pestilence across the planet. "In a world of intensifying global interconnectivity," as Nigel Clark observes, "we are multiplying vectors and niches for our microscopic nemeses far faster than we can physiologically or culturally adapt to their exertions."[2]

In this chapter, I will consider how just such a scenario of socioculturally intensified vulnerability to a lethal pandemic was prefigured by Mary Shelley in her apocalyptic novel *The Last Man* (1826), in which the virtual extinction of humankind unfolds, uncannily for today's readers, amid an oddly disordered climate in the closing decades of this century. In the case of an eco-catastrophe involving infectious disease, we are reminded of the vulnerabilities that inhere in our utter dependence upon an unruly biosphere that was not designed for our exclusive benefit. In a contemporary horizon of disease risk, moreover, reducing human susceptibility to contagion cannot be divorced from ethical questions concerning our treatment of other animals.

The term *epidemic* made its way into English from Hippocrates's *On Airs, Waters, and Places* (c. 400 BCE). This is not only the oldest surviving medical treatise in European culture; as its title suggests, it is also an early work of environmental medicine.[3] Composed of the prefix *epi* ("upon, at, or close upon, on the ground or occasion of") and *demos* ("the people"), the word *eipidemiou*, formerly meaning "toward home" or "native," is used in a new sense by Hippocrates in order to relocate the source of disease from the divine to the terrestrial plane. Countering the popular mythic conception of disease as dispatched by the gods, as in the illness that Apollo inflicts on the Achaean army at the beginning of Homer's *Iliad* (c. eighth century BCE), Hippocrates attributed infectious disease to the interaction between people and environment.[4] In his view, human health and sickness were conditioned by material contingencies such as the quality of air, water, and food, along with the vagaries of climate and the constellation of the planets, in their presumed effect on terrestrial flows and bodily "humors." While he believed that some illnesses, which he classified as "endemic," arose entirely from internal humoral imbalances, the outbreak and spread of an "epidemic" disease was conceived by Hippocrates as a type of eco-catastrophe, arising from a baleful conjunction of human corporeal vulnerability and prevailing environmental conditions.

Epidemic appears to have entered English in the fifteenth century from the Middle French *ypidemie,* with the first recorded vernacular usage of this term appearing in a report by Sir John Paston from 1472 concerning the illness that was at that time killing British soldiers on the battle fields of Brittany.[5] Although several other infectious illnesses were rife in Europe in the 1400s, especially in the growing towns and cities, the disease that loomed largest for Paston's contemporaries was the one that had caused incomparable carnage in Europe between 1347 and 1351 and continued to flare up with frightful frequency for the next 350 years. The "Black Death," as it was dubbed in the nineteenth century, is generally believed to have been caused by the bubonic plague. Although the last major outbreak in Western Europe occurred in Marseille in 1720–22, the persistence of plague as the paradigmatic pandemic in European cultural memory is evident in Shelley's naming of the primary agent of humanity's imagined demise in her novel of 1826 as "Plague." In the meantime, the development of antibiotics has, for the moment, transformed this dreaded killer into a treatable disease. The horror of the plague nonetheless continues to resonate in the popular imagination, haunting the Internet and the cinema and prompting authorities to downplay actual occurrences for fear of causing panic.[6]

In the wake of the triumph of the germ theory of disease, the Black Death might be seen as an eco-catastrophe of a somewhat different kind from that which Hippocrates conceived of under the rubric of epidemic, although environmental factors were certainly critical to its spread. Whether or not the primary pathogen in that pandemic was the *Yersinia pestis* bacterium that causes bubonic plague—and there is some debate about this[7]—there is no doubt that one or another of our microbial Earth others was in play. Microbes are believed to have evolved some four billion years ago, and they have played a crucial role in creating, altering, and sustaining that diverse collectivity of multitudinous life forms into which *Homo sapiens* only relatively recently emerged around two hundred thousand years ago. Sociable life on this planet began with microbial networking, and that of all other extant species, including our own, remains utterly dependent upon the lively interchanges of the myriad miniscule critters that not only surround but also dwell within and upon our bodies.[8] This dependence is both diachronic and synchronic, phylogenetic and ontogenetic, collective and individual: our species became what it is today through a process of ongoing evolutionary "symbiogenesis," as Lyn Margulis terms it, with these most ancient of our Earth others.[9] Every human infant, within hours of its birth, is colonized "by swarms of them, all intent on living off this new food source,"[10] and, in the process, providing essential protection to the growing child's skin and gut and helping to build up their immune system. The human body, it turns out, is a queer confederacy: we have, in fact, never been (wholly or exclusively) human. As Donna Haraway delights in informing us:

> Human genomes can only be found in about 10 percent of all the cells that occupy the mundane space that I call my body; the other 90 percent of the cells are filled with the genomes of bacteria, fungi, protists, and such, some of which play in a symphony necessary to my being alive at all, and some of which are hitching a ride and doing the rest of me, of us, no harm. I am vastly outnumbered by my tiny companions; better put, I become an adult human being in company with these tiny messmates. To become one is always to *become with* many.[11]

Yet this world of teeming microbial life within and without, to which our very existence is indebted, can also be the source of our undoing: several of our microbial companions can make us ill, and some are deadly, causing a catastrophic alteration to that most intimate *oikos,* the more-than-human household of the body that we like to imagine is our own. Yet even the most deadly microbes have also helped to form those of us who are alive today: for we are the ones whose forebears not only survived the depredations of past epidemics but also developed a degree of hereditary immunity to particular pathogens, some of which have in turn become less virulent through this ongoing process of symbiogenesis.[12]

The story of humans and microbes, fascinating though it is, is nonetheless only one strand in the epic tale of epidemics, which also entails the dynamic inter- and intra-actions of a whole host of other human and non-human agencies and processes. As Dorothy Crawford explains, "Epidemics strike whenever and wherever microbes find a large susceptible group of people to infect and can successfully forge a path between them."[13] Many such paths were opened up for the first time with the domestication of plants and animals in those parts of the world where farming was developed between 8,500 and 2,500 BCE. Since it enabled the evolution of new pathogens, the agricultural revolution appears to have led to an initial decline in human health and longevity compared with most hunter-gatherer societies (a decline tragically repeated wherever agrarian or industrial invaders have colonized the lands of hunter-gatherers).[14] The subsequent growth of towns and cities, bringing higher population densities, the buildup of refuse, and continuing close contact with some animals, both feral and domesticated, allowed microbes to flourish on a whole new scale. Catastrophic epidemics, along with a variety of endemic illnesses, became thereby a regular feature of human socioecological existence. Particular diseases only reach pandemic proportions, however, when a number of other factors coalesce. In the case of the Black Death, these included the conjunction of military conflict and particular sociocultural norms relating to housing, diet, and trade, with particular climatic conditions, animal and insect population dynamics, and the ever-agile agency of germs.[15]

Assuming, as do the majority of researchers, that the Black Death was in fact a plague pandemic, the story goes something like this. The *Y. pestis* bacterium, first identified in Hong Kong in the early 1900s by a young Swiss microbiologist and student of Louis Pasteur, Alexander Yersin, is a relatively recent pathogen, believed to have evolved between fifteen hundred and twenty thousand years ago, which generally gets around courtesy of fleas. There are around twenty-five hundred different types of flea, but the primary vector of mammalian infection, especially of humans, is *Xenopsylla cheopis*, which makes a living by sucking the blood of a variety of rodents and lagomorphs. Some of these flea hosts, including several of the fifty-odd species of plague carriers in North America, are merrily immune to *Y. pestis* and therefore do a very good job of keeping this particularly nasty pathogen alive and well in the ecosystems they inhabit. Others, however, such as *Rattus rattus*, the black rat, die in agony within days of being infected by a plague-carrying flea. The wee fleas, too, have a rough time of it. *Xenopsylla cheopis* has developed a special valve that allows it to feed several times without loosing the contents of its swelling stomach by allowing liquid in but preventing it from flowing back out. If it has the misfortune to suck the blood of a host infected with *Y. pestis*, however, the proliferating bacteria form a clump around this valve, deactivating its feeding tube. In its vain effort to feed, the flea disgorges the contents of its stomach, which are now likely to include some twenty-five thousand bacteria, into the body of its new host. Eventually, the flea will starve to death, but generally not until it has infected another host, if its prior one has died in the meantime. Infected fleas can wipe out an entire colony of black rats in around ten to fourteen days, and given that each rat is likely to harbor around three fleas, you then have a horde of desperately hungry bloodsuckers frantically looking for a feed. Human blood is definitely second best, but it will do in a crisis, so if there are any warm human bodies close by, as there always were in medieval towns and villages, trading vessels and military encampments, the ravenous fleas will find them. Infected fleas can live for some time without a host, moreover, especially in cool, moist conditions, so ships whose resident rats had been wiped out can still convey the disease to their next port of call, with or without the intermediary of flea-infested and perhaps already infected crew members.

Rattus rattus, for its part, appears to have set forth on its gradual colonization of much of the planet from its ancestral haunts in northern India in the foothills of the Himalayas. From there it spread both east and west by hitching a ride overland and across the sea as a stowaway on the caravans and ships of merchants and armies. Black rats were in North Africa by the end of the first century BCE, but it was several centuries before the first plague pandemic broke out in Europe. This was the Justinian Plague of 542–c.740, which probably originated in Africa and, not unlike the imaginary global pandemic in *The Last Man*, subsequently spread throughout the crumbling Roman Empire from Constantinople, producing an estimated death toll of some one hundred million people. By the Middle Ages, some adventurous black rats had made it all the way up through continental Europe to Britain. Because they are not particularly hardy, though, and are generally happier in the tropics, they could only find an ecological niche in these cooler climes by wintering close to human sources of warmth and shelter, such as thatched roofs, barns, and granaries (which had the added advantage of supplying ready meals). Every cottage acquired a little colony, and in Europe's growing towns and cities, large numbers of rats cohabited at even closer quarters with humans, especially poor ones, whose living conditions were inadequately ventilated, overcrowded, and unsanitary. Apart from their inroads into sometimes scant human food stores, though, this was not so much of a problem unless they became infested with plague-carrying fleas. This was more likely to occur if favorable climatic conditions and ample food supplies had generated a rodent and lagomorph population explosion, in turn causing wild species harboring infected fleas to forage more widely, bringing them into contact with those rats that had happily made a home for themselves among humans. During the Medieval Warm Period, crop yields increased, and by the mid-thirteenth century, human and rodent populations had both burgeoned.

Climate, then, appears to have been a further factor in the fatal triangulation of fleas, rats, and humans that is generally believed to have produced the carnage of the Black Death. But there were also several other ingredients that went into the making of this eco-catastrophe: namely, commerce, conquest, and urbanization. By the mid-thirteenth century, food production was failing to keep up with human population growth in some parts of Europe. As poverty began to rise, rural underemployment contributed toward a drift to the cities. Meanwhile, the constant movement of crusading armies, and, following the end of the Crusades in the late thirteenth century, the increase in trade between Europe and Asia via the Near East, fostered the spread of infectious diseases such as typhoid and smallpox, as well as creating "a virtual flea bridge."[16] These commercial activities were not always peaceful, sometimes occasioning skirmishes between European merchants and the armies of the massive Mongol Empire, which encompassed all of modern China, most of Russia, and much of Central Asia through to Iran and Iraq.

The pandemic of the mid-1400s appears to have broken out in 1346 somewhere in Russia, in the Golden Horde region of the Mongol Empire. From there, *Y. pestis* is believed to have found its way west via the Genoese trading port of Caffa (now Feodosiya) on the Black Sea, to which the

Mongols laid siege in 1347. When disease erupted among their ranks, the Mongol troops retreated, allowing the Italian merchants and their ships to head for home, taking the plague in tow. By the time the first trading vessels arrived in Messina on the coast of Sicily in October that year, many of the men aboard were already sickening. In view of their symptoms, as mysterious as they were unpleasant, the port authorities expelled all the ships' crews, who made for Genoa and Venice. The pestilence then spread swiftly to other trading ports, reaching France via Marseille and North Africa via Tunis by January 1348, penetrating inland along well-trodden trading routes, frequently assisted by people vainly attempting to flee from infection. During the summer, it crossed the Channel and entered England through the port of Melcombe Regis on the south coast. When it reached the amplification zone of London, the disease did away with around twenty to thirty thousand of its sixty to eighty thousand inhabitants. Moving northward at a rate of one to one and a half kilometers per day, it is estimated to have covered the length of England (five hundred kilometers) in around five hundred days.[17] In the meantime, the epidemic was also advancing south down the Iberian Peninsula, north into Scandinavia, and back into Eastern Europe, enveloping the whole continent in just three years. As Barbara Tuchman recalls in her account of "the calamitous fourteenth century": "In a given area, the plague accomplished its kill within four to six months and then faded, except in the larger cities, where, rooting into the close-quartered population, it abated during the winter, only to reappear in spring and rage for another six months."[18] In addition to Europe and North Africa, Asia too fell prey to this unprecedented pandemic, which is believed to have killed a third to a half of the world's population between 1346 and 1353. In parts of Europe, the death toll was even higher, with two-thirds or more of the inhabitants of some towns and villages succumbing. Recurrent outbreaks are believed to have put a brake on population growth for the next three hundred years.

The horror elicited by the Black Death, like the complex etiology of the pandemic itself, was compounded of several elements. For Europeans, who initially lacked any personal experience or cultural memory of the bubonic plague, this included its utter unfamiliarity and the sheer awfulness of its effects, not only for the sufferer but also for those obliged to witness the appalling stench and bodily disfigurement wrought by this dread disease. In humans, *Y. pestis* generally makes its way from the bite site to the nearest lymph glands, either in the neck, under the arms, or in the groin. As Crawford colorfully explains:

Although the immune system is alerted, this microbe has a veritable armament of devices ready to foil the attack. It grows happily inside the macrophages when they engulf and try to kill it, and it tricks the body into overproducing suppressive cytokines that knock out key immune cells. This strategy gains time, and the microbe can multiply to enormous numbers, causing the glands to swell into the characteristic buboes—huge, exquisitely painful abscesses. If the immune attack succeeds in restricting the microbe to the gland, then the victim stands a chance of surviving, particularly if the buboes rupture and discharge their stinking pus. But all too often *Y. pestis* is one step ahead, spilling out into the bloodstream, attacking blood vessels and causing bleeding into vital organs. Skin haemorrhages produce the typical dark spots, called "God's tokens" because they almost invariably herald the victim's death.[19]

If the pathogenic particles enter directly into a blood vessel at the bite site, the results are less abject, but more certainly and swiftly fatal, producing death from internal bleeding in a matter of hours, as opposed to several days of agonizing illness, but with a 20 to 50 percent chance of recovery.[20] Death is also assured if some of the bacteria escape from the glands and travel to the lungs, causing pneumonia. In its pneumonic form, moreover, the plague acquires the ability to move readily and directly from person to person, without rat and flea intermediaries, if any infected droplets of stinking blood-streaked sputum that get sprayed into the air when the sufferer coughs or sneezes are inhaled by somebody nearby. Like it says in the well-known nursery rhyme: "A-tissue, a-tissue, we all fall down."

Epidemic disease is one kind of eco-catastrophe that brings us up hard and fast against the limits of hospitality. The "categorical imperative of hospitality," as framed by Jacques Derrida, commands that I make a place for whoever or whatever turns up, "the absolute, unknown, anonymous other,"[21] without expectation of a return or consideration for my own well-being. In practice, however, this imperative must be held in tension with the responsibility of safeguarding the conditions that enable me to continue to act hospitably toward other others in the future. There are, then, some *arrivants*, strange strangers of a microbial variety, which you are not going to want to allow across the threshold of your body, if you can help it. If you knew about their animal vectors, then you would be quite justified in seeking to keep them at a distance as well (although how to do so is likely to lead to further ethical conundrums, as you quickly discover if you want to find a humane solution to freeing your home from a colony of black rats who have taken up residence in your roof or wall cavities, such as those that started making a ruckus right beside my desk when I was writing this chapter).

There is no evidence that anybody in the fourteenth century suspected that the pestilence was being spread by rat fleas. It is tempting to wonder whether the causal connection between the agonized deaths of their rodent cohabitants and the sickening of family members might not have been glimpsed earlier if rats had been considered worthy of ethical regard, rather than seen simply as a "pest." The sixteenth-century version of the German fairy tale of "The Pied Piper," in which the mysterious Piper lures away all of Hamelin's children because he has not been paid for ridding the town of rats, provides the only possible hint of the recognition of this link in Europe during the long centuries of repeated plague outbreaks. Many other animals were targeted, however, either as suspected disease carriers or as presaging an approaching visitation, including cats, dogs, geese, pigs, and sundry irritating insects, such as spiders, bed bugs, and grasshoppers (the real culprits evidently being too small and too omnipresent to attract notice).[22] Although the actual disease vectors were not understood, the suspicion of cats probably had an evidential basis. Both cats and dogs can harbor plague-carrying fleas, but whereas dogs have developed a fairly good immunity against *Y. pestis,* cats are very susceptible, and they can also become infected by eating infected rodents. If a cat contracts the pneumonic variant, moreover, it can easily pass it on to humans, as has occurred in a number of cases in the United States in recent decades.[23] At the height of the Black Death pandemic, we can safely assume that there must have been an awful lot of very sick felines about, and many of those who died at human hands might well have been spared greater suffering in the grip of the plague (the killing of cats nonetheless also removing a helpful rat predator). The massacre of healthy dogs, though, was a different story. As the human death toll mounted, anxiety grew around the packs of "masterless" canines roving the land. As Mark Jenner has suggested, their mass slaughter might well have functioned psychosocially as a strategy for reasserting Man's dominion over brute creation at a time when the certainty of human overlordship was being severely shaken.[24]

The withdrawal of hospitality toward domesticated animals in the face of this ghastly pandemic did not necessarily go hand-in-hand with an enhanced solidarity among fellow humans, however. On the contrary: as a creeping catastrophe that affects individuals and communities in a patchy way and at a variable pace, no pandemic is likely to engender the outbreak of mutual aid that is fostered by the "throwntogetherness," as Nigel Clark puts it, of more sudden and less widespread disasters.[25] To offer hospitality and a helping hand to another whose malady is assumed to be infectious takes an uncommon degree of courage and selflessness, especially if the disease in question is mysterious in its causation, repulsive in its manifestation, and typically fatal in its effects. In place of the "panic of empathy" elicited globally by witnesses to the Boxing Day Tsunami of 2004,[26] for example, the plague prompted something more like a panic of abjection, in which the healthy were afraid so much as to look upon the sick, for fear of being infected through the eye. While many physicians continued to visit, nuns to tend, and priests to perform Last Rights for the sick, Boccaccio's account of the plague in Florence in the *Decameron* is indicative of the perceived breakdown of human sociability wrought by the pandemic: "One man shunned another . . . kinsfolk held aloof, brother was forsaken by brother, oftentimes husband by wife; nay, what is more, and scarcely to be believed, fathers and mothers were found to abandon their own children to their fate, untended, unvisited as if they had been strangers."[27]

While this description of the dissolution of all forms of love—*agapic,* erotic, and even filial—is echoed in many other accounts of the time, it might well be exaggerated. The exacerbation of existing social tensions is nonetheless well attested. Not only were those who were perceived to benefit from the epidemic, including salve sellers, gravediggers, and, ironically, physicians, sometimes targeted; so too were those who had long been suspected of spreading spiritual contamination, as the poor and ill educated fell prey en masse to a particularly nasty paranoid delusion: namely, that the illness could be traced to the malice of the Jews, who were accused of poisoning wells and springs (a charge previously leveled against lepers). The pogroms began on Palm Sunday in 1348 in Toulon in southern France, where the townspeople attacked the Jewish quarter, killing forty people. In the following months, massacres spread beyond France to Spain and Germany, and in 1349 Jews also came under attack in Switzerland and the Low Countries. "Within three years of the arrival of plague in Europe, Jews had been exterminated in or hounded out of hundreds of towns and cities," according to Philip Alcabes, and in some German cities there were further attacks on Jewish communities, who had survived this foretaste of the Shoah, when plague returned there in the 1380s and 1390s.[28] While accusations against Jewish communities in association with the plague became less common in the fifteenth century, "Jews were expelled from Cologne in 1424 on this basis, and in 1488 a plague outbreak in Saxony was attributed to the arrival from Nuremberg of a converted Jew."[29] In Tuchman's analysis, the plague altered the position of Jews in Western Europe for centuries to come, deepening the incipient anti-Semitism that culminated in the Nazi death camps. The myth of "well-poisoning and its massacres had fixed the malevolent image of the Jew into a stereotype. Because Jews were useful, towns which had enacted statutes of banishment invited or allowed their re-entry, but imposed new disabilities. Former contacts of scholars, physicians, and financial 'court Jews' with the Gentile community faded. The period of the Jews' medieval flourishing was over. The walls of the ghetto, though not yet physical, had risen."[30] As in Kleist's fictitious earthquake in Chile, then, the eco-catastrophe initially wrought by this historical disaster was compounded by the narrative fabrication of a scapegoat.

But there were other stories and other responses. While secular authorities sometimes condoned this eruption of anti-Jewish violence, and certainly benefited from the seizure of Jewish property, the church officially opposed it. Pope Clement VI not only issued two edicts in 1348 prohibiting the killing and forcible conversion of Jews, he also denounced those who blamed the plague on them as having fallen under Satan's sway, pointing out that Jews too succumbed to the disease.[31] While some speculated as to whether the plague was sent by the devil, the theologically approved interpretation of the pandemic followed the script of the punishment paradigm, attributing it ultimately to divine displeasure toward a sinful humanity and presaging the Final Judgment. This dominant narrative informs the vernacular naming of the disease: the French *peste,* like the German *Pest,* carries the connotation of a scourge, while the English *plague,* derived from the Latin *plagare,* "to strike," implicitly construes the pandemic as a blow from on high, placing it in the biblical lineage of the various disasters said to have been visited upon the Egyptians on account of their refusal to liberate the enslaved Hebrews in Exodus.

As in the case of collective calamities wrought by geophysical extremes, the officially recommended response was prayer, penitence, and the mending of wicked ways. And in this case, too, the punishment paradigm provided the opportunity for various forms of social critique. Among the usual litany of sins, that of *superbia* (pride or arrogance), to which the growing urban elite was seen to be especially prone, was often highlighted. Accordingly, ordinances against the plague regularly listed modest dress among their moral prophylactics. Opinions differed as to whether God's wrath had been aroused by the waxing wickedness of humanity in general or whether specific groups were primarily at fault. One fifteenth-century chronicler, for example, attributed the outbreak to the crimes allegedly committed by the Genoese in Crimea, who are said to have joined the heathens in plundering a Christian city, outdoing even the Saracens in their mistreatment of fellow Christians.[32] The failure of neighbor-love and, in some cases, fear of the plague itself were also targeted, meaning that self-protective flight was construed by some as counterproductive in the long run. The prudent Martin Luther, by contrast, argued that since the impulse toward self-preservation was God-given, endeavors to remove oneself from the risk of infection were entirely justified, so long as this was compatible with one's family and communal responsibilities.[33]

Regardless of such theological debates, it appears that those who could flee generally did, and as these were primarily among the physically and financially better off, the poor, elderly, ailing, and disabled were all too often abandoned to their fate. As the crisis deepened, some joined roving groups of flagellants, engaging in bloody spectacles of prophylactic self-scourging and, in some cases, Jew bashing, while others indulged in drunken and disorderly outbursts of "apocalyptic hedonism."[34] In many areas, moreover, food scarcity increased for lack of labor to bring in the harvest and get it to market, leading to malnourishment, especially among the urban poor, compromising their ability to recover from infection and thereby adding to the death toll.[35] During later epidemics, this problem was exacerbated by the reduced crop yields and severe weather conditions of the Little Ice Age, which began to set in during the fifteenth century and, after a brief warming period, peaked right around the time of the last big outbreak in Western Europe in the mid-1660s.[36]

From the time of the Black Death through to the eighteenth century, mainstream religious understandings of the pandemic were held to be compatible with medical ones, and moral injunctions were regularly combined with practical measures intended to reduce the spread of the disease and deal with its consequences. Medical treatises and treatments remained largely indebted to Hippocrates and other ancient authorities, notably Galen, Ptolemy, and Avicenna Averroes and Albertus Magnus. Suspicion fell primarily on bad air ("miasma"), whether related to astrological phenomena or terrestrial conditions, such as the poisonous vapors believed to rise from swamps, seas, and underground. Observations of the differential rate of infection led some, such as the fifteenth-century French physician Jacques Despars, to postulate person-to-person infection through the intermediary of the air, bodily contact, or tainted objects.[37] Those, such as Benjamin Marten in his "New Theory of Consumption" (1720), who revived the ancient theory of *contagion vivum*, linking infection to the agency of the kind of "animalcules" recently rendered visible by Anton van Leeunhoek's microscope, nonetheless remained in the minority until the ascendancy of germ theory in the second half of the nineteenth century. Practices such as quarantining goods and people, and isolating the sick, which began to be institutionalized during the first plague pandemic, nonetheless testify to the recognition of certain material vectors of infection. The homes of the sick were required to be marked with a cross, plague-ridden towns and villages were sealed off, and by the early 1700s a massive nineteen-hundred-kilometer *cordon sanitaire* had been established along the border between the Austro-Hungarian Empire and the Turkish and Slavic lands to the east, which, not entirely unreasonably, continued to be feared as the source of infection. Plague only departed from Eastern Europe in the mid-nineteenth century, by which time a new and continuing, if currently contained, epidemic was breaking out in China.

Assessments of the long-term impacts of the plague in Europe vary, but there is little doubt that they were profound. Many historians believe that the Black Death hastened the decay of feudalism, as widespread depopulation increased both the demand for rural labor and the amount of land available, fostering the emergence of a class of yeoman farmers. Labor shortages meant that wages rose, contributing to the growth of the money economy. Meanwhile, the sphere of operation of the state was enlarged through such administrative measures as the establishment of state-run "pesthouses," the compilation of mortality lists, the creation of municipal health departments, the collection of plague taxes, and the increase in border control. In many respects, such responses to the experience and threat of plague epidemics pertain to the emergence of what Michel Foucault identifies in his *History of Sexuality* as a modern form of "biopolitics": a regime of governance that operates on and through the body, with a view to wedding social control to the maximization of productivity. More generally, as Alcabes observes, "The institutions that would contribute to the evolving public nature of civil society were shaped in no small part, by plague."[38] Equally importantly, it undoubtedly lent impetus to empirical investigations into the material dimensions of human health and sickness, hastening the emergence of modern medical science. In my view, the trauma of the plague, in conjunction with the rigors of the Little Ice Age, is also likely to have conditioned the way in which Sir Francis Bacon conceived of his "new organ of knowledge": namely, as a project oriented not only toward enhanced human knowledge of but also power over the troublesome natural world.

As Theodor Adorno and Max Horkheimer observe in their *Dialectic of Enlightenment*, the "happy match," as Bacon termed it, "between the mind of man and the nature of things that he had in mind is patriarchal: the human mind, which overcomes superstition, is to hold sway over a disenchanted nature."[39] The patriarchal and anthropocentric, or more precisely, "anthroparchal,"[40] underpinnings of modern scientific endeavor, as it was framed by Bacon and Descartes in the seventeenth century, has come in for considerable ecofeminist critique over the past three decades, beginning with Carolyn Merchant's landmark work on the Scientific Revolution, *The Death of Nature* (1980). It should be stressed that critical ecofeminists such as Merchant do not claim that women are naturally "closer to nature" or that modern science is inherently "masculine" and necessarily "bad."[41] Their critique is directed, rather, toward the cultural assumptions and social ideologies that infected and inflected the institutionalization of empirical inquiry into "Nature's secrets" in the modern era. The prehistory of these assumptions, which implicitly set Man, mind, and spirit apart from, and above, Woman, body, and matter, while identifying the truly human with the former, have been variously traced to Greco-Roman rationalism, medieval reinterpretations of the biblical notion of human dominion, and Renaissance humanism.[42] Yet the powerful appeal of the Baconian project of technoscientific mastery, which, as Merchant stresses, dovetailed nicely with the interests of mercantile and later industrial capitalism, also needs to be understood in light of the truly dreadful depredations of the plague over several centuries, during which Northern Europe was simultaneously plunged into a period of severe and unstable weather conditions. In view of the traumatic historical experience of utter subjection to some distinctly dire other-than-human agencies, the prospect of expanding the sphere of human self-determination by gaining greater control over the physical conditions of our existence must have seemed profoundly alluring (as indeed it probably does to most people today). What emerged from the work of those who followed Bacon, moreover, was in some cases not so much the triumphalism of conquest as the disquieting discovery of kinship: long before Darwin, for example, Edward Tyson (1651–1708) was startled and moved by the resemblance that he discovered between himself and the chimpanzee whom he studied, both living and dead.[43] As discussed in the last chapter, the rise of physico-theology from the end of the seventeenth century—interestingly, among a generation in Britain whose parents had witnessed the final outbreak of the plague in England (thus far) that had ravaged London in 1665—held out the promise that greater understanding of Nature's laws would enable humanity to exercise a better stewardship of creation: as wise rulers, that is, rather than as reckless tyrants.[44]

While physico-theological confidence in the stability, lawfulness, and beneficence of a divinely authored Nature was beginning to look a little shaky by the late eighteenth century, some writers and philosophers of the Romantic period were attracted by the idea that human moral and techno-scientific advancement could, in time, bring about an "active im-paradising" of the Earth.[45] Among them was Percy Bysshe Shelley, who, in his ecotopian poem "Queen Mab" (1813), for example, envisages an eman-cipated humanity living in harmony with other creatures, as "an equal amidst equals" (viii, line 226), in a universally habitable (and specifically, temperate) earth from which, echoing the eschatology of Isaiah, all wild-ness and discord have been eradicated, thanks to a felicitous marriage of Mind and Nature, in which the former has nonetheless retained its "om-nipotence" (line 236).[46] It is this vision of the pacification of the entire Earth under the sway of human mental sovereignty that Mary Shelley discloses as delusional and even self-defeating in her apocalyptic plague novel, even while honoring the beloved husband, who had been drowned in the Mediterranean Sea just four years before she penned it.

Mary Shelley was all too familiar with the depredations of disease. Her own mother, the early feminist Mary Wollstonecraft (1759–97), had died within days of giving birth of "womb fever" (*puerperal septicemia*, a common complication of childbirth, currently treatable with antibiotics). Mary and Percy's second child, William (1816–18), died of malaria, and their third, Clara (1817–18), of dysentery. Mary's niece Allegra (1817–22), the daughter of her stepsister, Claire Clairmont, and Lord Byron, died of typhus. Their acquaintance John Keats (1795–21), whom they greatly admired as a poet, died of tuberculosis the year before Percy drowned. And in 1824, their close friend Byron (1788–1824) died of an unidentified fever contracted while commanding a Greek army in the independence movement against the Ottoman Empire. At the time that Mary Shelley embarked upon *The Last Man*, moreover, a dreadful new disease was threatening to go global. Having broken out across India in 1817 a new strain of cholera had been spread to Arabia by British troops from the Raj in 1821 and was making its inexorable way toward the imperial homeland. Shelley, meanwhile, was living in London in a state of considerable grief and loneliness. In addition to the children lost to illness, her first daughter had died unnamed within days of being born prematurely in 1815, and Mary had also had a miscarriage from which she too nearly died, in 1822, shortly before Percy's drowning. One son only, Percy Florence (1819–89), remained to her, but he could not provide the companionship she craved, as indicated by a telling diary entry from May 14, 1824: "The last man! Yes I may well describe that solitary being's feelings, feeling myself as the last relic of a beloved race, my companions, extinct before me."[47]

By the time her new novel appeared in 1826, the topos of "the last man," to which she alludes in her diary, was already looking somewhat jaded. "Since 1823," as Morton Paley records, "the literary world had been preoccupied with a controversy about just who had invented the Last Man,"[48] following Francis Jeffrey's observation in the *Edinburgh Review* that the best imagery in Thomas Campbell's apocalyptic poem of that name had been lifted from Byron's "Darkness" of 1816. When Campbell countered that Byron had pilfered the concept from him, and that he had been prompted to get his own version out before yet another poet (Thomas Lovell Beddoes) published his, his claims were met with mirth. As one anonymous commentator observed in the *London Magazine,* Campbell's assertion that he was the originator of this topos was ridiculous, "the idea of the Last Man being most particularly obvious, or rather absolutely common-place, and a book with the taking title of *Omegarius* [sic.], or *The Last Man,* having gone the rounds of all circulating libraries for years past."[49] The book referred to here was actually entitled *Omegarus and Syderia, a Romance in Futurity,* published anonymously in 1806, and it was a translation of Jean-Baptiste François Xavier Cousin de Grainville's prose poem *Le dernier homme* (The last man) of 1805.

Mythic visions of the end of the world are ancient and transcultural, but interest in the figure of the last man around 1800 was stimulated also by new ways of thinking about the history of life on Earth emerging from empirical research. Investigations of rock strata had led some in the nascent field of geology to postulate planetary catastrophe as a vehicle of terrestrial transformation, while the fossilized evidence of now-extinct species suggested that such "revolutions" might have played an important role in the generation of the existing family of life. Even among those who posited a more gradual process of evolution, the recognition that entire species had died out in the past opened the possibility that humans too could one day become extinct. Kant, for example, was moved to speculate privately:

If our globe (having once been dissolved into chaos, but now being organized and regenerating) were to bring forth, by revolutions of the earth, differently organized creatures, which, in turn, gave place to others after their destruction, organic nature could be conceived in terms of a sequence of different world epochs. . . . How many such revolutions (including, certainly, many ancient organic beings no longer alive on the surface of the earth) preceded the existence of men, and how many . . . are still in prospect, is hidden from our inquiring gaze.[50]

In addition to this disquieting historical record, a number of alarming natural phenomena, in conjunction with emerging anxieties about the impact of human industrial activities, contributed to the apocalyptic imaginings of the Romantic period. Among these were the "Great Hurricane of 1780," the largest of three cyclonic storms to strike the Caribbean that year; a series of five strong earthquakes that shook the Calabrian region of Italy in 1783; a major eruption of the Loki volcano in southern Iceland on June 8 of that same year; earthquakes in Equador and Sumatra in 1797 and in Crete, in 1810; and the eruption of the Tambora volcano on the Indonesian island of Sumbawa on April 10, 1815. As Jonathan Bate has demonstrated, the bad summer that Byron and the Shelleys experienced when they were staying on Lake Geneva the following year can be attributed to the temporary global dimming occasioned by this massive eruption, which is also estimated to have killed some eighty thousand people in the immediate vicinity, as well as occasioning cooler temperatures, failed harvests, and food shortages in faraway Europe for several years afterward. It was in these unseasonably inclement conditions that Mary Shelley was coaxed into writing *Frankenstein* in response to a friendly competition as to who could write the best gothic tale. And, in Bate's view, it was at least in part this bleak summer that prompted Byron's apocalyptic vision of the complete extinction of all life on Earth in his "last man" poem, "Darkness" (1816).[51]

Shelley's *Last Man*, like the poems of de Grainville and Byron, is, as Paley puts it, an "apocalypse without millennium," in that the cataclysmic event upon which the novel turns does not follow the biblical script of redemptive violence. However, what makes Shelley's take on this tired topic both highly innovative and, from a humanistic perspective, particularly disturbing is that the ending that she envisages is reserved exclusively for humankind. De Grainville, Byron, and Campbell all locate their last men on a universally blighted planet. Shelley, by contrast, vouchsafes Earth's other-than-human life forms a renewed flourishing by having their self-proclaimed overlord excised from creation, with something approaching surgical precision, by means of a pandemic that is fatal for humans alone. Not surprisingly, the novel did not go down well with her contemporaries and was variously condemned as "a sickening repetition of horrors," the "offspring of a diseased imagination, and of a most polluted taste," and "an abortion."[52] Although it was reprinted in Paris in 1826 and Philadelphia in 1833, it did not enjoy anything approaching the success of her first novel, *Frankenstein* (1818), and actually went out of print between 1833 and 1965. Scholarly interest in *The Last Man* only took off in the closing decades of the last century, beginning with the landmark feminist discussions of the novel by Sandra Gilbert and Susan Gubar in *The Madwoman in the Attic* (1979) and Anne K. Mellor in *Mary Shelley: Her Life, Her Fiction, Her Monsters* (1988). In addition to being republished in several new critical editions,[53] *The Last Man* has now also made its way, albeit in a substantially altered guise, into popular culture in James Arnett's 2008 film of that name, one of countless more-or-less fanciful and angst-ridden imaginings of humanity's demise to greet the new millennium. As Barbara Johnson observed in 1993, albeit for somewhat different reasons from those that I will advance here, this novel, which was so untimely in its day, has become "ardently timely" for our own era:[54] a time, in my analysis, in which the likelihood of a planetary pandemic of cataclysmic proportions, notwithstanding the wonders of modern medicine, has only increased in tandem with, and to a considerable extent as a consequence of, the number and diversity of fellow creatures who have come to suffer at human hands.

Not unlike "The Earthquake in Chile," Shelley's novel features a narrator whose perspective is subtly subverted by the tale he tells. The story is narrated in the first person by an Englishman named Lionel Verney, who, as we discover at the end of three long volumes, is writing in the year 2,100 in the depopulated city of Rome—an apt place to reflect, as he does both explicitly and implicitly, upon both the unrealized promise and the fatal pathology of a civilization that traces its origins to Greco-Roman antiquity; a civilization that had now been abruptly terminated by the demise of the collective entity that it had elevated to quasi-divine status: namely Man.

Verney's narrative begins autobiographically, somewhat in the manner of a bildungsroman, or novel of experience, with the story of how he and his sister, Perdita, who had been orphaned and impoverished at an early age, were befriended by the gracious son and daughter, Adrian and Idris, of the last English monarch, formerly a close friend of their dissolute father. Foiling the plans of the erstwhile queen, now Countess of Windsor, who had tried unsuccessfully to persuade her republican son to reclaim the throne and who now sought to marry her daughter into the Austrian royal family from whence she herself hails, Idris elopes with Lionel. Perdita, meanwhile, marries a close friend of Adrian's, Lord Raymond, recently returned as a military hero from a new Greek war of independence against the Turks. Adrian remains single, having been rejected by the beautiful and exotic Greek princess Evadne, who is enamored of Raymond, the trauma of which renders him temporarily deranged. Following Adrian's recovery, they all spend several years of private felicity on the former royal estate at Windsor, England having peacefully transitioned to a republic following the king's abdication in 2073. This happy period of pastoral retreat ends with Raymond's appointment as Lord Protector, drawing the protagonists into the political life of the nation and causing the narrative to morph into the genre of political romance. Raymond institutes an ambitious program of reform, but his administration is derailed by a chance reunion with Evadne, now widowed and living in poverty in London, who turns out to be the anonymous creator of the architectural designs for the new national gallery that he aspires to have built. Raymond commits himself to restoring Evadne to society, but his secret, albeit chaste, visits to her are discovered by Perdita, who assumes their liaison to be adulterous. In his fury, Raymond abandons not only his wife but also his role as Protector, returning instead to the Greco-Turkish war, with Adrian in tow. The first volume ends, following Adrian's wounding and repatriation, with a Greek victory; but this good news is overshadowed by reports of Raymond's disappearance.

In the second volume, the narrative horizon expands yet further from the national to the international scene, with Lionel and a remorseful Perdita in search of Raymond in the contested borderland between the Eastern and Western worlds. Securing Raymond's release from Turkish imprisonment, Lionel returns with him to Athens, only to join him on a new military campaign, the objective of which is the capture of Constantinople. Raymond succeeds in taking Stanboul, as it is known to the Turks, but at great cost: not only does he die in the explosion that is mysteriously triggered by his forced entry into the city, but this also appears to open the way for the Plague, which, in consort with starvation, had killed all the inhabitants of the besieged city, to begin its westward advance. At this point, the narrative takes a decidedly gothic turn. Raymond's death amid "fire, war, and plague" had been prophesied by Evadne, whom Lionel encounters dying on the battlefield, dressed as a soldier. When Perdita commits suicide rather than be wrested away from Raymond's graveside by Lionel, the narrator is left to return to England alone. A year of peace throughout the world, and the advancement of egalitarian and democratic sociopolitical reform in England, appears to open the way for the realization of Adrian's humanistic vision (one that bears a distinct similarity, it might be noted, to that of the author's deceased husband). Elsewhere, however, the Plague has been spreading. When it crosses the English Channel, the radical democrat Ryland, who had succeeded Raymond as Protector, abandons his post in the vain hope of saving his own skin, and the selfless Adrian assumes command of his dying nation. Lionel, whose oldest son succumbs to the Plague, also contracts the disease but recovers and joins Adrian in his efforts to limit its spread and maintain a hospitable social order in the midst of the unfolding calamity.

The third volume begins with the death of Idris and the departure of the remnant English for warmer climes in southern Europe, where they imagine that it will be easier to survive in the wake of the collapse of their wider society. Their numbers dwindle as they journey across the increasingly depopulated continent. Finally, only Adrian and Lionel, together with the latter's infant son, Evelyn, and Raymond's and Perdita's orphaned daughter, Clara, remain alive. Ironically, having survived the depredations of the pandemic, which has finally come to an end, little Evelyn dies of typhus, while Clara and Adrian drown attempting to sail from Italy to Greece. At the time of writing, Lionel believes himself likely to be the titular "last man." He nonetheless hopes that this might not be so and, in the final pages of the novel, describes his intention to set out on a boat, together with a canine companion, some provisions, and a few books, to circumnavigate Earth's continents in search of other survivors.

Verney's narrative, long-winded as it is, is not the whole text of *The Last Man,* however. Whereas his tale is composed for the most part in the past tense, it is prefaced by a fictional "Author's Introduction," which foregrounds the novel's orientation toward a possible future. According to this frame narrative, the work was inspired by the author's discovery of fragments of prophetic verse in several languages, both ancient and modern, traced on "leaves, bark and other substances," that she and an unnamed companion had found—along with the "perfect snow-white skeleton of a goat," which had evidently fallen through the opening above—deep in the cave of the Cumaean Sybil on the Bay of Naples. Having "made a hasty selection of the leaves, whose writing one at least of us could understand," the two then set about "deciphering these sacred remains," a task that the author was subsequently left to pursue alone, following the loss of her "matchless companion." While acknowledging that these fragments "were unintelligible in their pristine condition," the author nonetheless insists that, despite the not inconsiderable work of selection, translation, linking, and ordering involved in this editorial process, "the main substance rests on the truths contained in these poetic rhapsodies, and the divine intuition which the Cumaean damsel obtained from heaven."[55] Verney's past, then, is presented to Shelley's readers as their potential future. Shelley, presumably, does not expect us to take her fictitious "Author's Introduction" for real, but she does implicitly claim for this early work of speculative fiction a prophetic dimension. As such, it does not aspire to predict so much as to warn. In transforming the archaic verse fragments into the form of a modern prose novel, the author displaces the voice of the ancient female seer into that of a future male narrator, whose perspective is disclosed as both partial and conflicted. However, as Stephen Goldsmith recalls, the Sibyl too was double voiced, in that her prophecies were said to be have come from the male god Apollo, "who literally inspires her. Passing through the Sibyl, his breath transforms her into his medium."[56] Similarly, in *The Last Man*, Verney's voice becomes the medium through which Mary Shelley imparts a vision that the fictional author attributes to the legendary Sibyl, one that is in many respects at odds with the worldview professed by the fictitious narrator himself.

Verney opens his account with a nostalgic recollection of the world that is no more:

> I am the native of a sea-surrounded nook, a cloud-enshrouded land, which, when the surface of the globe, with its shoreless ocean and trackless continents, presents itself to my mind, appears only as an inconsiderable speck in the immense whole; and yet, when balanced in the scale of mental power, far outweighed countries of larger extent and more numerous population. So true it is, that man's mind alone was the creator of all that was good or great to man, that Nature herself was only his first minister. England, seated far north in the turbid sea, now visits my dreams in the semblance of a vast and well-manned ship, which mastered the winds and rode

proudly over the waves. In my boyish days she was the universe to me. When I stood on my native hills, and saw plain and mountain stretch out to the utmost limits of my vision, speckled by the dwellings of my countrymen, and subdued to fertility by their labours, the earth's very centre was fixed for me in that spot, and the rest of her orb was as a fable, to have forgotten which would have cost neither my imagination nor understanding any effort. (*LM*, 5)

Verney's idealized image of England is structured around a series of interlinked oppositions: land versus sea; bounded places ("nook," "ship") versus undifferentiated space ("shoreless ocean"); the domesticated ("plain and mountain . . . subdued to fertility") versus the wild ("trackless continents"); mind ("mental power") versus matter (geographical "extent"); Man versus Nature, which as "first minister" is ambiguously construed both as a law-giver and as subservient, "ministering" to human wants. These oppositions compose a worldview in which the human subject—one marked as English, of "superior mental power," and implicitly masculine—is construed as the lord and master of all he surveys. Introducing himself in terms that are at once ethnocentric, androcentric, logocentric, and anthropocentric, Verney's self-stylization provides a textbook example of what feminist ecophilosopher Val Plumwood terms the "logic of colonisation," underpinning dominant constructions of human identity within Western modernity.[57] In this, Verney's voice mimics that assumed in much of the male-authored "last man" poetry of the 1820s. As Steven Goldsmith has observed, these texts typically imagine the end of humanity in such a way as to "reassuringly confirm . . . the epistemological status quo" by salvaging human consciousness in an immaterial beyond, even as they imagine the obliteration of the human species.[58] Shelley's novel, by contrast, ends up undoing every binary that is implicit in its ideologically loaded opening. In this way, the subaltern wisdom of the Sybil, as appropriated by the implied female author, might be seen to undercut the privileged consciousness of her male narrator, allowing a radically different view of human identity to emerge from a narrative that stages a catastrophic "return of the repressed."[59] In my reading, however, what "returns" is not "nature" or "the feminine," as in Jane Aaron's reading, but a gender-bending monster, largely of human making.

As a truly apocalyptic event, which, recalling James Berger's definition, in its disruptive moment clarifies and illuminates "the true nature of what has been brought to an end,"[60] the catastrophic pandemic reveals the narrator's earlier view of England's splendid isolation to have been utterly illusory. While England is the last nation of the world to succumb to infection, its socioeconomic order, underpinned as it was by the "busy spirit of money-making, peculiar to our country" (*LM*, 200), has already largely collapsed due to the introduction of quarantine regulations that have interrupted international trade. Moreover, while the narrator persists in demonizing the frequently feminized but ambivalently gendered Plague as an external agent of humanity's demise, even likening it at one point to the satanic "Arch-Felon" of Milton's *Paradise Lost* (195), it is made clear that the disease only reaches pandemic proportions on account of the interconnectivities engendered by commercially motivated colonial conquest. Recalling that the Britain of Shelley's day had been enriched by the only recently outlawed slave trade, it is perhaps not insignificant that she identifies the African continent as the original source of the pandemic. Moreover, Verney is shown to become infected through direct bodily contact (the only such instance in the novel) with "a negro half clad, writhing under the agony of disease," who was among the many immigrants given refuge in Windsor Castle and who held him "with a convulsive grasp" (268). Revealing not only England's dependence on the rest of the world but also the shared corporeal or rather "trans-corporeal" vulnerability of erstwhile masters and slaves, colonizers and colonized, Shelley's Plague, as Kevin Hutchings has observed, "because of its leveling effect . . . becomes, to a certain extent, an emblem of social justice carried out on a global scale."[61] Verney is almost the only character who is shown to recover from infection. While his revulsion toward the dying African American has distinctly racist overtones, it is, as Anne K. Mellor suggests, perhaps precisely "from this unwilling but powerful embrace of the racial other . . . [that] Verney . . . becomes immune to the plague."[62] Although Verney insists that the "plague was not what is commonly called contagious, like the scarlet fever, or extinct small-pox" (185), the physical intimacy of this embrace appears to effect a kind of immunization.[63] As mentioned previously, the disease from the East that was most worrying to Europeans in the 1820s was cholera, which was beginning to go global as a consequence of British colonial policies that were, in turn, entwined with the process of industrialization in Britain.[64] The association between imperialism and disease was beginning to be widely recognized at this time, but, in Alan Bewell's analysis, *The Last Man* was "one of the first major works on the historical ecology of disease," which discloses "the important role empire has played in the global spread of disease."[65] While the original outbreak of Shelley's fictitious Plague is traced to Africa, the colonial venture that provides the conduit for the entry of the disease into Europe is located in the Near East. Having expelled the Islamic invaders from Greece, Raymond, who aspires to "subdue all Asia" (*LM*, 43), frames his exploits as a struggle of "civilization" against "barbarism" (121). Verney nonetheless reveals that "every European nation" had a commercial interest in the success of the Greek cause (127).

Verney's account of the military campaign that he witnesses also undercuts Raymond's imperialistic glorification of his mission by foregrounding the high price of warfare in terms of both human morality and the fertility of the land. The decisive battle is fought on the plain between Kishon and Rodosto, a part of Thrace that "had been so long a scene of contest, that it had remained uncultivated, and presented a dreary, barren appearance" (*LM*, 143). Surveying the carnage that remained in its wake, Verney writes, "I turned to the corpse-strewn earth; and felt ashamed of my species" (144). This passage echoes Adrian's reflections on the earlier campaign in which he had participated, when an entire town was massacred and he witnessed a Moslem girl being raped by two Greek soldiers, "perhaps good men among their families," whose "brutal appetites . . . were changed by the fury of the moment into incarnated evils" (128).[66] Ironically, the war that is being prosecuted in the name of "civilization" is disclosed as brutalizing the combatants. Similarly, Verney comes to recognize that in participating in Raymond's bid to liberate Constantinople, his "mind had yielded itself a willing slave to the state of things presented to it by its fellow-beings; historical association, hatred of the foe, and military enthusiasm held dominion over me" (144). Verney's insight into the oppressive and blinding force of ideology is facilitated by the expansion of his consciousness that attends his contemplation of the "evening star, as softly and calmly it hung pendulous in the orange hues of sunset" (144). Similarly, if less beneficently, it is the more-than-human horizon opened up by the advancing Plague, which—not unlike the Spanish flu epidemic of 1918, which helped to hasten the end of the First World War—intervenes in the epochal struggle between East and West, disclosing the parochialism of this human-all-too-human conflict.

It is among the battle-dead, in the gathering darkness of nightfall, that Verney is accosted by the mortally wounded Evadne. Hearing of her demise and dying curse upon him, Raymond becomes increasingly melancholy, while starvation and disease proceed to lay waste to the besieged inhabitants of Stanboul. Significantly, Raymond disregards not only the

better judgment of his friend, the entreaties of his wife, and the trepida-
tion of his troops, but also the resistance of his horse and the opposition of
his dog, to ride triumphantly into the disease-ridden city, thereby triggering the explosion that kills him outright and releasing the contagion that
proceeds to ravage the rest of the world. Verney, who abductively intuits
more than he admits consciously, prefigures this outcome in the dream
that assails him when he succumbs to his bodily needs and falls asleep
while searching for Raymond amid the rubble.[67] Here, his friend appears
to him "altered by a thousand distortions, expanded into a gigantic phantom, bearing on its brow the sign of pestilence" (LM, 161). When Verney
sleeps, it seems, the Sibyl speaks, disclosing the socioecological character
of the pandemic, which the narrator has such difficulty confronting consciously. That Raymond bears the sign of Plague on his forehead suggests
metonymically not only that the human mind is dependent upon "our animal mechanism" (234) but also that it can become a fatal liability: namely,
if our "mental creations" (315), such as, in this case, Raymond's desire to
win fame by planting "the Grecian standard on the height of St. Sophia"
(155), are privileged over our bodily being and earthly environs, which
for Raymond have become no more than "a tomb, the firmament a vault,
shrouding mere corruption" (149). This overvaluation of ideation, or the
realm of the symbolic, and the frequently mentioned "self-will" that it en-
genders, proves fatal for a number of other characters as well, including
his wife, Perdita, who commits suicide rather than be separated from his
graveside, and their daughter, Clara, who drowns with Adrian in a storm
while attempting a rash sea crossing to visit her parents' tomb in Greece.

Surviving this disaster also, thanks not to any mental effort or feat of
willpower but rather to the "instinctive love of life" that "animated" his
creaturely being (LM, 354), Verney finds enduring consolation neither in
wild nature, which is flourishing anew in the absence of human domination, nor amid the material remains of human (and specifically Western)
civilization in the depopulated city of Rome. Significantly, his attempt
to befriend a family of wild goats is met with fear and hostility. There is
a contrastive echo here of the skeletal remains found in the cave of the
Cumaean Sybil, of which the author observes: "Ages perhaps had elapsed
since this catastrophe; and the ruin it had made above, had been repaired
by the growth of vegetation during many hundred summers" (2–3). The
individual "catastrophe" of this lone goat's fall to its death, together with
the reparation of the breach effected by the vegetation, both prefigures

and contrasts with the collective human catastrophe prophesied by the Sybil and narrated by Verney, in which other-than-human life is shown to be recovering well, following the demise of a fallen humanity. That the animals in question in both cases should be goats, however, also carries a further connotation: that of Arcadia. In the wake of the collapse of civilization, Verney briefly fantasizes an Edenic "return to nature"; but the goats wisely recognize him as a potential predator, shattering his anthropomorphic illusions. The narrator does nonetheless find, or rather, is found by, an other-than-human companion. Having previously been inspired by Adrian to abandon his "savage" existence as an untutored shepherd and poacher in the Lake District and having gained admittance "within that sacred boundary which divides the intellectual and moral nature of man from that which characterises animals" (21), Verney ends as he began: alone, with a dog. There is a crucial difference, however, in that his new modus vivendi is neither savage nor civilized, but integrally natural-cultural, albeit confined to the miniature more-than-human world of the boat, in which he and the dog who has joyously befriended him are left circumnavigating earth's coastlines in search of other survivors. The demise of Man (as defined in accordance with the logic of colonization), it is hinted, might just open the way for the emergence of a new kind of human-nonhuman collectivity, albeit not in an idealized world, such as Percy Shelley envisaged in "Queen Mab," from which all conflict and difficulty had been expunged, but in a queer passage toward an uncertain future.[68]

As well as disclosing the transnational, transpecies, and trans-corporeal connectivities that are in play in both the etiology and the outcome of the pandemic, the capacious form of this novel allows Shelley to explore diverse human responses to the unfolding catastrophe with a degree of detail and insight that should qualify *The Last Man* as compulsory reading in all of the currently burgeoning disaster management courses. These range from opportunistic looting and apocalyptic hedonism through to pragmatic self-organization on the part of communities and selfless kindness among some individuals. New structures and styles of leadership emerge, as the wheeler-dealer politics of everyday governance are displaced by the moral guidance provided by the selfless Adrian, who only now assumes the role of Protector that his friends had hoped he would take on earlier, working tirelessly to prevent panic and criminality, to maintain public hygiene and civil order, and to protect the healthy and aid the sick. As Vicky Adams observes, Adrian's ethic of care stands in stark contrast to Raymond's heroic drive to mastery, which is manifest not only on the battlefield but also in his autocratic and technocratic efforts to manufacture a perfect commonwealth.[69]

While nationalist and racist prejudices condition initial reactions to the outbreak, including Verney's, and resurface in the face of an influx of refugees, these are ultimately rejected by the narrator and other (if not all) survivors, in favor of the recognition of a common humanity. Faced with escalating conflict between the English and a rag-tag army of marauding Irish and Americans, Adrian manages to persuade both sides to lay down their weapons, exhorting them, over the body of a slain combatant, to "throw down those tools of cruelty and hate; in this pause of exterminating destiny, let each man be brother, guardian, and stay to the other" (*LM*, 241). As Peter Melville observes, in its representation of England as an asylum, the novel is "committed to representing a form of hospitality that is fuelled less by optimism than it is by an irrepressible obligation to welcome the other even when all hope is lost, even when to do so might lead to one's destruction."[70] In practice, however, there are limits to the asylum that can be offered: Adrian arranges for some of the "invaders" to be housed in deserted villages, but others are sent back to Ireland, and "any increase of numbers prohibited" (241).

Meanwhile, Ryland's endeavors to legislate an egalitarian society are trumped by the pandemic, as the propertied are persuaded to fell their forested hunting grounds for dwellings and turn their parks and flowerbeds over to subsistence food production. As the mortality rate rises, moreover, the "products of human labour" become more evenly distributed: "We were all equal now; magnificent dwellings, luxurious carpets, and beds of down were afforded to all" (*LM*, 253). This equality, wrought by catastrophe, is nonetheless shadowed by the Malthusian equivalence engendered by the disease, obliterating individuation by reducing all members of the population to the status of a statistic in the growing death toll: "We were all equal now; but near at hand was an equality more levelling, a state where beauty and strength, and wisdom, would be as vain as riches and birth" (253).[71] As centralized governance breaks down, Verney is deputed to foster improvisational forms of what would today be termed "adaptive governance" under the leadership of able local figures, who would never have had the chance to enter government under normal conditions, including nonelite youths and women (215–16).

Gender assumptions, along with sexual norms, are put under pressure in other ways, too. Verney, for example, is forced by grief at the death of his wife to acknowledge emotions that he had previously considered exclusively womanly (*LM*, 285). He also comes to accept the homoerotic depths of his feelings for Adrian: while repressing his "girlish ecstasies" and not daring to "embrace" him, Verney nonetheless admits to having thrown himself on the ground before his friend to "kiss the dear and sacred earth he trod" (323). Experiencing the vulnerability attendant on the bodily dimension of human being also leads Verney to open his heart to other-than-human suffering (248). And as he witnesses the colonization of erstwhile human spaces by a plethora of flourishing and newly liberated plants and animals, he is finally brought to question the anthroparchal "arrogance" of calling ourselves "lords of creation, wielders of the elements, masters of life and death" (184).

Shelley's subversion of the patriarchal and anthroparchal assumptions announced in the opening paragraph—one that acquires a distinctly ironic undertone in light of the rest of the narrative—does not culminate in a simplistic reversal of the reason-nature dualism, however. In my reading, it points rather to the necessity of a process of ecological enlightenment, in which the nonhuman is resituated as agentic, communicative, and ethically considerable, while human consciousness is recognized as embodied and interconnected with a more-than-human world that is neither fully knowable nor entirely controllable. Ecological enlightenment entails overcoming the "pathogenic" denial of our own human animality.[72] But it also necessitates the cultivation of the human capacity for mindfulness: the capacity for critical self-reflection on one's own "mental creations," which is facilitated by complex works of literature such as this one, in its subtle subversion of a patriarchal and anthroparchal symbolic order in denial about its own conditions of possibility and ultimately self-destructive tendencies.

Eerily for readers now living in the climatically changing century in which this novel is set, Verney relates how containing the spread of the pandemic and coping with its impacts is rendered more difficult because of the disordered weather conditions that accompany its inexorable progress over several years. These include unusually hot summers, as well as extreme cold snaps, violent storms, and massive sea surges. Together with the solar eclipse that precedes the entry of the Plague into Europe and the triple meteor shower and consequent tidal wave that the remnant English witness while waiting for sufficiently calm seas to cross the Channel en route to milder climes, these weather surprises are read by some in the novel as signs of the Second Coming, giving rise to a millennial cult led by a false prophet on an ego trip. Importantly, however, these expectations, which the text initially also invites its readers to form, are disappointed, as Shelley pitches her own this-worldly prophetic vision against otherworldly apocalypticism. No explanation is given for the unseasonable and extreme weather, which seems to have settled down again when the narrative concludes. As Gillen D'Arcy Wood has observed, the disordering of the climate in *The Last Man* is reminiscent of the conditions that Shelley had experienced in the wake of the Tambora volcanic eruption: conditions that are now believed to have played a key role in the emergence and spread of the new strain of cholera that was advancing on Europe at the time that she was writing this novel.[73] While Shelley and her contemporaries knew nothing of the only recently established connection between the climatic impacts of this eruption and the approaching epidemic, of which her own half-brother William was to become one of the last victims to die in the London outbreak of 1832, her adherence to the atmospheric theory of disease could well have predisposed her to associate the extreme weather of 1816 to 1818 with the mounting depredations of cholera.[74] However, the text can also be seen as suggestive of an anthropogenic origin for the wild weather that accompanies the spread of her fictitious Plague. Despite the fact that Raymond's modernization drive entails the recruitment of "machines to supply with facility every want of the population" (*LM*, 84), Shelley's late-twenty-first century appears minimally industrialized: transport, for example, is still by horse, coach, sailing boat, or hot air balloon. Since the advance of the pandemic is attributed primarily to the medium of the "empoisoned air" (186), it could well be associated, whether figuratively or causally, with the anthropogenic air pollution that was already being produced by the "Satanic mills" of Shelley's day. As James McKusick notes in an early ecocritical reading of *The Last Man:* "As the manufacturing cities of England disappeared into a thick haze of photochemical smog, it becomes possible to imagine that human activities might alter the climate and eventually destroy the Earth's ability to sustain human life"— as did Blake, in McKusick's reading, in his prophetic verse epic, *Jerusalem* (1804–20).[75]

While Shelley's novel explicitly refutes the violent logic of millennialist apocalypticism, it also implicitly undermines the hyperseparation of "nature" and "culture," materiality and morality, characteristic of the Modern Constitution. Today, nature-culture dualism is impeding our ability to recognize our own hand in the kind of weather extremes that beset the diseased society of *The Last Man*. These extremes are increasingly being powered by the "murderous engine" (*LM*, 366), as Verney calls the Plague, of the fossil-fueled process of industrialization that was set in motion during Shelley's lifetime. Anthropogenic climate change, moreover, has its own epidemiological implications: among other things, it is engendering the spread of tropical diseases, such as mosquito-borne malaria, dengue fever, Rift Valley fever, and yellow fever. Several types of insect-borne brain infections are also expected to become more prevalent over a wider area, including Australia and throughout Asia.[76] A further critical factor in the growing potential for a new global pandemic, though, is the underlying malaise that afflicts human relations with other living beings, including those that coconstitute our own bodies, as human populations and consumption levels continue to rise under the conditions of global capitalist modernization.

This malaise is most clearly manifest in those destructive incursions into densely forested environments, especially in the tropics, that are exposing ever more humans and their domesticated animals to viruses that have evolved a symbiotic relationship with other free-living forest species, but to which their new hosts have no hereditary immunity. The felling of Queensland's eucalypt forests, for instance, is destroying the native habitat of Australian flying foxes (or "fruit bats"), driving them into agricultural and urban areas and thereby opening opportunities for the viruses they carry to spread to other species. One of these, which does not cause illness in the bats themselves, was dubbed Hendra virus after the Brisbane suburb where it was first identified in 1994, having fatally infected several horses and their handlers; another is Lyssavirus, which can be contracted directly by humans and is most likely to be found in bats that are sick or stressed (for instance, by changes in their environment or by the methods used by humans to expel them from theirs).[77] Epidemiological mapping of the epicenters of new deadly viral infections indicate that they have all emerged from rainforest biomes. Ebola, Marburg, and HIV, for instance, all hail from the African rainforest or its hinterland. As Frank Ryan observes, this suggests that "interference with rain forests, and deforestation in particular, is the most dangerous activity with regard to the emergence of new epidemic viruses."[78]

We are placing ourselves and other animals at grave risk in other ways as well, notably through the industrialization of animal husbandry. The emergence of bovine spongiform encephalopathy, commonly known as "mad cow disease," as a consequence of feeding herbivorous cattle sheep brains infected with scrapie, is probably the most obscene instance of the

commercially motivated mistreatment of food animals, while its association with Creutzfeldt-Jakob disease in humans is indicative of the ways in
which such mistreatment can rebound upon the societies that perpetrate
it. Equally concerning is the widespread use of antibiotics, not only to
counter the enhanced incidence of illness attendant upon factory farming
practices but also to increase rates of growth in livestock, which is contributing to the development of drug-resistant "superbugs."

The other major cause of antimicrobial resistance is the overprescrip-
tion of antibiotics for humans and their domestic companions. This is
a particularly revealing case of the "hazards of domination." As Marie-
Hélène Huet argues with respect to shifts in the interpretation of disease,
especially cholera, in the course of the eighteenth and nineteenth centuries, Enlightenment rationality, in disburdening God and the stars of
responsibility for causing epidemic illness, "yielded a world of shadows
where dreams of controlling a rebellious nature gave rise to a scientific
project itself fraught with perils and anxieties."[79] In the twentieth century, the discovery of antibiotics and the development of preventive and
early remedial treatments for several viruses, while significantly reducing
mortality from formerly common infections, gave rise to a dangerous delusion that disease could be entirely eradicated from human life. During
the heroic postwar period of medical advance, moreover, antibiotics stood
alongside antibacterial cleaning agents as weapons in a wider war against
"germs." Not only is this leading to the emergence of increasingly invin-
cible enemies; it also causes a good deal of collateral damage, taking out
beneficial bacteria as well, unsettling our inner ecology, and rendering us,
and other animals, more susceptible to superbug infection. Meanwhile,
effluents from urban areas, farms, and slaughterhouses are introducing
antimicrobial-resistant biota into free-living animal populations. These
are most likely to become a problem in the wider environment when, once
again, other stressors are in play and biodiversity is compromised.[80]

If, as Ryan concludes, "in our exploitation of all life on earth, in our
intrusion into every crevice of the biosphere, we have become a threat to
ourselves,"[81] then it is high time that disease prevention and treatment are
reconceived along ecological lines as a multispecies project. Among other
things, this would entail the conservation of wildlife habitat, the cessation
of factory farming, protection of our own microbial messmates, and the
stabilization of human population and consumption to levels that would
allow for the continued flourishing of diverse other-than-human lives.
Such multispecies practices of disease mitigation and amelioration imply

the acknowledgment of our transcorporeal connectedness with one another and other others, both in life and in death; and they would find support in the ethos of more-than-human flourishing toward which Shelley's narrator is belatedly propelled by the catastrophe of which he is, perhaps, the lone human survivor. Disease alone is unlikely to extinguish all human life on this planet. However, if a virus with the morbidity of Ebola or Hendra were to acquire the contagious properties of influenza, "fulminating in the amplification zones of our modern cities" and "fanned by the wind of modern airline travel,"[82] the fictitious scenario imagined by Mary Shelley could well become something approaching a historical reality, with the socially disadvantaged suffering worst and first. From the grim perspective of those who ponder the present prospects for such an eventuality, a further source of vulnerability has come into view—namely, the complacent human self-enclosure described so vividly by Albert Camus in his plague novel of 1947:

> In this respect our townsfolk were like everybody else, wrapped up in themselves; in other words, they were humanists; they disbelieved in pestilences. A pestilence isn't something made to man's measure; therefore we tell ourselves that pestilence is a mere bogey of the mind, a bad dream that will pass away. But it doesn't pass away and, from one bad dream to another, it is men who pass away, and the humanists first of all, because they haven't taken their precautions. Our townsfolk were not more to blame than others, they forgot to be modest—that was all—and thought that everything was still possible for them; which presupposed that pestilences were impossible. They went on doing business, arranged for journeys, and formed views. How should they have given a thought to anything like plague, which rules out any future, cancels journeys, silences the exchange of views? They fancied themselves free, and no one will ever be free so long as there are pestilences.[83]

Camus's plague might have been metaphorical, coding for the insidious spread of fascism, but his narrator's observations on the perilous hubris of humanism hold good for more literal variants of pestilence as well.

3

BREAKING WAVES

In the "Classical Walpurgis Night" scene of Act Two of the second part of his epic drama *Faust* (1832), Goethe stages a debate between two of the earliest philosophers in the Western tradition regarding the formation of the earth. While Anaxagoris (c. 500–428 BCE) celebrates the fiery volcanic forces that raised the mountains, his pre-Socratic predecessor Thales (c. 624–545 BCE) professes a preference for the creative element of water: "In moisture all that lives originated" (act 2, scene 10, 7856).[1] When Mephistopheles fronts up with a half-formed test-tube baby, fruit of a failed alchemical experiment by Faust's former student Wagner, who holds the old-fangled sexual process of reproduction to be beneath human dignity, Thales proceeds to put his theory to the test by consulting the sea god Nereus as to how Wagner's disembodied brain child might acquire a corporeal existence. Nereus duly instructs him to take the hermaphroditic Homunculus, who appears only as a pulsing light, to Proteus. Manifesting intermittently as a dolphin—with some coaxing from Thales, who is not keen on talking to an entity that he cannot locate—Proteus declares that the Homunculus must be entrusted to the creative agency of the ocean if he wishes to become a man (while remarking misanthropically that things would be all downhill from there). Thales, giving a proto-evolutionary spin to Proteus's words, accordingly exhorts Homunculus to "seek the beginnings of creation" in the watery deep, in order to "move onward by eternal norms / Through many thousand thousand forms / And reach at last the human state" (act 2, scene 10, 8322–26). For Goethe's Thales (if not for today's genetic engineers) there was no bypassing those generative processes that originated in, and were sustained by, earth's life-giving oceans:

> In water all things began to thrive!
> By water all things are kept alive!
> Grant us your bounty for ever, great ocean:
> Send us clouds, for if you did not,
> Abundant streams, for if you did not,
> And rivers in meandering motion,
> And great waterways—for if you did not,

Where would the mountains, the plains, and the world be then?
By you fresh life lives and is sustained again.
(act 2, scene 10, 8435–43)

Ultimately, however, it is not Thales's wise words but the sexual appeal of
the sea nymph Galatea, who appears Venus-like in a seashell chariot, that
draws Humunculus into the waves. As s/he bursts orgasmically out of the
confines of the test tube, and flame and water are conjoined, the scene
culminates with a chorus of Sirens singing the praises of Eros, to which
"all" respond with adulation for the four elements:

Hail to the mild and gentle breeze!
Hail, caverns rich with mysteries!
Fire, water, air, and earth as well:
You elements all four, all hail!
(act 2, scene 10, 8484–87)

In the wake of Charles Darwin's persuasive postulate of "natural selection"
as the primary driver of adaptation and speciation, most modern evolutionary biologists would doubtless reject Goethe's talk of "eternal norms"
as smacking of natural theology. There is nonetheless general agreement
today that earth's first living cells did indeed emerge in the ocean, as Thales
had postulated, and as the early evolutionary thinkers of the Romantic
period, Goethe among them, concurred. As Erasmus Darwin (Charles's
grandfather) phrased his version of this theory in *The Temple of Nature; or,
The Origin of Society* (1803) (a work that is inclined to make one glad that
scientists generally no longer try to share their findings in verse):

Organic Life beneath the shoreless waves
Was born and nurs'd in Ocean's pearly caves;
First forms minute, unseen by spheric glass,
Move on the mud, or pierce the watery mass;
These, as successive generations bloom,
New powers acquire, and larger limbs assume;
Whence countless groups of vegetation spring,
And breathing realms of fin, and feet, and wing.[2]

While the natural philosophers of the Romantic period thought they
had found material evidence for Thales's postulate in the microscopic
organisms that they mistakenly held to form spontaneously in standing
water, the idea that life originated in the sea has considerably more an-

cient antecedents in the mythic creation stories of many cultures. These include the "earth diver" narratives of several Native American and Central Asian peoples,[3] as well as the Babylonian myth of Marduk, the warrior god, who is said to have created heaven and earth out of the slain body of the primordial mother, goddess of the watery deep, Tiamat. This matricidal creation narrative was radically rewritten by the priestly authors of Genesis 1, whose divine agent (a heavenly collective referred to as Elohim) acts far more peacefully, and perhaps even collaboratively, in summoning a differentiated world of day and night, sea and sky, land and water, plants, animals, and finally humans, out of the "surging watery deep" (tehom).[4]

Remembering the watery world from which each of us emerged into the air at birth, it is hardly surprising that aquatic accounts of life's origin should have such widespread appeal for placental mammals such as ourselves with a penchant for storytelling. Yet the indispensability of that eagerly awaited first breath to the continuation of life beyond the womb points up the profoundly ambivalent place of water in the existence of all landlubbers. For creatures whose inner aquifers, so to speak, require regular replenishment, a ready source of fresh water is clearly essential to survival. For many terrestrial species, moreover, bodies of water, whether fresh or salt, also provide a crucial source of nourishment, as well as a welcome place to bathe. Among such water lovers are those human communities—or, more accurately, more-than-human collectives—across the world and throughout the ages who have created seasonal or permanent abodes on the shores of rivers, lakes, or seas. But for all who breathe air, even a small quantity of water relative to their size carries the risk of drowning; and rivers, lakes, and seas are not always placid neighbors. This is not such a problem if your way of life is mobile and flexible, allowing you to simply avoid flooded ground or get out fast whenever you spot the signs foreshadowing immanent inundation. The practice of permanent settlement, however, turns the labile ways of water into a hazard, not only for human residents but also for many of the nonhumans who share their space. In order to mitigate flood risk, settled societies have developed various techniques to manage their aqueous environs. But these have always come at a price and frequently engendered further hazards.

Consider, for example, the case of Ancient Mesopotamia. It was the propensity of the great rivers Tigris and Euphrates to periodically overrun their banks and shift their course, which helped to produce the rich alluvial soils that attracted early agriculturalists to this region as the climate began to warm and stabilize following the end of the last glacial maximum.

Grains that had probably first been domesticated up in the hills where they grew wild began to be cultivated down on the alluvial plains over ten thousand years ago. By around 5,500 BCE, with the rise of the first walled—and often warring—city states, an irrigation system had been developed that facilitated the expansion of agriculture to the drier southern reaches of the Mesopotamian basin, while the building of levees helped mitigate the ever-present flood risk. In time, however, this resulted in the buildup of silt and rising levels of soil salinity, which in turn led to repeated agricultural crises from around 3,000 BCE, contributing to the collapse of one center of Mesopotamian civilization after another. In Evan Eisenberg's analysis, a faint suspicion "that their greatest triumph, irrigation, was bringing about their greatest disaster, salinization,"[5] can be traced in ancient Sumerian poems that turn upon the conflict between the tricksterish water deity, Enki, and the mountain-dwelling fertility goddess, Ninhursag. Similarly, another work from the eighteenth century BCE, the *Epic of Atrahasis,* recounts how the gods punished humans for making too much of a racket by causing the salty sea to rise up through the earth: "During the nights the fields turned white. The broad plain brought forth salt crystals, so that no plant came forth, no grain sprouted."[6]

The changes in land use and ecosystem functioning that occurred over centuries and even millennia in such ancient centers of riverine agricultural development were dramatically concertinaed in the context of European colonization from the sixteenth to the nineteenth century, the consequences of which, in conjunction with the dramatic impact of industrialization, continue to unfold in the present. One place where this is proving particularly problematic is on the lower reaches of the Mississippi. This is another of the world's great rivers. Toward its mouth in the Gulf of Mexico it had long been in the habit of depositing piles of sediment along its banks, which formed natural levees of around three feet in height. These would be breached from time to time, but it appears that the Native American peoples who took up residence by the river tolerated occasional flooding as part of the deal that enabled them to benefit from the Mississippi's many gifts of food, water, and fertile soils. As Nancy Tuana emphasizes in her interactionist account of the catastrophic impact of Hurricane Katrina, these indigenous inhabitants in turn reshaped their environs, not least by the deposition of shell middens, which fostered the growth of new plant communities. Among them were the stands of cyprus and oaks, which attracted those European and Euro-American colonists in the eighteenth century, for whom the trees beckoned as a profitable commodity. Meanwhile, the river itself was refunctionalized as a transit corridor for cotton, sugar, grain, and other goods from upstream to the port city that grew up around its mouth. As New Orleans expanded, its buildings plastered with lime quarried from the shell middens left by generation upon generation of the region's displaced prior occupants, water was pumped out of the swampy low-lying land appropriated for new housing and industries, while artificial levees were constructed to contain the mighty river.[7]

Those charged with the task of creating and maintaining this regime of draining and disciplining the aqueous environs of the city are known as the Army Corps of Engineers. For around two centuries, their battle with the river has been ongoing, and they appear unlikely to win a final victory. In 2008, Andrew Pickering sketched the story of this protracted campaign as follows: "As the levees rose, the river rose as well; flooding continued; the levees had to be raised further, and so, back and forth, right up to the present. As a result New Orleans became a walled city, surrounded by a ring of earthworks thirty feet high." To make matters worse, the river that now flows, in places, above the city, wants to move. According to Pickering, it is now thirty feet above one of the lesser rivers it drains into, the Atchafalaya: "Left to itself, the entire Mississippi would spill into the Atchafalaya, reaching the Gulf a couple of hundred miles west of its present destination, and leaving the existing lower reaches of the Mississippi a mere trickle."[8]

Within the prevailing settler culture of the United States, the role accorded to the Army Corps of Engineers is scripted by the master narrative of human domination over Nature. By contrast, Pickering reconceives their struggle with the Mississippi as a "dance of agency," understood as a "decentred and open-ended becoming of the human and non-human,"[9] in which the river has repeatedly responded to the strictures placed upon it in ways that have prompted yet further interventions. As Adrian Franklin has observed, Pickering's dance metaphor is suggestive of a tango.[10] The trouble is that, in refusing to respect the moves the river wants to make in this dance—one that has been conducted on the patriarchal assumption that the man always leads—the Army Corps of Engineers is forever running the risk of coming a cropper, at the expense of the more-than-human collectivity of the city that it has been ordered to protect. To make their task trickier still, as nobody who witnessed the devastating impact of Hurricane Katrina should need reminding, New Orleans is also vulnerable to the cyclonic storms and sea surges that are regularly generated by the interaction of particular atmospheric flows with the warm waters of the gulf, waters that are currently getting warmer as a consequence of anthropogenic climate change and increasingly likely to deliver a far bigger hurricane than the one that made lethal landfall in Louisiana on August 29, 2005.[11]

In order to trace the historical background to the campaign of discipline and draining that the Army Corps of Engineers has been waging on the Mississippi, we need to head back across the Atlantic to Europe. The geographical focus for my consideration of this history is the Low Countries of northwestern Europe, and in particular the west coast of North Frisia, now part of the German state of Schleswig-Holstein. This is the setting—and, indeed, one of the primary actants—in a literary work that engages with this history in a particularly illuminating manner: Theodor Storm's novella *Der Schimmelreiter* ("The rider on the gray," or, in the translation used here, *The Dykemaster*[12]), which tells the tragic tale of Hauke Haien, a fictitious dykegrave and dyke builder, who ends up leaping to his death in a watery grave in the great flood of 1756.

The landscape of Storm's natal North Frisia has been shaped and reshaped many times over in an open-ended and decentered process of geocultural becoming, such as Pickering traces on the Mississippi. In brief, the story goes something like this: the favorable, if highly labile, environmental conditions that attracted human settlers to the Frisian salt marshes—first gatherer-hunters, then a succession of herders, salt harvesters, peat cutters, and farmers—were created by a dynamic interplay of oceanic, climatic, geological, and biotic factors. The terrestrial changes introduced by the people who laid claim to the land altered the impacts of sea and storm in ways that called forth further human interventions along the coast, which in turn impacted upon social relations. Prior to human settlement, the coastline had morphed dramatically over the millennia as a consequence of rising and falling sea levels. In addition, smaller changes were frequently wrought by the winter storm surges to which the southern North Sea coast is particularly susceptible. These typically occur when the wind changes from the south or southwest to the northwest, causing a confluence of the currents forced up into the North Sea from the English Channel with those simultaneously being forced south from the North Sea between Scotland and Norway.[13]

Prior to the eleventh century, peasant farmers in North Frisia built their dwellings on small knolls (*Wurten* or *Warften*), accommodating themselves to regular flooding in exchange for the nutrients that the sea left in the soil. By the early Middle Ages, some had begun to extend the amount of land under cultivation by the construction of summer dykes that were dismantled after the harvest. With the development of permanent dykes, however, this dance of people, plants, animals, wind, and sea changed its character significantly. By the thirteenth century, as environmental historian David Blackbourn explains, the "golden ring" that surrounded the Frisian marshes ensured that "the flood waters, instead of spreading out a few inches deep over the marshland behind the tidal mudflats, built up against the dykes and battered at them, giving rise to the familiar image of the angry, growling sea."[14] This also engendered greater social stratification as rich farmers, whose family wealth was based on the drainage and colonization of landward marshes and bogs, joined with other men of high social standing (town merchants and professionals) to take charge of dyke building and maintenance, while impoverished or displaced peasants joined the ranks of their paid laborers.[15] The dykes demanded continuous attention, and during times of war, famine, or plague, they were commonly neglected, making them more susceptible to failure. Meanwhile, as the drained marshes dried and peat was cut from the moors, the land shrank and sank, resituating the dyked fields below sea level. In seeking to extend and fortify their settlements against the sea, the North Frisians had in effect made themselves and their domestic animals more vulnerable to major disaster, as light to moderate more-or-less annual flooding was replaced by a catastrophic deluge around once a century. Their attempt to break the landward passage of the North Sea waters, in other words, had caused far greater waves to break into and over their dwelling places than those with which earlier inhabitants of this region had learned to dance.

The first recorded of these "floods of the century" occurred in 1164, and it was followed by those of 1287, 1334, 1362, 1511, 1570, 1634, 1717, 1756, 1825, and 1855. The Christmas 1717 storm surge, followed by further flooding in 1718 and 1720, remains the worst on record in terms of fatalities, claiming the lives of around eleven thousand people and some ninety-five thousand domestic animals.[16] There has been a run of big floods in the twentieth century, with the highest water level yet recorded in Storm's hometown of Husum peaking at 5.66 meters in 1976. Higher, stronger dykes and tidal barriers, in conjunction with more reliable forecasting of extremes, have reduced fatalities. Whether and for how long these techno-scientific improvements can keep pace with today's anthropogenically rising sea levels and more frequent and intense extremes remains to be seen. But beyond a certain point, dykes can be built no higher without destabilizing the very ground upon which this increasingly dicey dance of distributed agency has been enacted over the past millennium.[17]

The control of water was integral to the making of modern Germany, and Storm's fictitious dyke builder is exemplary of the quest for aquatic mastery that got under way around the middle of the eighteenth century. While the technical innovation that Storm attributes to his protagonist— the construction of a more gently sloping seaward side of the dyke to reduce water pressure and hence erosion—was actually developed in the Netherlands in the early sixteenth century, it had not yet been widely adopted in Schleswig at the time when Hauke Haien's story is set. After 1750, moreover, the hydrological projects that were undertaken through-out the German region were far larger, with correspondingly greater im-pacts, and primarily oriented toward enhancing the wealth and power of territorial states. Chief among these was Prussia under Frederick the Great, who drained more marshland and fen than any other ruler of his day.[18] In Schleswig, following the catastrophic 1717–20 floods, coastal pro-tection was unified under the authority of the state, in accordance with the principles laid out in Albert Brahms's *Anfangsgründe der Deich und Wasser-Baukunst* ("Principles of Dyke and Aquatic Engineering," 1754–57). Brahms (1692–1758), a dykegrave on the Frisian Wadden Sea and a pioneer of modern German coastal engineering, advocated building dykes with a convex shape on both the landward and the seaward sides.[19] These administrative and technical innovations helped reduce the death toll on the mainland during the 1825 storm surge, when floodwaters peaked higher but claimed fewer lives than in 1717. In North Frisia the leading dyke builder of the mid-1700s was Jean Henri Desmercieres (1687–1778), who created several new "polders" or *Kooge*—areas of fertile marshland re-claimed from the sea—using the improved sloping-sided dyke design. Des-mercieres's dyke-building enterprise is one of the likely models for Hauke Haien's; but whereas Storm's protagonist is a resident farmer, his historical counterpart was a capitalist entrepreneur. A director of the Royal Bank in Copenhagen, Desmercieres acquired permits from the Crown to finance the building of new dykes by paid laborers, in order to then sell off par-cels of the newly acquired land at a tidy profit, part of which returned to the Crown in taxes. Throughout the 1700s, there were also repeated— and, significantly for my reading of *The Dykemaster*, costly and largely unsuccessful—attempts to dam the so-called Königstief (King's Deep), the deepest and most dangerous of three watercourses that flowed across the "New Koog" on the Hattstedter Marsh near Husum. From the early nineteenth century, measures to control inland waters and drain marshland also intensified.[20]

The practice of ever more intensive and extensive damming, dyking, and drainage created an increasingly sharp divide between sea and land, watery waste and cultivated soil, in place of what had once been a natural-cultural amphibious zone, where the wild and the domesticated, fresh and saltwater, human and nonhuman agencies, had previously intermingled promiscuously (if not always harmoniously). This material division rendered palpable, and thereby reinforced, the long-standing nature-culture dualism within European thought. As discussed in the first chapter, this binary was also in the process of becoming entrenched as the organizing principle of the modern system of knowledge, severing the "natural" from the "human," or, as the Germans put it, the "natural" from the "spiritual" sciences, under the Modern Constitution. By the time Storm wrote *The Dykemaster,* this onto-epistemological bifurcation had contributed to a further discursive divide: namely, between disasters wrought by "nature" and those caused by "man."

In his historical reconstruction of changing interpretations of North Sea storm surges from the sixteenth to the nineteenth century, Manfred Jakubowski-Tiessen identifies the 1825 flood as a turning point in this development. Around midnight on February 3, 1825, the North Sea rose once again, whipped up by a powerful storm rendered all the more lethal by a sudden wind change from the southwest to the northwest. The surging waters of that night's high tide breached the barriers that had been extended and fortified since the last major North Sea floods of 1717–20, inundating farms, villages, and towns along the coast from Belgium to Jutland, devastating hundreds of square kilometers of agricultural land and even tearing off huge chunks of peat moor, which were strewn across the ruined fields by the receding tide. Eight hundred people are believed to have died that night, along with some forty-five thousand domestic animals.[21] In Theodor Storm's hometown of Husum, according to the pillar that stands in the harbor as a memorial to this history of weather- and sea-borne disaster, the floodwaters of February 1825 peaked at 5.10 meters.[22]

For participants in the Protestant revivalist movement, this great flood provided the occasion for a reactionary reassertion of the biblical paradigm of divine punishment with a millenarian agenda—a view occasionally still voiced today by monotheistic fundamentalists and represented in Storm's novella by the members of the local tailor's revivalist conventicle. This perspective was opposed by more mainstream Christians on familiar physico-theological grounds, according to which such events could not be attributed directly to divine intervention, but were a function of the natural world that God had graciously enabled to come into being, and doubtless served some ultimately good purpose that was as yet veiled to us. However, the increasingly widespread view was that which found expression in phrases such as the "fury of nature," "raging battle of the elements," and, more soberly, "natural occurrence of flood."[23] The shift that Jakubowski-Tiessen traces, namely toward an identification of the unruly elements as the sole agent of destruction, is consistent with Blackbourn's findings for the German region as a whole, in which Nature is increasingly cast "as an adversary to be manacled, tamed, subjugated, conquered."[24] It is this dominological view that informs Hauke Haien's engineering scheme, a view that is subtly challenged within the complex narrative weave of Storm's multivalent text.

Storm was an impressionable seven-year-old in 1825, and in her biography of her father, Gertrud Storm describes this as the first "great event" of his life.[25] It also had a big impact on the aging Goethe in Weimar, leading him to "look upon the elements as gigantic adversaries with whom we have to fight unceasingly, conquering them in particular cases only by courage and guile and the highest energy of our spirit," as he wrote in his "Essay on Meteorology" (1825).[26] This reminder of the chaotically destructive agency of the elements also precipitated his return to *Faust, Part Two*, which he had begun, but then abandoned, in 1816, eight years after the publication of *Part One*.[27] In the final version, completed in 1831 and published posthumously the following year, Goethe's archetypically modern tragic hero metamorphoses into a hydrological engineer.

Unlike his legendary and literary predecessors, Goethe's Faust does not seek wealth, fame, and power, but aspires rather for a perpetual process of self-realization, powered by a sense of permanent dissatisfaction with the present. Accordingly, his bargain with Mephistopheles entails this pledge:

> If ever to the moment I shall say:
> Beautiful moment, do not pass away!
> Then you may forge your chains to bind me,
> Then I will put my life behind me
> (act 1, scene 7, 1699–72)[28]

In *Part One,* it is the pretty village girl, Gretchen, who pays the price for Faust's classically modernist project of ceaseless self-development.[29] Having been left to deal with an illegitimate pregnancy alone, she is driven to the desperate solution of infanticide and subsequently dies in prison awaiting execution. Scandalously, the play ends with her redemption by an unconventional deus ex machina, who mercifully foils Mephistopheles's bid to claim her soul. Having recovered from his feelings of grief and guilt about the death of Gretchen, the Faust of *Part Two* sets his sights on a higher quest, namely for the love of the legendary epitome of female beauty, Helen of Troy. It is in the process of preparing to raise her from the Underworld that Mephistopheles and Faust participate in the Classical Walpurgis Night, in which the subplot of the Homunculus is played out. In the third act, the union between Helen and Faust is eventually achieved and even issues in a child, Euphorion. When their son, Ikarus-like, flies too close to the sun and falls to his death, however, Helen too returns to the Underworld. Left distraught by their loss, Faust externalizes his urge for self-transformation into a quest to remake the world around him, eliminating in the process all traces of the premodern *oikos*, to which his first love, Gretchen, had belonged.

The celebration of the sea with which act 2 of Goethe's cosmic drama closes stands in stark contrast to the distaste that befalls the aging and embittered Faust at the beginning of act 4 as he looks out upon what he perceives as the "barrenness" of the waves that eternally return upon the shore in a "useless" expenditure of "elemental energy" (act 4, scene 14, 10212–19). Assuming an agro-industrial standard of productivity, Faust is insouciant to the other-than-human life that flourishes in the liminal zone of the shoreline. Determined to assert himself against the waves by reclaiming the "dreary waste of dismal sand" (10215) for some more useful purpose, he blinds himself also to the cost entailed in the Mephistophelian realization of his new project to "ban the lordly sea" and "curb its force" (10229). As we discover in the dialogue between the Wanderer and his kind hosts, the shore-dwelling Philemon and Baucis, at the start of act 5, this cost was borne not only by the more-than-human life of these coastal wetlands but also by those forced to perform the labor of turning them into a "garden" (act 5, scene 17, 11085): "All night long we heard the cries—/A canal was built by morning" (11129–30). Behind the diabolical means that created what is, for Faust, a "paradisal scene" (11086) stand the historical realities, not only of land reclamation at home but also of slavery and colonial conquest abroad: the "undivided trinity/Of war and trade and piracy," applauded by Mephistopheles as Faust's ships return to harbor laden with plunder from overseas (11187–89).

Faust is dismayed when he learns that his appropriation of Philemon's and Baucis's dwelling place in order to create a viewing platform, from which to admire his achievements, had cost them their lives. He nonetheless remains committed to his Promethean project, to which he now gives a utopian spin: Goethe's tragic hero dies dreaming of the expanded living space for a new breed of human battlers against the elements, which he will have created through his ambitious dyke, dam, and drainage scheme. Scandalously, Mephistopheles fails to make off with his soul, having been lustfully distracted by the alluring boy angels whose ministry helps to facilitate Faust's unorthodox redemption by something referred to in the closing words of the drama as "eternal Womanhood" (act 5, scene 23, 1210). But, in keeping with his self-designation in *Part One* as the "spirit of perpetual negation" (act 1, scene 6, 1338), he does foreshadow the eventual ruination of Faust's endeavors:

> And yet it's us you're working for
> With all your foolish dams and dikes;
> Neptune, the water-devil, likes
> To think of the great feast there'll be
> When they collapse.
> (act 5, scene 21, 11544–48)

Indeed, according to one reading, Faust's hastily built canals are already collapsing, a phenomenon that was well known to Goethe and referred to at the time as "hydrological terrorism."[30] If so, the ending is profoundly ironic, as the "putrid puddle" (11559–60) that Faust is set on draining as he dies is not a remnant of the original coastal wetlands, but an unintended consequence of his attempted mastery of this aqueous terrain.

Goethe's two-part drama constitutes an extremely dense text, and it has invited a wide range of divergent readings. I have had a few goes at it myself in the past, but the interpretation that I currently find most persuasive is Heather Sullivan's "non-equilibrium ecocritical reading."[31] Sullivan's fresh approach is informed by "affinity studies," which resituate human agency within "a complex entanglement of cultural and physical patterns, or as part of flows between 'open systems.'"[32] On this open systems understanding, no entities stand alone and unconditioned, no actions are entirely free, and no events are monocausal. All things, including human subjects, are formed and transformed through their dynamic interrelations with other things, and their agency is always in some sense "distributed," as Peter Taylor puts it, emerging "within the interpersonal, cultural and natural flows around it."[33] Attending to Goethe's poetic discourse of interweaving flows, along with the triple framing of the dramatic action of *Faust*, which reveals the protagonist's quest as, first, a literary fiction ("Dedication"), second, a staged performance ("Prelude in the Theater"), and third, the subject of a Job-like gamble between Mephistopheles and God ("Prologue in Heaven"), Sullivan reinterprets the tragedy as "questioning rather than exemplifying human control over nature-culture."[34] From this perspective, the dyke becomes legible as "a metaphor for the Faustian consciousness that blindly sees its own agency but not its inevitable affinities and 'enabling conditions,' and thus believes that it can close the open systems of flow."[35]

Storm's last great work, completed just months before he died in 1888, also features a Promethean dyke builder, whom some within the narrative take to have a similarly sinister associate. Storm was fascinated by *Faust*, especially the remarkable second part, and a number of critics have discerned similarities between the protagonist of his novella, the North Frisian Hauke Haien, and Goethe's archetypal modernizer.[36] Despite certain variations in emphasis and interpretation, these earlier comparisons share a broadly anthropocentric agenda, according to which human reason and will are assumed to be pitted against the blindly destructive forces of "nature" (along with the irrational impulses of dim-witted or unenlightened humans).[37] When reconsidered from a material ecocritical perspective, however, the Faustian echoes in Storm's text acquire a very different salience. Taking my cue from Sullivan's reading of Goethe's drama, I will argue here that Storm's protagonist is "Faustian" in the sense that he too falls prey, not so much to the violence of the elements or the backwardness of his compatriots, but to the characteristically modern anthroparchal illusion of unidirectional self-determined human agency. Moving beyond the point where *Faust. Part Two* concludes, namely to the disastrous return of the sea as prefigured by Mephistopheles, this text also reveals the complex entanglement of diverse human and nonhuman agencies and processes in the unfolding of the catastrophic flood with which it culminates. This is a story that raises increasingly urgent questions about human interrelations and intra-actions with those elemental forces that have only been rendered more unruly by the project of technological mastery that was intended to keep them at bay. By contrast with Faust's epic drama, no horizon of transcendence opens at the end of Storm's tragic novella.[38] However, it is possible to discern an implied alternative to the Faustian project within this text—one that opens the prospect of a post-anthroparchal pathway toward a different, more ecological mode of enlightenment.[39]

In the postwar era, both within and beyond the world of literary schol-arship, the predominant view of Storm up until the 1980s was of a senti-mental and apolitical *Heimatdichter,* a provincial poet of place. As his more recent biographers have disclosed, however, he was by no means entirely at home in the provinces; nor was he altogether hostile to the changes that were afoot in the wider world. According to Georg Bollenbeck, the letters that he wrote to his friends in the years following his return to Husum in 1842 indicate that he often experienced his hometown as lonely and stifling.[40] Storm's views on marriage, sexuality, and the status of women, informed by his reading of the left-Hegelian Ludwig Feuerbach, were de-cidedly modern, if not as radical as those of the Young German movement. During the 1840s, he also became a public supporter of the democratic nationalist cause of independence for Schleswig-Holstein, positioning himself in his articles for the Schleswig-Holstein press on the left wing of the nationalist party (Landespartei).[41] Following the defeat of the move-ment in 1851, Storm refused to sign a declaration of loyalty to the Danish throne, leading to the withdrawal of his license to practice as a lawyer in Schleswig. From 1853 to 1864 he therefore lived in voluntary exile in Prus-sia and Bavaria. Prussia's annexation of Schleswig enabled him to return to Husum in 1865 to work as a district magistrate until retiring to Hade-marschen in 1880.

Theodor Storm's last novella is also his best known, both within and beyond the German-speaking region. It was enthusiastically received at the time of publication and has since generated a considerable body of secondary literature, along with over forty translations and at least three film versions,[42] including one from the Nazi era, which totally elides the complexity and ambivalence of the written narrative in construing its pro-tagonist as a modernizing Führer-figure. *Der Schimmelreiter* also rates a mention in Blackbourn's *Conquest of Nature,* where it is said to relate the "the heroic efforts of Haike Hauen [*sic*] to preserve a dyke in the face of selfishness and indifference, efforts which eventually cost him his life." Blackbourn adds that "more than a trace of the heroic tone, mixed with pride in the latest technology, has found its way into the modern literature on coastal defences and the need for vigilance against the threat of natural disaster from the sea."[43] Blackbourn evidently assumes that the implied reader of this text is meant to applaud the protagonist's dyke-building prowess. Indeed, this was the dominant reading of the novella for at least a century, and not just among literary critics: on June 10, 1961, the minister president of Schleswig-Holstein announced that his government had acceded to popular pressure to name a newly created polder below the North Frisian town of Bongsiel the "Hauke Haien Koog," in recognition that Storm's fictional hero embodied nothing less than the "poetic ideal of the work of dyke-construction."[44] By the mid-1960s, however, more equivocal views were beginning to be voiced, at least among some scholars, foremost among them Jost Hermand, who reinterpreted Storm's novella as at once a product and a critique of the ideology of the ruthless Übermensch current in late-nineteenth-century imperial Germany.[45] Other, more fine-grained investigations have followed, indicative of the ambivalent perspective on the protagonist that emerges from a close reading of the novella in hermeneutic horizons less favorable to the figure of the Faustian modernizer.[46] The unconditionally positive view of Hauke Haien nonetheless persists, as can be seen, for instance, in David A. Jackson's afterword to Denis Jackson's 1996 English translation. Jackson eulogizes Storm's fictional dyke builder as "a true humanitarian hero," who "forms a trinity with Socrates and Jesus Christ as a searcher after truth." Like the latter, moreover, he not only dies as a martyr for his cause but also suffers the indignity of being "turned into a ghost" by those who fail to recognize the humanitarian significance of his legacy.[47]

In likening Hauke to Socrates and Jesus, Jackson endorses the view of the fictional narrator, a wizened schoolmaster who recounts Hauke's story to the journalist whose article is subsequently recalled and retold by the second frame narrator. While Jackson discerns a degree of ambivalence toward Hauke on the part of the schoolmaster, he endorses the generally sympathetic view of the protagonist as a progressive enlightened humanist that emerges from his account. This view presumably also motivates Denis Jackson's decision to entitle his translation *The Dykemaster*. For it is in the schoolmaster's eyes that Hauke is to be remembered first and foremost as that: not only as a noteworthy overseer, that is, but as one whose engineering genius made him a master of the whole dyking enterprise, embodying the triumph of human reason over the destructive forces of nature. This interpretive choice is a dubious one, in my view, as it elides the ambiguous evaluation of the protagonist that is generated by the complex narrative structure of the text and inscribed into the German title.

To begin with, it should be noted that this is a case of the unreliable narrator, amplified to the power of three: the schoolmaster admits that he has a particular take on the tale and that he has cobbled it together out of other peoples' accounts, privileging those of "rational people" (*D*, 65) but also incorporating aspects of the "superstitious" version of the story, of which he strongly disapproves, along with details, such as Hauke's train of thought in deciding to build his new dyke, to which there were no witnesses and that must therefore be highly speculative. The schoolmaster's story is recounted in an article published in the 1830s by a journalist, whose first-person narrative begins with a description of his encounter with a mysterious horseman as he rode along a North Frisian dyke one afternoon in October, in "fierce weather" (13). Reporting this eerie encounter to a gathering of the local dyke committee in the inn where he has taken refuge, he learns that this will have been the ghost of Hauke Haien, who is said to haunt the dyke when a new breach threatens, plunging into the breach pond that was formed at the place where he and his horse had died in the great flood of the previous century. The current dykemaster directs the journalist to the schoolmaster to hear the whole story, while remarking that his old housekeeper, Antje Vollmer, would tell it very differently. Her version is suppressed; but the article implies that it should not be too lightly dismissed, as the schoolmaster's narration is subsequently interrupted by two further sightings of the ghostly rider by various members of the dyke committee. This article, moreover, is being recounted by another first-person narrator, writing in the 1880s, who claims that he has never forgotten it, even though he read it fifty years earlier. Unless he was blessed with a photographic memory, we have to assume therefore that this too is a retelling, presumably with its own slant: "I cannot guarantee the truth of the following account," he cautions, "nor could I vouch for the details should anyone wish to dispute them." (13) The only thing we learn about this frame narrator is that he still shudders when he recalls his over eighty-year-old great-grandmother's hand caressing his hair as he read the article. This unpleasant detail has remained oddly unremarked in most of the secondary literature. But this reader, for one, is inclined to wonder how the second frame narrator's revulsion toward his great-grandmother's tender touch might color his remembrance of the old women who figure in the article—Antje Vollmer in the first frame narrative and the decidedly witchy Trin' Jans within the story of Hauke Haien—compounding the schoolmaster's marginalization of their stories and perspectives.

The uncertainty surrounding the true identity of the protagonist and the correct interpretation of his life story is also implicit in the German title. As the "rider on the gray" (*Schimmelreiter*), Hauke is *both* the malign ghost of Antje Vollmer's version *and* the enlightened dyke builder of the schoolmaster's. In the former account, only glimpsed indirectly, he is a sinister figure, whose horse is not entirely of this world, having been acquired, by his own admission (as reported by the schoolmaster), from a gypsy with a claw-like hand who laughed "like the devil" as Hauke led him away (*D*, 72). According to Hauke's stable boy, the purchase of the gray coincided with the disappearance of the mysterious skeletal remains and ghostly apparition of a horse that he and the farmhand Carsten had seen on Jevershallig, one of the small, undyked islands close to the mainland. And, while this is not recalled explicitly in the text, according to North Frisian folklore, the devil (and, before him, the Norse God Odin) rides a gray. In the schoolmaster's account, by contrast, this demonic transaction reads more like an animal rescue operation: the horse, as Hauke points out to his "prudent wife," who is worried about the expense, had been "starved and ill-treated" (70) and is skinny, dull eyed, and lame. Once he has been nurtured back to good health, the gray, whom only Hauke can handle and who becomes "at one" with his rider (73), is enlisted in the dykemaster's construction scheme, becoming an ally in his control over other (socially subordinate) men, in the service of his containment of the watery deep:

> Appointed foremen walked up and down, and when it blew a gale they stood with wide-open mouths hollering their orders into the wind and weather; among them rode the dykemaster on his grey, which he now rode all the time, and the animal flew to and fro with its rider as he swiftly and coldly rapped out his orders, praised the workmen, or, as happened from time to time, dismissed a lazy or clumsy worker without mercy. (80)

What the schoolmaster's tale lets slip here are the historical interconnections between the domination of nature and particular forms of social oppression, as discerned by Adorno and Horkheimer in *Dialectic of Enlightenment* and since explored further by an array of ecological socialist, feminist, and postcolonial theorists.[48] In their critique of capitalist modernization, Adorno and Horkheimer also highlight the psychosexually repressive dimension of this dominological endeavor, notably in the guise of the Puritan work ethic, which, as Max Weber had previously demonstrated, proved so conducive to the "spirit of capitalism." Hauke has this in abundance: as dykemaster, his life of "unremitting toil" (*D*, 59) meant that Elke's efforts in the early years of their marriage to lie awake waiting for him to come to bed went unrewarded, and they remained childless for many years. Hauke's rational self-mastery is also hinted at in his designation as the "rider on the gray": namely, in the echo of Socrates's metaphorical charioteer in Plato's *Phaedrus,* tasked with reining in the horse of carnal passion and forcing it to walk in step with that of moral impulse.[49]

Rather than obliging the reader to accept one or the other of these contrasting takes on the tale, and the opposing onto-epistemologies from which they emerge, the double framing of Storm's narrative opens up the possibility that neither Antje Vollmer nor the schoolmaster is in possession of the final truth of the matter. The deconstructive conclusion that has been drawn from the narrative's onto-epistemological undecidability is that this highly self-reflexive though ostensibly "realist" text is not actually concerned with "reality" at all, but solely with the practice of narration itself.[50] While I agree that this is, among other things and importantly so, a story about storytelling, my reading of *The Dykemaster* suggests that what it discloses is that reality certainly matters, but that there is more to reality's material manifestations than meets the eye; more than has as yet been explained by science; and more, perhaps, than can ever be revealed by its methods or captured by human sign systems, whether mathematical or verbal.[51] Epistemologically elusive though it might be, the material world is nonetheless also shown to be powerfully agential, with a proclivity for interrupting human ideations and undertakings. To attend to this dimension of the text is to discern the lineaments of a third take on the tale, one that is neither mythic nor rationalist but ecological in a material feminist vein.

The first step toward this alternative reading of Hauke Haien's story involves attending more closely to the many-nonhuman entities that figure in the narrative. The more-than-human character of the collective that inhabits and coconstitutes the coastal region memorialized in *The Dykemaster* is established in the opening of the journalist's tale in his description of the "crows and gulls, which, constantly cawing and cackling, were being driven inland by the storm" (*D,* 13–14)—a reminder that nonhumans too must contend with the unruly elements. These opening bird calls are echoed in the schoolmaster's description of Hauke's last ride along this same dyke in the tempest with which his story concludes. But whereas in the frame narrative the encounter between birds and rider is almost tender, with the low-flying birds' long wings being said to have "almost brushed" the journalist and his "trusty mare" (14), in the schoolmaster's tale, Hauke's powerful stallion crushes a gull under its pounding hooves. Identifying the victim as Claus, one of his intellectually disabled daughter's companion animals, Hauke expresses pity for the tame creature who had found death where it had presumably sought shelter. This recalls, but also differs from, the journalist's fellow feeling for the wild birds he encounters, with whom he had "every sympathy" (13) as they too struggle against the strong gale.[52] Whereas Hauke's feeling is one of pity for a dependent, the journalist's is more like solidarity with (other) animals, possessed of their own interests and agency.

Hauke's movement of pity for Wienke's pet also stands in stark contrast to the utter disdain for animal life that he displayed as a teenager: during his long solitary hours on the old dyke, he is said to have "heard neither the splashing of the water nor the cries of the shore birds and seagulls which flew around or above him and nearly brushed him with their wings, their dark eyes flashing into his" (D, 19). In his mental preoccupation with the problem of improved protection against the sea, Hauke ignores the sensory perceptions that might have revealed these birds to him as fellow creatures. Declining to meet their gaze, he denies also their ethical considerability, and takes to honing his throwing skills by killing "little grey sandpipers" with stones hurled from the dyke as they "called and scurried across" the mudflats (24). As there is no indication that the birds supplied a dietary supplement for Hauke and his widowed father—unlike Trin' Jans's old Angora tomcat, to whom he was in the habit of tossing one of his catch on the way home—the reader is left to assume that this was an act of wanton and perhaps sadistic violence. Moreover, having on one occasion scored something more beautiful and exotic, which the schoolmaster identifies as possibly a kingfisher, Hauke breaks his deal with the cat. When the tom endeavors to take by stealth what he had come to consider his by right, Hauke becomes infuriated and remorselessly strangles him to death.

Neither the schoolmaster nor many, if any, of Storm's interpreters appear to rate the fate of Hauke's nonhuman victims as worthy of consideration in their own right. In good Kantian fashion, the killing of the cat is only acknowledged as wrongful because of the indirect harm caused to its human owner: the old Angora, we are told, was Trin' Jans's "pride and joy . . . her sole companion and the only thing that her son, a seaman, had left her after meeting with sudden death on this coast" (25). In her dismay, the old woman curses Hauke. This curse would no doubt be considered portentous within the mythic account of his tale; Trin' herself observes on the birth of his defective daughter that he is being punished, although what for exactly remains unclear. As narrated by the schoolmaster, however, the primary interest of this episode is psychological: his father is said to have agreed with Hauke's own analysis that this violent outburst could be put down to pent-up adolescent frustration, for which the good Protestant solution is meaningful employment. In killing a fellow predator in a fit of "rage like a wild beast's" (24), so this story goes, Hauke is forced to confront his own aggressive instincts, which are thenceforth to be sublimated in the labors that he now embarks upon: first as the old dykemaster's farmhand, then as his accountant, and finally, having married his daughter and thereby acquired sufficient property to qualify, as the new dykemaster.

To be fair, the casual cruelty of the adolescent is replaced by a more compassionate attitude in the adult dykemaster, who also displays an unconventionally immanental view of the divine. According to the schoolmaster, Hauke had worked out his own enlightened understanding of religion, in which God is taken to be omnipresent but no longer omnipotent (nor, in this pessimistically Schopenhauerian version of physico-theology, in the least bit comforting). In seeking to dispel his daughter's fear of the mythic "sea devils" of whom she had heard in the tales of Trin' Jans (whom Elke had installed in the Haien barn, along with her companionate seagull and a footstool made of her old cat's coat), Hauke insists that the figures she can glimpse out to sea from his new dyke are "just poor hungry birds . . . catching the fish which come up in those waters when the mist is clearing. . . . They're all living creatures, just as we are; there is nothing else; but God is everywhere" (*D*, 99). The quasi-mythic worldview, by contrast, is shown to lack an ethical regard for individuals of any species, prioritizing instead the survival needs of the human collective. The men working on Hauke's dyke might be happy to share their lunch with the scavenging gulls; but Hauke has to intervene to prevent them from burying a puppy in the dyke wall as a living sacrifice, in accordance with local tradition. Declaring that he "won't have any such crime [or sacrilege: *Frevel*] on this dyke" (88), Hauke risks further antagonizing the local men, on whose labor his plan is dependent, by rescuing the cute "little golden-haired dog" (88) and taking it home to his daughter, Wienke, as a pet.

While this enlightened intervention exemplifies the ethical promise, for nonhuman as well as human others, of the rational questioning of superstitious practices that are recognized as cruel, Storm's text also reveals what stands to be lost in the course of the dykemaster's modernization drive. Morally objectionable and dubiously efficacious though it might be, the practice of animal sacrifice bears the trace of an archaic, pre-Christian ethos of reciprocity with the nonhuman world, according to which a return must be made for what is taken: in this case, land from the sea through the construction of a dyke. In terms of the distinction formulated by environmental philosopher Freya Mathews, this pertains to a "deontic" worldview, as distinct from the ethics based on empathy with individual others that gained prominence within the civilizations of the Axial Age (c. 900–200 BCE) and has continued through into modernity.[53] From the latter perspective, it is entirely unjust that, in accordance with the mythic logic of symbolic substitution, it is another living creature who should be made to pay the price: "A child's best of all; but when there's none to be had, a dog will do!" as one of the workmen tells Hauke. The "impudent laugh" (*D*, 89) that accompanies this assertion nonetheless suggests that this practice has lost any religious significance it might have once had and is being perpetrated, at least in part, to aggravate the rationalist dykemaster, lending a cynical element to the cruelty of the act that Hauke interrupts. However, Hauke's modernist assumption that land is there for the taking as a mere resource for human use—an assumption that owes much to the lingering legacy of the biblical notion of human dominion (Genesis 1:28), which is perpetuated within Hauke's enlightened deism[54]—is also problematic. With the disenchantment of nature, the sea no longer needs to be propitiated, having been redefined as so much meaningless matter to be exploited for its edible and tradable resources and otherwise kept in check technologically. Forms of symbolic exchange, such as ritual sacrifice, are banished in the passage to modernity; but, as Adorno and Horkheimer emphasize, the enlightenment itself administers the ongoing sacrifice of animals in the service of exclusively human interests in a new, desacralized guise, notably in scientific research laboratories.[55]

The survival needs of nonhuman species are also regularly sacrificed to the modern cause of human socioeconomic "development" through the destruction of wildlife habitat. This was the case with the massive expansion of water-control projects designed to bring ever more land under cultivation in the German region from the mid-eighteenth century. In this connection, it is surely not insignificant that the slaughtered bird that Hauke was so keen to keep from the cat is identified as possibly having been a kingfisher, as this beautiful and once sacred species was (and remains) one of many endangered by the destruction of wetlands and natural river systems. The ecological cost of the modern regime of "discipline and drain," as Rod Giblett puts it,[56] was a matter of considerable concern to some of Storm's contemporaries. The North Frisian Wadden Sea is particularly rich in bird life, and according to Blackbourn, bird protection so-

cieties were formed earlier in the German region than in most other countries and were strongly supported. Moreover, the study of aquatic species
and habitats was pivotal to Germany's pioneering contribution to modern
ecological ideas.[57] In this context, Hauke's prowess in the business of dyke
building appears in a more ambivalent light. As an enlightened adult, with
a more highly developed ethical sensibility, Hauke might no longer be
taking pot shots at the shorebirds; but the project that he undertakes as
dykemaster instantiates a model of technocratic and anthroparchal modernization that will prove devastating for many species of wildlife.

In the schoolmaster's narrative, Hauke's suicide is explicitly framed as
Also characteristically modern is the institution of pet ownership that
Hauke inaugurates within his family. Unlike Trin' Jans's familiars, who
retain a greater degree of independent agency, while performing certain services for their human benefactor (such as keeping her warm at
night and killing rodents, in the case of the cat), the bourgeois pet, in Val
Plumwood's analysis, often functions as little more than "a servile toy . . .
lacking both autonomy and mystery, often conceived in humanised terms
as a childlike or inferior self."[58] In *The Dykemaster,* moreover, pets are also
shown to pay for their privilege by sharing in their masters' vulnerability
to the unintended consequences of the attempted domination of nature.
As already noted, Claus, who was formerly Trin's familiar but has since
become Wienke's pet, is killed by Hauke's horse. Meanwhile, her pet dog,
Pearl, having escaped ritual sacrifice, ends up being drowned—along with
Wienke and her mother and the horse pulling their trap—as Elke, defying
the elements, attempts to drive out to her husband on the dyke, only to
be engulfed by the floodwaters rushing in through the breach. The dykemaster's gray too goes down with his suicidal master. Here again there
is a contrastive echo of the opening of the journalist's article. While the
latter's horse is allowed to take the initiative in seeking food and shelter
for herself and her rider at the inn ("My horse of *its own accord* had already
started down the track on the side of the dyke that led me to the door
of the house" [*D,* 15; emphasis added]), Hauke's stallion is clearly forced
against his will to plunge with his rider to their death: "Another jab of the
spur; the horse's shrill cry rose above the noise of the storm and the thundering of the waves; then, below, from out of the plunging water, a muffled
sound, a brief struggle" (115).

In the schoolmaster's narrative, Hauke's suicide is explicitly framed as
a sacrifice of sorts: "Take me, Lord God," the dykemaster is said to have
called out, "but have mercy on the others!" (*D,* 115). While this prayer
goes unanswered so far as his immediate family is concerned, the fact that

his new dyke holds, and has continued to provide protection for the local community for nearly a century, is taken by the schoolmaster (and, once again, by most of Storm's interpreters) as a vindication of the project to which he has dedicated his life and in the service of which, so this version of the story goes, he dies. Within the marginalized mythic account, meanwhile, Hauke's death, together with that of his Satanic horse, would presumably be interpreted as belatedly realizing the sacrificial rite that he had previously scorned, their bodies becoming the "living thing" that is required to help strengthen the dyke wall and plug the breach.

There is a sense, however, in which both rider and horse had long been subjected to a different kind of sacrificial regime—namely, that which Adorno and Horkheimer refer to as the "introversion of sacrifice" ordained by the quest for rational mastery: "The subjective spirit which cancels the animation of nature can master a despiritualised nature only by imitating its rigidity and despiritualizing itself in turn."[59] It is consistent with this analysis of the baleful dialectic of enlightenment that Hauke's very name identifies him with the sovereignty of reason: this is the Frisian form of Hugo, and it derives from the Middle High German *huge/hoge*, meaning mind. The kind of reason with which Hauke is particularly gifted, moreover, is shown to be primarily calculative.[60] This is evident in the mathematical genius that enables him, with the assistance of his grandfather's Dutch version of Euclid's geometry, to correctly diagnose the weakness in the traditional dyke and to design a superior model. More troublingly, though, Hauke's calculative thinking is also evident in his mixed motivations for pushing ahead, against considerable opposition, in having it constructed:

> Another calculation occupied his thoughts: the foreland belonged to the community here, shared out among its individual members according to their property-holding within the district, or acquired by some other legal means: he began to count up how many shares he had acquired from his father, how many from Elke's father, and how many he had bought during his marriage, partly with a hope of future profit and partly to develop his sheep breeding business; it was already an impressive amount; for he had also bought Ole Peters' entire holding when he was devastated by the loss of his best ram during a flood. . . . What excellent pasture and cornfields there would be, and of what value, when it was all enclosed by his new dyke! (*D*, 62)

Having profited from another's loss during a previous flood—not coincidentally, that of Ole Peters, his archrival, both personally and professionally—
it is presumably in part to protect these pastures and cornfields, in which
he has a predominant interest, that Hauke subsequently prevents the men
acting under Ole Peters's orders from artificially breaching the new dyke
in the storm of 1756. As he clearly anticipated, this ensures that the old
dyke would breach instead, inundating the old polder and endangering
"the lives and property of the people upon it" (101), but not his own fine
home, which was built on higher ground, the lights of which he can still
see blinking reassuringly above the flood.

A degree of calculation even enters into Hauke's marriage: it was their
shared gift for mathematics that created the bond between Hauke and
Elke, but it was as the old dykemaster's daughter, and sole heir, that she
was initially of interest to him ("if he were to go to old Tede Volkerts, he
would take a much closer look at her to see what kind of girl she really
was" [D, 28–29]). Moreover, having achieved his ambition of replacing
her ineffectual father as dykemaster, with the assistance of the inherited
property that Elke transfers to his name, Hauke's calculation of future
gain motivates that sacrifice of present pleasure (his wife's as well as his
own) already noted with regard to his unrelenting work ethic. His horse
too is made to share in this sacrificial regime: literally, as his independent
agency is subordinated to his rider's objectives, even unto death; and figuratively, as symbolizing the subordination of the body and its impulses to
the dictates of reason (a trace of which is perhaps also visible in the shriv-
eled form of the rationalistic schoolmaster and the "unsuccessful court-
ship that got him stuck here in his hometown" [17]).

Hauke's suicide, as Chenxi Tang has observed, both echoes and contrasts with that of another famous suicide in German literature: namely,
the protagonist of Goethe's *Sorrows of Young Werther* (*Die Leiden des jungen
Werthers*, 1774). Tang argues that these suicides arise from apparently an-
tithetical views of nature, which are actually two sides of the same coin,
sharing a common ground in the reification of Nature as society's Other
within Western modernity. While Werther, the proto-Romantic, seeks un-
mediated oneness, Hauke "incarnates the urge of enlightened man to exert
his power over nature from a distance" by means of purposive-rational
action, entailing a "body politics of self-mutilation."[61] What these texts disclose also, in Tang's analysis, is how each of these interlinked extremes
necessarily implodes: Werther's suicide restores him to "the absolute still-
ness and immediacy of nature" but is at the same time an inscription of

his own body that will in turn become the stuff of further mediation and interpretation; Hauke's suicide is a final act of self-mastery, but one that returns the dyke builder to the "deep, engulfing immediacy of nature" in the very waters he had sought to keep at bay.[62] What Tang overlooks in Storm's text, however, are the multiple narrative actants that are shown to resist Hauke's drive for domination. To bring these elements of resistance into critical focus is also to move beyond the theoretical impasse of the "dialectic of enlightenment" and toward an ecological materialist alternative to the problematic modern paradigm of either seamless oneness or distanced mastery.[63]

It is, to begin with, Hauke's own body that rebels, responding to the stress of overwork by falling sick. The illness to which he succumbs is itself significant: identified as "marsh fever," it acts as a reminder that human corporeality is, as Stacy Alaimo puts it, better described as "trans-corporeality," interlinking the only partially separate self to others and the environment via material flows that are largely invisible and often uncontainable. Moreover, this particular illness, namely malaria, had become prevalent in this region as a consequence of the expanding colonization of the littoral zone enabled by dyke building. Outbreaks of malaria begin to be mentioned with increasing frequency in local chronicles from the late Middle Ages, as growing numbers of farmers moved down from the *Wurten* and onto reclaimed marshland. The native malarial mosquito of this area is *Anopheles atroparvus,* which thrived in the brackish water of the Wadden Sea mudflats, while the construction of canals provided it with welcome new breeding grounds. Certain cultural assumptions increased peoples' vulnerability, in particular the avoidance of what were thought to be disease-bearing oceanic exhalations by retreating into heated, smoke-filled interiors, in which the mosquitoes also liked to hang out. Malaria retreated in the course of the nineteenth century, due in part to the introduction of potatoes, and with them pigs, for which *Anopheles atroparvus,* happily for humans, has a preference. More significant, though, were the better drainage systems that enabled the intensification of farming practices in association with the process of industrialization, which now, unhappily for many, human and otherwise, threatens this entire coastal region with rising sea levels.[64]

It is while he is still in a weakened state following this illness that Hauke encounters a further locus of resistance: at the point where the old and new dykes meet, the former was being weakened by a colony of mice who had made their homes in the wall, thereby rendering it more susceptible to erosion from the watercourse that he had blocked in order to create what has now become known as the "Hauke Haien Polder." To address this problem, Hauke would have to overcome yet another source of resistance, namely that of his fellow townsmen, whose hostility toward him had been enhanced by his harsh treatment and disregard for local custom in the building of the new dyke and who would now be unwilling to commit to the labor and expense entailed in shoring up the old one.

In his moment of tragic *anagnorisis*, as recounted by the schoolmaster, Hauke identifies his guilt as a lack of follow-through in his project of aquatic mastery: "'I confess, O God,' he suddenly cried out into the storm, 'I have failed in the duties of my office!'" (*D*, 113). Storm himself appears to have shared this view of his protagonist's fault, noting in a letter to Ferdinand Tönnies that when Hauke returned to inspect the damage more closely he was beguiled by the lovely spring morning into considering the problem less serious than it was.[65] Hauke was, as the schoolmaster puts it, "unaware of how Nature can deceive us with her charms" (103). This might be seen as indicative of the would-be autonomous man of reason's blindness to those environmental influences on his mood and state of mind, to which Storm's own poetry bears eloquent witness and that have since been amply theorized in the field of ecological aesthetics.[66] However, the text also hints that his project was flawed from the outset: namely, in the description of Elke's initial response to Hauke's plans.

In addition to her concern that this will entail "perilous work" against considerable local opposition, Elke warns that "ever since I was a child I have heard that the watercourse cannot be blocked, and for that reason should never be touched" (*D*, 63). Unlike the superstitious practice of infant or animal sacrifice that she also recalls in this conversation, this turns out to be a well-founded convention grounded in traditional environmental knowledge and consistent with the history of costly and unsuccessful attempts to block the Königstief near Husum, referred to earlier. Hauke evidently loves and respects his wife, but their relationship is not an equitable one, and he refuses to be swayed by her concerns. In overriding Elke's warnings, he reverts to the hubris that he had displayed as an adolescent: "'You're no good,' he would shout into the noise of the wind; 'just like human beings!'" (20). In addition, he is evidently seeking to protect the sole authorship that he aspires to in this work, through which he wishes to demonstrate that he has earned the position of dykemaster by his own efforts, rather than by inheriting it through marriage. Elke, meanwhile, dutifully suppresses her concerns out of loyalty to him (a loyalty that will later cost her and their more-than-human household their lives).

When she is gravely ill following the birth of their child, Elke nonetheless appears to prefigure the catastrophic flood in which Hauke drowns. Trin' Jans also has a vision of rising floodwaters on her deathbed. From the perspective of the suppressed mythic version of the narrative, these visions would be seen as supernatural and accorded predictive potential, while from a rationalistic perspective they would be dismissed as feverish fears or optical illusions. Viewed biosemiotically, however, they might appear rather as insightful abductions, arising from the recognition, below the level of rational consciousness, of those signs that suggested another disaster was in the making. Blocking the watercourse, moreover, might be read as the environmental analogue of the inhibition of those affective and bodily (specifically, seminal) flows, which Elke had also vainly sought to overcome in her rationalistic and workaholic husband. From an ecological materialist perspective, then, it is here, in the illusion of individual self-determination, puritanical self-denial, and the attempted mastery of nature, that Hauke's deeper fault lies and from which the tragedy unfolds—a tragedy that is neither a divine judgment nor a natural disaster, but a socio-ecological calamity, in which many nonhuman, as well as human, lives are lost. By contrast with both the dykemaster's instrumental rationality and the mythic thinking of the townsfolk, Elke manifests a relational mode of reasoning, oriented toward collective flourishing rather than either unidirectional control or seamless oneness and informed by affective insights and collective memories, as well as by logical deduction and empirical experience. To follow this mode of reasoning would be to endeavor to understand and negotiate the multiple flows that weave through our collective lives—corporeal, affective, and environmental—rather than trying to shut them off in the pursuit of a singular predetermined goal.

In his "Essay on Meteorology," Goethe arrives at the conclusion that "where man has taken possession of the earth and is obliged to keep it, he must be forever vigilant and ready to resist." This does not hold out the prospect of any kind of ultimate mastery, however. Rather, in his analysis, "the elements are to be viewed as colossal opponents with whom we must forever do battle; in each case we can overcome them only through the highest powers of the mind, by courage and cunning." Having instanced the potential violence of the elements, Goethe concludes: "These observations depress us when we realize how often we must make them after a great and irretrievable catastrophe. It elevates our hearts and minds, however, when we realize how man has armed himself against the elements, defended himself, and even used the enemy as his slave."[67] By pursuing this struggle in a Faustian manner, however, with scant regard for its impacts on more-than-human others and insufficient respect for the agency of natural systems, such as riverine and tidal flows, modern societies have created a situation in which the elements are getting wilder, sea levels are rising, and floods are becoming more frequent and more extreme.[68] There is no doubt that those nations that can afford to will erect higher and stronger barriers against the encroaching waters; indeed, some are already doing so. A bigger and, in the long term, more important challenge, though, would be to reshape our socioecological practices of human and nonhuman cobecoming in ways that would enable future generations to interact more safely and sustainably with earth's life-giving and, potentially, life-taking waters.

4

PROLIFERATING FIRE

In the previous chapter, I argue for an ecological materialist alternative to the Faustian project of discipline and drain. Turning to the matter of fire, however, demands a reconsideration of the mythic prototype that stands behind the figure of Faust: namely, Prometheus, the Titan who is said to have stolen fire from the gods to either empower or engender fire-wielding humans. Bent on mastery and denying dependence, the "modern Prometheus," as Mary Shelley subtitled *Frankenstein,* is a defiantly self-made man who aspires to remake the conditions of human existence on his own terms. This is the Prometheanism of the industrial age, under-writing the project of human self-assertion not only against divine and terrestrial overlords but also against the troublesome forces of nature. It has engendered new kinds of human subjectivity and new possibilities of human self-realization, along with new practices of subjectification and relations on inequity. In availing himself of technologies powered by the combustion of ancient biomass, moreover, the modern Prometheus is re-fashioning the Earth and its atmosphere in ways that are fast becoming calamitous.

Yet it is important to recall that the Greek myth of Prometheus long predates industrial modernity. In fact, as Stephen Pyne never ceases to re-iterate in his passionate histories of anthropogenic fire, mythic narratives about the human acquisition of the flame, often by stealth and in defiance of "a fire-hoarding potentate,"[1] have been passed down over the millennia in virtually all cultures throughout the world. Inscribed in these stories is a profound insight into what, if anything, is universally constitutive of the human condition. The ability to keep and, later, start the flame is humanity's primal technology, and it has played a critical role in the development of all human cultures, the colonization of new climes, and the mediation of our relations with the nonhuman world:

> For all the manifest feebleness of this species, fire compensated,
> and more. It made palatable many foodstuffs otherwise inedible
> or toxic; with smoke or heat, it made possible the preservation of
> foods that would soon spoil; it promoted a cultivation of indigenous

forbs, grasses, tubers and nut-bearing trees; it stimulated hunting; it hardened wooden tools, made malleable shafts to be rendered into arrows or spears, and prepared certain stones for splitting; it kept at bay the night terrors, promoted and defined the solidarity of the group, and made available the evening for storytelling and ceremony. It even allowed humans to reshape whole landscapes as, in effect, humans slowly began to cook the Earth. Everywhere humans went, fire went also as guide, labourer, camp follower, and chronicler.[2]

Meanwhile, fire etched itself deeply into those stories and ceremonies, songs and beliefs, that were first shared around the campfire, becoming an indispensable ingredient, at once material and ideational, of human life: "Remove fire from a society, even today, and both its technological and its social order will lie in ruins. Strip fire away from language, and you reduce many of its vital metaphors to ash."[3] From this perspective, rejecting the Promethean gift altogether is not an option; what is required instead is a more ecological way of engaging with it.

While the use of fire might have made us human, it was not the exclusive property of *Homo sapiens sapiens*. Some of our *Homo erectus* ancestors were evidently already wielding firesticks in China and Java following their migration out of Africa some seven hundred thousand years ago, as were our cousins the Neanderthals in Ice Age Europe. The domesticated fire that defines our humanity might therefore be considered a hominid inheritance, gifted to us by our prehuman ancestors. Moreover, it is only on account of certain peculiarities of this planet that things on Earth's surface can be burned at all. To get the chemical reaction that manifests as flame, you need free oxygen, combustible material, and a source of ignition. Among the other planets in our solar system, Mars has traces of oxygen, Saturn's moon Titan has a gaseous fuel (methane), and Jupiter receives sparks of lightning. As far as we know, however, only Earth has all three ingredients and the means to combine them. And those means, as Pyne explains, are biotic: "Marine life pumped the atmosphere with oxygen, and terrestrial life stocked the continents with fuels."[4] And once the biosphere really got going, with oxygen and carbon dioxide cycling nicely between plants and animals, oxygen stabilized in Earth's atmosphere at just the right level: too little, and no lightning strike would engender anything more than a bit of sullen smoldering; too much, and the entire biosphere would be consumed by flame. If humans have become uniquely fire creatures, as Pyne puts it, it is because we have evolved on a uniquely fire planet.

Having taken up the firestick, humans everywhere proceeded to refashion the ecosystems that they colonized, fostering biotic adaptations to the particular fire regimes that they introduced. When humans began to dance with fire, other beings got caught up in the whirl. Wherever humans ventured, the life cycles of plants and animals became attuned to the rhythms of anthropogenic fire, while those who could most readily adapt to this new biotic ballet fared better than those who could not. In many parts of the world, but perhaps nowhere more so than on the continent that the British dubbed Australia, multispecies collectives gradually came into being through this process of pyro-symbiogenesis that actually required the element of anthropogenic fire for maximal flourishing. As a protean element that acquires the properties of weather, wind, terrain, and fuel, however, fire is not a tool in the conventional sense, and it has always been an unruly companion, never totally at the command of even the most skilled human practitioners. For this reason, Pyne terms our acquisition of fire power "the first of humanity's Faustian bargains."[5] It is surely no coincidence that so many myths of the end of the world, "from the Aztecs to the Stoics, from the Christian Apocalypse to the Nordic *Ragnarok,*"[6] feature fiery conflagrations. While Pyne is right to stress that these are also narratives of new beginnings, they bear the knowledge of fire's powerfully destructive force. The new kinds of agency that humans acquired by entering into alliance with this "queer"[7] companion were therefore far from risk free and brought with them a new burden of responsibility. Fire could be engaged carefully and skilfully in ways that favored human sustenance, while also benefiting those other-than-human lives with which ours was entangled; or it could be wielded heedlessly "like the spray cans of environmental vandals."[8] The use of fire might be an anthropological constant; but human fire cultures and histories vary significantly.

Not all ecosystems, moreover, are equally fire prone, or fire adapted. Temperate Europe, for instance, is uncommonly inhospitable to free-ranging fire. It was only in the company of fire that modern humans, like Neanderthals before them, were able to colonize such cooler climes. But after the climate had restabilized at the end of last glacial maximum, Europe's temperate regions never developed the regular cycle of wet and dry times that is found virtually everywhere else on Earth, with the notable exception of Antarctica. While the latter is dry all year round, albeit locked (thus far) in snow and ice, temperate Europe is (or has been) perennially wet and therefore lacks a natural fire season. Here, as elsewhere, though, humans engaged fire to remold the landscape, slashing and burning to open up the dense forests that grew in the wake of the retreating ice sheets, thereby enabling the spread of pastoralism and farming. The resulting moorlands and fields were then also regularly fired in order to keep woody weeds in check and to fertilize the soil with ash. Useful though it has been for such human purposes, however, fire never became an ecological necessity in temperate Europe.

During the Enlightenment, moreover, a new breed of Northern European town-based agricultural expert advocated the cessation of the one use of free-burning fire that had remained common on the land. Faced with the necessity of increasing food production for a growing population, and committed to putting agriculture on a "rational" basis, the would-be "improvers" condemned traditional field rotation and fallow-firing practices as archaic and wasteful. Over the course of the eighteenth century, free-burning fire became associated with itinerancy, backwardness, and social unrest. Fire belonged in the hearth, not on the ground. Notwithstanding the year-round sogginess of northern European lands, this intensification of crop production would have impoverished the soil had the suppression of crop rotation and fallow-firing not been compensated by the introduction of new fertilizing agents appropriated from other places and times: guano from the Peruvian islands and, when supplies of that began to dwindle, phosphates extracted from pulverized rock. The replacement of ash and dung by superphosphates was part of that much bigger shift whereby the controlled burning of flammable materials harvested on the Earth's surface was, as Pyne puts it, "sublimated" into the controlled combustion of ancient biomass extracted from beneath the ground (and, later, the sea).[9]

In parts of continental Europe, meantime, the push was on to drive free-burning fire out of forests as well. Toward the end of the eighteenth century, German concern about dwindling forest resources (the so-called *Holznot*) led to the development of an early version of "sustainability" (*Beständigkeit*) in forest management. Forests hold an honored place in German culture, not least thanks to Tacitus's influential treatise on the Germanic tribes who were able to largely resist Roman imperialism, thanks in no small part to their densely wooded abode. The Roman historian depicts these typically tall, strong, and frequently fair-haired peoples, whose womenfolk fought alongside the men, with ambivalent fascination as forest-dwelling noble savages.[10] In the early decades of the nineteenth century, German Romantic poets, storytellers, and painters, such as Joseph von Eichendorff, the Brothers Grimm, and Caspar David Friedrich, leaning on Tacitus, sought to reenchant the bosky beauties and twilit terrors of the German woods. Within the rationalist ranks of German forestry, however, more instrumental values generally ruled the day. Accordingly, much of Germany's ancient mixed woodland was gradually converted into a standing reserve of preponderantly fast-growing, commercially attractive species, waiting in neat, straight lines to be sustainably harvested for the timber industry.[11] One of the central tenets of the conservation philosophy of German forestry, which became definitive of European forestry more broadly, was the protection of the nutrient-rich humus by the total exclusion of fire. This principle probably made good ecological sense in the dark, dank forests of temperate Europe. But it was not suited to those anthropogenically fire-adapted parts of the world to which it was exported as part of the arsenal of European imperialism.

Nowhere would the "marriage" (to recall Bacon's metaphor) between the Mind of European man and the Nature of the colonial earth prove to be more of a mismatch than in Australia; and nowhere else has it bred such fearsome monsters. For it was here that Europeans, at the height of their enlightened pyrophobia and at the dawn of the industrial age, were brought face to face with the most pyrophitic geocultural landscapes on the planet. The consequences were—literally and horribly—explosive; and the lessons that have slowly, painfully begun to be learned within Australian settler society—not least by paying greater respect to Aboriginal pyrotechnics—now hold significance for other societies around our periously warming planet as well.

How Australia became so flammable is an exemplary tale of pyro-symbiogenesis. The first long, slow move in this dance of distributed agency was made by the lithosphere: when the supercontinent of Gondwana broke up around forty-five million years ago, the segment that became Australia drifted north toward the tropics, getting hotter and dryer along the way. Ice ages came and went; earthquakes and volcanoes altered the face of the land; species evolved and disappeared, and when a land bridge was formed to the smaller islands to the north, new ones arrived. Among them, eventually, were human beings. By the time they got here, almost certainly by boat, and probably around fifty thousand years ago, many Australian plants had already learned to dance with fire. Only a small percentage of the ancient Gondwanan species survived in the tropical rainforests of the north and in remnant temperate rainforest regions of the southeast. Throughout most of the continent, plants had adapted to increasing aridity by developing small, hard, and sometimes spiny leaves ("scleromorphy"), while the trees that predominated throughout Australia's sclerophyll forests and grassy woodlands were eucalypts: "fire weeds," Pyne terms them, with no disrespect intended, not only because most have evolved an extraordinary capacity to withstand fire but also because they actually require it in order to germinate. "During Greater Australia's lonely latitudinal drift," writes Tom Griffiths, "the continent became embraced by fire just as its abandoned partner, Antarctica, loitering at the pole, became overwhelmed by ice."[12]

The nature and extent of the environmental impact of the early human colonization of this continent remains a matter of heated debate, but it currently appears unlikely that Aboriginal peoples caused the disappearance of any or all of Australia's megafauna, and if their hunting practices did play a part, so too did climatic changes.[13] What is without doubt, however, is that the first Australians ultimately got the hang of living on a largely arid, fire-prone continent and that most of Australia's megadiverse plants and animals eventually learned to dance along with the sophisticated fire regimes that they established. The outcome of this process of pyro-symbiogenesis was not only a peculiarly pyrophitic biota but a human society that had become extraordinarily adept at what Rhys Jones famously termed "fire-stick farming."[14]

That the "natives" were forever lighting fires was abundantly clear to the British invaders and other colonists who arrived in Australia in growing numbers from 1788 onward (along with their ark of comestible and companionable biota and some seriously pesky stowaways, mainly of the microbial and rodent variety). What was not visible to them then, and is only now beginning to be more widely appreciated among non-Indigenous Australians today, was the knowledge and skill, labor and love, that went into Aboriginal place-making across the entire length and breadth of the continent. The fullest account to date of Aboriginal place-making, or "land management," as he terms it, is to be found in Bill Gammage's magisterial study *The Biggest Estate on Earth: How Aborigines Made Australia* (2011). According to Gammage's extensive research, those rippling fields of succulent grasses and grassy woodlands, into which the colonists poured their hard-hoofed sheep, and the open, parklike forests, where they grazed their cattle and sited their sawmills, had been carefully crafted and painstakingly maintained by human agency in a felicitous alliance with fire. By means of this partnership, upon which the flourishing of a great many indigenous plants and animals came to depend, Australia had effectively been fashioned into "the biggest estate on earth."[15] In the eyes of the newcomers, however, it was as "wild" as the natives and theirs for the taking. And take it they did, without having the faintest idea what they had got themselves in for, especially once the dire impact of their disordering of Aboriginal fire regimes began to make itself felt around the middle of the nineteenth century.

The violent dispossession of Australia's first people and the widespread degradation of the lands that they had evidently learned to care for so sustainably for millennia strikes me as all the more appalling in view of the likelihood that this modus vivendi was hard won, involving much trial and error over a very long period of time. Possible evidence for one phase of this extended learning period comes from the work of paleoecologists and paleoclimatologists who have unearthed the record of a rapid increase of wildfire in southeastern Australia around fifty-seven hundred years ago, coinciding with a sudden intensification of the El Nino Southern Oscillation, with its roughly decadal alternation of dry and wet periods. Intriguingly, sites that have been investigated in the Sydney basin by Manu Black and Scott Mooney show a marked and ongoing reduction of intense blazes from around three thousand years ago. As this did not coincide with an alteration in the ENSO system it has led them to speculate that the melioration of fire activity could be indicative of cultural adaptation to the changed climatic conditions: specifically, the development of controlled burning practices, which finally put a brake on the propensity of the bush to erupt in massive wildfires, at least in this region, for the first time in some twenty-five hundred years.[16]

Among the European colonizers, some were certainly astute enough to recognize the strategic nature of Aboriginal burning. In the 1840s, for example, Surveyor-General T. L. Mitchell observed during his expedition into the tropical interior that the Australians' apparent pyromania was actually an extremely effective form of pyrotechnics:

> Fire, grass, and kangaroos, and human inhabitants, seem all dependent on each other for existence in Australia; for any one of these being wanting, the others could no longer continue. Fire is necessary to burn the grass, and from those open forests, in which we find the large forest-kangaroo; the native applies that fire to the grass at certain seasons, in order that a young green crop may subsequently spring up, and so attract and enable him to kill or take the kanga-

roo with nets. In summer, the burning of long grass also discloses vermin, birds' nests etc., on which the females and children, who chiefly burn the grass[,] feed. But for this simple process, the Australian woods had probably contained as thick a jungle as those of New Zealand or America.[17]

Although their land-use practices were radically different, some of the new settlers also appear to have learned a thing or two about fire from the people whose land they had stolen. In her memoir of growing up in rural New South Wales in the 1860s and '70s, Mary Gilmore describes how her grandparents had been taught by the local Wiradjuri people to use bushes to "beat out a conflagration." Even in her day, she recalls, "'Send for the blacks!' was the first cry on every settlement when a fire started."[18] While the emphasis here is on fire suppression, the new Australians soon took to setting fires as well: itinerant "swagmen," following paths that had been made over countless generations by Aboriginal feet, lit "billy" and camp-fires wherever they stopped along the way; "squatters" (a term originally coined to refer to those who illegally appropriated grazing land beyond the official line of British settlement but subsequently used for graziers in general) learned to improve their pastures by taking up "the aboriginal method," as E. H. F. Swain disapprovingly termed it, of seasonal burning; "selectors" on the smallholdings (many still very large by European standards) made available by government policies to encourage closer settlement in the 1860s used fire, in conjunction with the ax, to open up the "scrub" for farming and then to burn off the stubble after the harvest; and miners used fire to gain access to prospecting sites. In those parts of the country where the temperate climate made closer settlement a realistic venture, Aboriginal fires were gradually but surely extinguished during the course of the nineteenth century, as the firestick was wrested into colonial hands.

Compared with Aboriginal fire, however, colonial fire was lawless and generally ill fitted to existing ecosystems and climatic conditions. The same could be said for those new land-use practices that presupposed a relatively regular seasonal cycle with reliable rainfall. Over the millennia, the first Australians had perfected a flexible and mobile way of life that was well suited to the nonannual weather patterns, erratic rainfall, and frequent extremes that characterize the climate of much of the continent.[19] Unfamiliar with the quirky ways of the colonial earth, the new-comers from historically agrarian, now industrializing Europe—to the puzzlement and no doubt occasional amusement of the locals—built permanent homes beside rivers that alternated, seemingly haphazardly, between desiccation and flood. They also ran big mobs of sheep on pasture that was never going to last the next dry period; put cattle on fire-prone forested hillsides; and cleared land to plant grain crops in thin, nutrient-poor soils that took off and blew away when the rains stopped altogether, as they are prone to do in southern Australia, for years at a time. The newcomers pathologized these entirely normal long dry periods by calling them "droughts" and framed their calamitous impact on their land, stock, and livelihood as a "natural disaster." In dry sclerophyll forests and grassy woodlands, the suppression of Aboriginal burning fostered the efflorescence of a highly combustible understory, while the wet sclerophyll forests of the southeast, which were formerly wont to go up only on rare summer days of extreme heat and high winds following long dry periods, also became more readily combustible, as the discarded crowns of huge trees felled for timber were left lying around and drying out under the thinned canopy, and waste wood and sawdust from the mills piled up about the homes of timber workers and their families, located deep in the forests being logged. And all along the expanding edge of settlement, whole stands of ring-barked eucalypts stood slowly dying, their bleached trunks bearing ghostly witness to the prolonged agony of colonization. In Pyne's analysis, the impact on fuel loads was uneven. "The big change," though, "was that most of the country was unsettled. . . . Once tended by the firestick, it now lay sullen, ready for a spark." That spark came from the feral fires of the colonizers themselves: "These fires, like rabbits, ran wild, and the shockwaves of settlement sparked, with eerie fidelity, a chronicle of conflagrations."[20]

These conflagrations have principally afflicted the southeastern quadrant of the continent, from Adelaide to Gippsland and Sydney to southern Tasmania. This was the temperate region that lent itself most readily to closer settlement. But it is also the region that is prone to the biggest and most violent wildfires, not only in Australia but on the whole planet. This is where I live, in the still heavily forested hills east of Melbourne known as the Dandenong Ranges (from a Woiwurrung phrase thought to mean "lofty mountains")[21] in a pretty little valley called The Patch. First cleared for subsistence farming during the depression of the 1890s, it is now a generally well-heeled village with a good government primary school; a small local store and post office; two excellent plant nurseries, thanks to the luscious volcanic soil; and a host of nonnative, mainly deciduous trees and exotic shrubs, along with plenty of wildlife, native and otherwise, including a fabulous array of birds, as well as wombats and wallabies, possums and antechinus, rabbits and foxes, rats and mice. Just over the rise behind our partly timbered house is a protected area of breathtakingly beautiful wet sclerophyll bush called Sherbroke Forest, with strips of remnant temperate rainforest threaded through its perennially damp gullies, many of them watered by underground springs. It is, then, with even less equanimity than I have managed to muster elsewhere in this book that I write the next part of this narrative.

Multiple factors and actors conspire to make southeastern Australia so peculiarly fire prone. In addition to the pyrophitic character of its vegetation and long dry periods, topography and winds play a significant role. Hot winds build as they billow across the vast deserts of Central Australia, descending upon the southeast from the North and West, fanning the flames of any fires they encounter along the way and driving them at speed in a southerly or southeasterly direction. Then, when the cold change comes through to quell the heat wave, as it inevitably does eventually, strong southeasterly winds, potentially up to 120 kilometers per hour, spark multiple new heads, as well as joining the long flanks of flame into a massive fire front. The impact of this aerial "double-punch," as Pyne terms it, is particularly severe in the mountain ash (*Eucalyptus rengans*) forests of the southern portion of the Great Dividing Range (including Sherbroke Forest). All eucalypts have evolved to burn, bearing year-round foliage flush with volatile oils; many types of eucalypt, including *Eucalyptus regnans*, also shed their bark, which dangles in long strips that turn into fuses, ferrying ground fire up to their oil-laden crowns. And in the case of mature mountain ash, which are the tallest flowering plants in the world, rivalling America's redwoods, that is a very long way up indeed. The wet sclerophyll forests where they tower over an understory of tall acacias and, below them, a dense array of ferns and shrubs, burn considerably less readily and frequently than other kinds of Australian bushland. Unlike the types of eucalypts that dominate dry sclerophyll forests and grassy woodland, which merrily regenerate by putting out masses of new branchlets all up their scorched trunks, mountain ash are killed by major blazes. But they also require a good conflagration every four hundred years or so in order to reproduce: the hard seeds that fall from their burning crowns burst open in the intense heat and germinate in their parents' ashes, moistened by the rains of the cool change and bathed in the sunlight that now falls unimpeded in the absence of the forest canopy. Once they get going, crown fires in mountain ash forests burn more explosively than any other wildfires in the world, building into a roaring tornado of flame that generates its own weather and can be seen from space. Long strips of bark and huge balls of flame and gases break away and are carried by the wind to start spot fires kilometers away from the fast-moving front, the radiant heat of which can cause anything flammable within a radius of four hundred meters, including fur and flesh, to combust instantaneously. The energy released by the 2009 Victorian firestorm is estimated to have been the equivalent of fifteen hundred Hiroshima atomic bombs. The heat generated was such that large domestic water storage tanks were seen by survivors, in the blitzed region around Kinglake where 119 people died, to simply evaporate, along with all the precious water needed to defend life and property.[22]

"Black Saturday" 2009 is the most recent, and thus far most intense, of Australia's megablazes, the "fires of regime change," as Pyne terms them, which followed the unsettling engendered by European colonization. The first, "Black Thursday," which also affected large swathes of Victoria, arrived on February 6, 1851. It coincided with the start of the Gold Rush and was linked, at least in part, to the disruptive impacts of grazing. It was followed by "Red Tuesday," February 1, 1898, which blazed in the Otway and Dandenong Ranges in the wake of decades of ring-barking and clearing. Smoke from these fires drifted into the Victorian Parliament, discomforting the assembled statesmen as they argued over the details of Australian federation. "It seems appropriate," as Richard Evans observes, "that the Australian nation was shaped in this setting: the founding fathers in their three-piece woollen suits gasping for breath."[23] Next up, again in Victoria, was "Black Sunday," February 4, 1926, which originated in forests reserved for timber harvesting and swept through Gippsland, the Dandenong Ranges, the Yarra Valley, and the Kinglake area. There were also more localized fires in the Dandenongs on February 4, 1913, and February 22, 1923. Embers from the 1913 fire set some homes ablaze in The Patch, and most of the mountain ash that now grace Sherbrooke Forest germinated in the wake of these fires or the later ones of the 1920s. According to Pyne, however, all of these blazes "paled before the Black Friday fires of 1939 that seemed to sweep all the wreckage and violence of settlement into one colossal maelstrom."[24] In Victoria on February 13 of that year, a massive firestorm burned out around 1.4 million hectares, destroying nearly five million cubic meters of timber in the central highlands alone; devastating several towns; killing countless animals, both wild and domestic, along with seventy-one people; and leaving many more injured, traumatized, and homeless.²⁵ Ash from this inferno fell across the sea in Tasmania and even New Zealand.

Firestorms such as these were utterly outside the experience of settler Australians, who also had to contend with the smaller, more localized, but nonetheless potentially devastating bushfires that became a virtually annual occurrence, especially during dry periods. Fire acquired emblematic status in colonial Australia, alongside drought and flood, as a malign force against which hardy settlers were called upon manfully to do battle in their conquest of the wayward colonial earth. Their struggle with the elements, above all with the ever-present threat of summer bushfires, formed the troubled terrain on which colonial Australians conceived the egalitarian ideal of "mateship." The utopian impulse underlying this cultural formation can be discerned in texts such as "The Fire at Ross's Farm" (1891), by one of the great Australian balladists of the late nineteenth and early twentieth centuries, Henry Lawson (1867–1922). What looks like an Antipodean version of the tragic tale of Romeo and Juliet, to which the singer explicitly alludes, turns into a narrative of male bonding across class lines, as Sandy the Scottish squatter finally rides up with his men to join the selector, Ross, with whom he has long been at odds, and his own son, Robert, who is enamored of the humble selector's daughter, in protecting the smallholding of his erstwhile enemy:

> "Here's help at last," young Robert cried,
>   And even as he spoke
> The squatter with a dozen men
>   Came racing through the smoke.
> Down on the ground the stockmen jumped
>   And bared each brawny arm,
> They tore green branches from the trees
>   And fought for Ross's farm;
> And when before the gallant band
>   The beaten flames gave way,
> Two grimy hands in friendship joined—
>   And it was Christmas Day.²⁶

The blessings of Christmas are invoked in the closing lines of this ballad to celebrate a human community created in the shadow of disaster. But the bounds of this community are very narrowly defined. Class differences, it is true, have melted away in the heat of the blaze. But this egalitarian community is exclusively masculine and white: "pretty Jenny Ross" features only as the prize for which the squatter's son is fighting, while the total absence of Aboriginal figures is not even meliorated by the recollection that it was Indigenous landholders who had inducted settler Australians into the use of those green branches to quell flame. Moreover, while Lawson does spare a thought for some of the nonhuman victims of the fire—the bees that "fell stifled in the smoke / Or perished in their hives," and the stock that joined the kangaroos in "flying for their lives"—the world of white, male mateship that he invokes here is only brought into being by means of the identification of a common enemy in the pyrophitic proclivities of the colonial earth. Lawson's anthropo-, andro-, and ethnocentric community of equals is created by casting fire as a monstrous foe:

> Like sounds of distant musketry
> > It crackled through the brakes,
> And o'er the flat of silver grass
> > It hissed like angry snakes.

The serpentine character that Lawson's fire acquires on the grassland recalls yet another natural adversary of settler Australians: the varied venomous snakes, which, like fire, infest southeastern Australia in especially great abundance. In light of the cultural connotations that have accrued to snakes through the reception of the biblical Fall narrative, Lawson's zoomorphism also imbues bushfire with an implicitly demonic dimension. Elsewhere, this mythic framing gives rise to the image of the bush as the haunt of a fire-breathing dragon, as in the poem entitled "Drought," by the schoolteacher Joseph Kelly, which was published in the *Queanbeyan Age* on December 28, 1865, under the pseudonym of "Bushman": "Fiery and hot, like a dragon's breath, / Bloweth the parching north-west gale." Kelly's demonization of the settler's scourge is reinforced in the following lines in the image of the "red sun" that "sinks in a sea of blood, / With an angry and ominous frown," while "lurid pillars of vivid light, / In tow'ring column o'er the tree-tops rise," and a "low sad moan from the flame-capped hills, / Like the plaint of one who in sorrow grieves, / Creeps through the woods and by silent rills, / And waketh the wail of the withering leaves." Having recalled the toll that the drought had already taken on stock and crops, bringing famine, sickness, and death upon embattled farming families, Kelly devotes his final three stanzas to exhorting his readers to pin their hope of salvation on "That Holy One whose blood was spilt / To cleanse us from sin and its loathsome slime." Kelly's imagery positions the naturally arid and fire-prone country of the Queanbeyan area, where Australia's federal capital would later be constructed, within the frame of a cosmic battle of good and evil, as articulated through the emphatically British myth of St. George and the dragon. In so doing, the poem assimilates this Australian place to a European cultural imaginary in a manner that militates against any accommodation to its old ways, such as might have been facilitated by entering into a respectful dialogue with the local people and their country. For Kelly, drought and fire can only connote disorder, and the response that he recommends is a renewal of faith in a monotheistic deity, who "will never withhold his children's bread."[27] The counterpart of Kelly's pious response to the hostility toward the godly "tiller" that he attributes to malign forces at work in the colonial earth is the quest for technological mastery. Indeed, this response too is inherent in Kelly's evocation of the dragon; for although he calls his readers explicitly to prayer, implicitly his poem awakens the desire for a slayer.

The mythic figure of the dragon also features in a bushfire narrative published a hundred years later by one of Australia's best-known children's authors, Colin Thiele. Here, though, it is deployed to a distinctly different purpose—one that was conceived in the wake of the 1939 firestorm and first articulated, powerfully and influentially, in the report that was commissioned to inquire into it.

Judge Leonard Stretton's *Report of the High Commission to Inquire into the Causes of and Measures taken to Prevent the Bush Fires of January, 1939, and to Protect Life and Property and the Measures to be Taken to Prevent Bush Fires in Victoria and to Protect Life and Property in the Event of Future Bush Fires,* to give this important document its full title, is, among other things, a great work of Australian environmental literature.[28] The opening paragraph is worth quoting in full:

In the State of Victoria, the month of January of the year 1939 came towards the end of a long drought which had been aggravated by a severe hot, dry summer season. For more than twenty years the State of Victoria had not seen its countryside and forests in such travail. Creeks and springs ceased to run. Water storages were depleted. Provincial towns were facing the probability of cessation of water supply. In Melbourne, more than a million inhabitants were subjected to restrictions upon the use of water. Throughout the countryside, the farmers were carting water, if such was available, for their stock and themselves. The rich plains, denied their beneficent rains, lay bare and baking; and the forests, from the foothills to the alpine heights, were tinder. The soft carpet of the forest floor was gone; the bone-dry litter crackled underfoot; dry heat and hot dry winds worked upon a land already dry, to suck from it the last, least drop of moisture. Men who had lived their lives in the bush went their ways in the shadow of dread expectancy. But though they felt the imminence of danger they could not tell that it was to be far greater than they could imagine. They had not lived long enough. The experience of the past could not guide them to an understanding of what might, and did, happen. And so it was that, when millions of acres of the forest were invaded by bushfires which were almost State-wide, there happened, because of great loss of life and property—, the most disastrous forest calamity the State of Victoria has known.

This dramatic opening is followed by a stark sentence standing alone: "These fires were lit by the hand of man."[29] Stretton then returns to his gripping account of the unfolding of the catastrophe, before proceeding to a searing indictment of settler Australian society's reckless irresponsibility in relation to its fire-prone environment. This was, in his analysis, no natural disaster. Not only were the vast majority of the two hundred–odd fires that had started to burn across Victoria from as early as August 1938 deliberately or carelessly lit by graziers, selectors, timber workers, campers, motorists, or bushwalkers, the conditions in which they expanded and eventually joined up were also, in part, anthropogenic. The conclusion that Stretton draws with respect to one small mill community, in which all but one person, along with their harnessed horses, perished, holds good for the catastrophe as a whole: "The full story of the killing of this community is one of unpreparedness, because of apathy, ignorance and perhaps of something worse."[30]

The unpreparedness that Stretton's report discloses is located at all levels of society, up to and including government bodies. While acknowledging the multiplicity of factors that combined to generate this conflagration, including the peculiarities of the southeastern Australian climate and landscape, Stretton asserts that the "major, overriding cause, which comprises all the others, is the indifference with which forest fires, as a menace to the interests of all, have been regarded."[31] In addition to the general dearth of public awareness and social responsibility regarding fire safety, Stretton targets the lack of a coordinated forest management and fire-control policy among the relevant state authorities, the interests and agendas of which frequently conflicted. Such legal regulations as did exist under the aegis of the Victorian Forests Commission (established in 1918) were largely unenforceable, while local volunteer fire-fighting units were woefully ill equipped and understaffed. Within the areas of greatest risk, moreover, virtually no measures had been taken to protect life and property in the event of fire. Following the fires of 1926, dugouts had been recommended for all sawmill settlements, but few had actually been constructed, presumably because the cost had to be borne by the mill owners, who also feared litigation should anyone sheltering in such a refuge perish of smoke asphyxiation. Not surprisingly, then, virtually all those who died on "Black Friday" were timber workers and their families, living deep within Victoria's mountain ash forests, surrounded by the woody waste generated by the sawmillers' assault on the majestic "forest monarchs": this financially motivated dereliction of the duty of care toward employees is a telling instance of the "something worse" hinted at near the beginning of the *Report*.

Among Stretton's many recommendations is not only the mandatory construction of dugouts but also the gradual relocation of sawmilling operations to towns beyond the defined boundary of the forests being logged. He also recommended that the Forests Commission do more for the reclamation and rehabilitation of these forests, observing that their disturbance by timber-getters had made them more susceptible to fire and warning also of the grave threat of erosion in the absence of reforestation. As it turned out, 1939 brought an end to the heyday of logging in Victoria's mountain ash forests, which set about regenerating without human assistance, to the delight and amazement of forester A. H. Beetham, who found that nearly 2.5 million seedlings per hectare had sprung out of the ash in one of the worst affected areas. This discovery contributed to the development of a scientific understanding of the process whereby very occasional intense conflagrations facilitate the renewal of these tall forests, where mountain ash had been energetically logged for decades in complete ignorance of their life cycle.[32]

Stretton's *Report* represents a significant advance in settler Australia's appreciation of what it means to live in a peculiarly pyrophitic land with a highly variable climate. In recommending the identification of different zones across Victoria with varying levels of fire risk, "according to conditions of topography, climate, habitation and populace," together with the specification of "prohibited" and "permitted" periods for burning, Stretton observes that extended dry periods are endemic to this continent, occurring "in cycles at intervals of from six to ten years," generating days of "acute danger," on which there should be a "black-out" for all activities, including sawmilling, which could spark fires.[33] Recognizing that the "forests are not static," he also calls for a regular review of policy.[34] While remaining true to the mantra of European forestry, according to which "the problem of fire prevention and suppression should be the first consideration of every forester,"[35] the *Report* acknowledges that, under Australian conditions, prevention necessarily entails controlled burning in some areas—albeit not within the mountain ash forests themselves—to be undertaken under the overall direction of the Forests Commission.

In addition to recommending a raft of further administrative, legal, and practical changes, such as the formation of a multidisciplinary committee to coordinate the regulation of land use across different government departments, the creation of state and local fire authorities, the storing of water reserves for use in firefighting, and the improved resourcing of both the Forests Commission and rural fire brigades, Stretton also called for a concerted educational campaign: "Probably the best means of prevention and protection is that of education, both of adults and of children. It is with the children of today that future forest safety lies."[36] The *Report* itself, hailed by Tom Griffiths as "the greatest literary legacy" of the 1939 firestorm, became for many years a prescribed text in the curriculum of matriculation English in Victorian secondary schools.[37] For younger children, however, something else was required, and in 1965, Colin Thiele eventually provided it in his cautionary tale for late primary to early secondary school children, *February Dragon*.

Thiele was one of Australia's most prolific and popular children's writers from the 1960s through to the 1990s. Born in 1920 into the rural and still predominantly German-speaking community founded by Old Lutheran religious exiles in the Barossa Valley, near Adelaide, in the mid-nineteenth century, Thiele began publishing poetry during the Second World War while serving in the Royal Australian Airforce in northern Australia and New Guinea. After the war, he became a secondary school teacher in Adelaide, while also writing scripts, stories, poems, and features for ABC radio. In 1956, he was appointed to a lectureship at Wattle Park Teachers' College, where he became principal in 1965. By this time he had published two major works of children's fiction: the autobiographical *Sun on the Stubble* (1961), which was serialized for ABC television in the 1990s; and *Storm Boy* (1963), which won the Netherlands Award of the Silver

Pencil and was made into a successful feature film in 1976. Many of his other books for children, of which he wrote sixty-four in all, won awards in Australia or abroad, and in 1977 Thiele was made Companion of the Order of Australia for services to literature and education.

As well as continuing to write poetry and fiction for adults, Thiele produced several landscape histories with a distinctly preservationist agenda: *Range without Man* (1974), *The Little Desert* (1975), and *The Bight* (1976). The question of humanity's relations with the natural world is critical to much of Thiele's work, earning him the Environmental Award for Children's Literature in 1977 and a place in Michael Pollak and Margaret Mac-Nabb's celebratory study *Hearts and Minds: Creative Australians and the Environment*.[38] Despite the continuing popularity of his writing, Thiele's death in 2006 was overshadowed by that of TV personality Steve Irwin. This is ironic, since both could be seen as animal advocates, but whereas Irwin was famed for pitting himself against Australia's most dangerous, eventually falling prey to a stingray, Thiele's tales consistently privilege human-nonhuman friendship, mutuality, intimacy, and cobecoming. Biophilia figures significantly in much children's literature.[39] For Thiele it provides the hook on which he hangs his environmentalist message, from the tale of Mr. Percival, the hand-raised pelican who is both orphaned and later killed by hunters in *Storm Boy*, through the penguin whose flock falls victim to an oil spill in *Pinquo* (1983), to the dolphin threatened by unrestrained fishing in *Speedy* (1991). It is regrettable, although perhaps not surprising, that the significant achievements of the elderly writer, who had for many years been enfeebled by arthritis, should have been eclipsed at the time of his death by Irwin's macho spectacles (of which his accidental demise was without doubt the most memorable).

February Dragon, which received a commendation from the Children's Book Council of Australia in 1966, was written at the request of the South Australian Bushfire Research Centre, in the hope that a "harrowing" tale might do for bushfire prevention what *Storm Boy* had done for the protection of wildlife in the Coorong wetlands at the mouth of the Murray River.[40] Despite the reforms that had been introduced following the Stretton report, first in Victoria and then in other states, several more major blazes had ravaged parts of southern Australia by the mid-1960s, albeit not on the scale of Black Friday. South Australia was also affected badly by the fires of 1938–39, which were followed by further outbreaks in 1943–44, 1951, 1955, 1958, 1959, 1960, and 1961. Although some of these fires burned in the northeast of the state, the most vulnerable areas in South Australia have tended to be in and around the Adelaide Hills, on the Eyre Peninsula, and in the southeast.[41]

For Thiele, as for Stretton, the primary culpability for destructive bushfires was to be found within settler Australian society. His "dragon," then, might be endemic to the Australian bush; but, unlike Kelly's, it is shown to only become a threat when lured out of its lair by wanton human firelighting. Here, though, it is not graziers, farmers, sawmillers, and miners who are seen as the main culprits, but holidaying townsfolk. As I discuss below, this is, in part, indicative of historical changes in social practice. However, it is also consistent with Thiele's pronounced antiurban bias. According to Brenda Niall, an "uneasy relationship with the land" pervades Australian children's literature from the 1830s through to the 1980s.[42] This uneasiness has assumed diverse forms, however, and in the case of Colin Thiele, along with a number of other postwar Australian children's writers, what is most troubling is not the land per se, but the encroachment of urban-industrial values and practices into erstwhile rural and wild places. In this, Thiele's writing can be seen to perpetuate the ambivalently nostalgic and sociocritical legacy of Romantic neopastoral in the tradition of early Wordsworth and John Clare.[43] What differentiates Thiele from other Australian children's writers in the neopastoral mode, such as Joan Phipson and Nan Chauncy, is his sober recognition of the irretrievability of the rural world that he recalls so fondly from his own childhood. As Niall notes, the opening and closing vignettes of *The Sun on the Stubble* signal simultaneously the end of childhood and the end of an era.[44] Similarly, the catastrophic bushfire in *February Dragon* not only destroys the protagonists' idyllic childhood home; it also ruptures a way of life, which, it is intimated, is already threatened by other forces and will never be restored.

Thiele's narrative is focalized through the perspective of three siblings growing up on a small farm fifteen miles from the nearest town (Gumbowie) and adjoining thirty to forty miles of uncleared bushland, partly state forest and partly privately owned, known to locals as "The Big Scrub." Unlike many of Thiele's other narratives, this one is not given a precise geographical location, possibly with a view to making its core message more readily generalizable to other places where small towns and farming communities adjoin native forests. However, the reader learns that this is hilly country around the South Australian border with Victoria, close to one of the main highways linking Melbourne and Adelaide. From the description of the terrain and plant community, this is most likely to be the Princes Highway, which would localize the setting to the vicinity of the highly fire-prone dry sclerophyll forests of the southeastern corner of South Australia. The vulnerability of the protagonists' home—along with the lively and not necessarily benign agency of the other-than-human entities that surround and infest it—is signaled from the beginning: "The gum trees and wattles, blackbutts, she-oaks, and native pines came jostling down the slope almost to the back door."[45] The children's affiliation with the forest is hinted at in their surname, Pine, which has in turn given rise to the nicknames "Resin" (Melton, twelve) and "Turps" (Crystal, ten). The youngest, Colin (six), is known as Columbine, a transliteration of his first attempts to say his own name. These Pines might not be "native," but their lives are shown to be tightly braided with the bush.

February Dragon lacks the structural complexity of the adult fiction discussed in previous chapters. However, the shared name of the youngest sibling and the author implies a certain doubling of the narrative voice. This is reinforced by the introduction of Mr. Pine as "Dad" at the beginning of the second chapter: "Everyone called the house 'Bottlebrush Barn,' which was the name Dad gave to the humpy he had built there after the war, when he first started clearing the land" (*FD*, 14). Behind the authoritative third-person narrator, then, lurks a situated first-person speaker, whose story admits a personal slant. The pastoral world in which Thiele locates his protagonists certainly recalls the one in which he was raised. This is a hybrid place, where the borders between the domesticated and the wild, human and animal, animate and inanimate, are shown to be porous and shifting.

Bottlebrush Barn is introduced in the second chapter as a "wonderful place for pets," and the animals that the children categorize as such are many and varied: in addition to a big black tom cat, called (for want of a better name) "Puss'll-Do," three dogs, five calves, two lambs, thirteen piglets, half a dozen goats, two ferrets, and a galah, there is Pinch, a possum who had been rescued from its mother's pouch after she had been killed by a car, and a couple of free-living regular visitors—a kookaburra, dubbed Jacky, who had taken to flying with a crash into the Pine parents' bedroom window on a daily basis to signal that it was time for Mr. Pine to get up and provide him or her with some juicy morsels, and "Gus," a rather intimidating five-foot-long bull goanna, who made occasional raids on the vegetable patch and, in one instance, the chook shed. In company with the hens, Mrs. Pine was not at all happy about Gus's rare appearances and sought to fend him off with a broom; but the children were thrilled, and their father was prepared to tolerate him, observing that "as long as he's about we won't be bothered by snakes" (*FB*, 20).

All of these animals are accorded their own agency, interests, and communicative capacities. They are therefore more like "familiars," as defined by Plumwood, rather than the pampered and infantilized creatures known as "pets" in bourgeois society, which are often little more than accoutrements and extensions of their owner's ego. The "familiar" is "an animal with whom we can form some kind of communicative bond, friendship, protective relationship, companionship or acquaintance."[46] Jacky and Gus, like the succession of wombats, Birubi and Victor, with whom Plumwood herself formed such a relationship, are wild familiars: free-living animals in their local surroundings whom the Pine family see sufficiently often to come to know them individually. Moreover, since some of the "pets" would conventionally be considered livestock, it is clear that the pattern of interspecies relations on Bottlebrush Farm does not conform to the dualism of use and respect that conventionally governs the differential treatment of economic and companion animals in modern societies: whether or not those lambs end up being valued primarily for their wool, and even if the calves and piglets later have their lives cut short for purposes of human consumption, the implication is that they will be well treated while on the farm.

Interactions between humans and animals drive most of the adventures in the children's lives, and none of them are entirely harmonious. While the goanna might be tolerated on the farm, foxes are not, and Resin is nearly badly injured by falling out of the cabin of his father's truck at the climax of a fox hunt in pursuit a big male (who gets away). Even well-meaning human interventions are shown to sometimes go awry, as when "Old Barnacle," the local store owner, applies too much turpentine to the Pines' retired sheepdog Woppit's mangy back, causing the dog to tear out of town, upending a picnic table that had been set up by passing motorists on the side of the road adjacent to the Big Scrub, in order to seek relief by plunging into Heaslip's dam (an artificial pond created for grazing animals). However, "events on Bottlebrush Farm didn't always start with living things like animals and reptiles. Sometimes they were caused by implements, tools, or bits of farm machinery" (*FD*, 92), such as the water drum that Columbine nearly drowns in when trying to extract a tennis ball that had flown in there and was loitering on the far side from where he had hauled himself up, just out of his grasp.

The potentially resistant agency of inanimate objects is emphasized throughout the narrative by the persistent use of anthropomorphic or zoomorphic imagery, such as that quoted earlier with reference to the vegetation of the Big Scrub. This passage continues, "Just as it looked as though they were going to trample over the farmyard and the sheds and Mrs. Pine's vegetable garden, they side-stepped, and veered off along the edges of the cleared land, sweeping and tossing their leaves in the spring wind" (*FD*, 14). The counterpart of this vitalizing strategy is a persistent depersonification of humans. While the school bus "whooped happily," for example, the children on it "would shoot out onto the footpath like gravel from a tip truck" (17). Whereas this somewhat disturbing simile serves to subtly associate school attendance with incorporation into the urban-industrial world, most of the imagery used to describe humans is delight-fully zoomorphic. In the opening chapter alone, for example, "Barnacle" is said to be "sharp as a possum's tooth" and to respond to the "bug-eyed" children purchasing sweets with an "airy snort," while "Turps rubbed one bare leg against the other like a human grasshopper" (7–8). In addition to undoing human-animal, animate-inanimate dualisms at the level of narrative discourse, *February Dragon* also shows how a human and an animal can together become something other than what each is singly in the description of Turps and her beloved pony Ginger (a gift for her eleventh birthday) competing at the Gumbowie Show: "the chestnut flanks and streaming tail of the horse shining in the afternoon sun, and Turp's blonde hair and light brown riding breeches blending so well that the horse and the girl seemed to be a single creature" (89). Ginger, however, "didn't jump well," and, although Turps crouched so far forward in the saddle that "she seemed to lie along her neck like a golden lizard" (89), horse and rider fall at the last jump. Both are shaken, and although neither is seriously hurt, this incident serves as a further reminder that human-nonhuman interconnectivity, which is shown to be the very stuff of life, is nonetheless far from risk free for either party. As it turns out, their positioning within the human world significantly increases the vulnerability of most of the children's "pets" and other farm animals to the "rampage" of the February Dragon.

Columbine, Turps, and Resin, along with Thiele's child readers, receive their first lesson in fire safety when their father explains to them that the entrancing show of "scattering sparks like a catherine wheel," which they once saw shooting out from a passing car, was "the most dangerous thing in Australia": namely, a burning cigarette butt that "could have set the whole country alight, turned the gum trees into torches, the pines into giant sparklers, and the hillsides into rivers of fire" (*FD,* 22). This message is subsequently reinforced when Resin and his friend "Burp" Heaslip are discovered by Columbine and their two courting schoolteachers, "Miss Strarvy" (Mr. Harvey) and "Lemon" (Miss Lemmen), stamping out sparks from the misappropriated pipe they are illicitly smoking in the Big Scrub. But the children are also taught that bushfires can start in many other ways as well. As their father seeks to impress upon them, these include: "Campfires, broken exhaust pipes, bad spark arresters on tractors and railway trains, magnifying glasses and empty bottles, hot ashes, incinerators, welding gear, lamps, electrical faults. But most of all from silly people with cigarettes and matches" (23). While several of the sources of risk listed here relate to rural activities, it is telling that Thiele's exemplar of silliness with cigarettes and matches is one of those city slickers who sometimes took the scenic route past their farm when driving between Melbourne and Adelaide, desirous of seeing Australia "by the back roads and bush tracks." Alienated from any corporeal or affective connection with the land through their motorized mode of transportation, however,

> most of them didn't really see Australia at all. They swept past with engines roaring, tyres whirring, and radios blaring, so that they didn't ever have a chance to see the sun shining through the green fern in the creek, or to feel the soft tickle of moss on a log with the tips of their fingers, or to smell the faint scent of a wild-flower as small as a spider's eye, or to hear the talk of crickets under the bark, or the itching and clicking of insects like beetles' castanets at the end of a still summer day. (21)

Oblivious to the more-than-human life of the country they were speeding through, such motorists are also construed as negligent in its care.

Thiele's targeting of townspeople as the primary agent of feral fire in the Australian bush is not simply a matter of the antiurban bias noted earlier: it also reflects changing social practices and perceptions. While the rural population had slowly begun to become more conscious of their responsibility for averting the wildfires to which they themselves were particularly vulnerable, the growth of private car ownership after the war had made the bush newly accessible to urbanites as a scenic playground. Just days before another major bushfire broke out in the Dandenongs in January 1962, the chief officer of the Country Fire Authority, A. W. Larkins, was reported as saying: "The worst offenders are city and townspeople who, when in the country, light fires in the vicinity of properties where the fire-conscious country people will not even allow the general smoking of cigarettes during the dangerous summer months."[47] As Griffiths points out, the 1962 disaster in the Dandenongs, close to one of Melbourne's expanding suburban fringes, in which four hundred homes were destroyed and eight people died (along with thousands of cattle, sheep, and household pets), "signaled a new kind of bushfire in Australian history. The bush had come to town. But the town had also come to the bush, insinuating its commuters and their homes among the gums."[48] Although there had long been a rail connection between the city and the Dandenongs, the growth in private car ownership contributed to the increasing population of commuters living in the hills outside Melbourne (as it had also in the equally fire-prone Adelaide Hills). Meanwhile, for those out on a day trip to the country, "picnicking and 'boiling the billy' were the major ways that city folk interacted with the bush."[49] And it is a recreational fire of precisely this sort that unleashes the dragon of Thiele's narrative.

In this case, the culprit—although neither she nor any of the other characters realize it—is the children's aunt Hester, "a telephone post of a woman, with a tall thin body, and cheeks as hard and smooth as porcelain insulators" (*FD*, 53). Married to the rural manager of the Instant Insurance Company, she resides in the regional city of Summertown, some thirty miles from Bottlebrush Farm, and clearly takes a condescending view of the inadequately modernized conditions in which her sister lives on the land. Thiele tends to be hard on aunts, and this one, as Brenda Niall comments, is a facsimile of Aunt Emily from Adelaide in *The Sun on the Stubble*: snobbish, prissy, and imperious, she is "equally loud-mouthed, 'gabbling and clacking,' all jangling ear-rings and suburban self-importance."[50] The suburban world that she and Uncle Stan and cousin Angelina inhabit is one in which the boundaries between the human and nonhuman are assiduously patrolled and where natural entities are either ornamental or useful, but preferably devoid of their own agency, interests, and communicative capacity. This is a world of "white picket fences and . . . small trapped beds of flowers and handkerchief lawns" (124), of pedigreed white Persian house pets (87) and equally well-groomed daughters, who "mince . . . up in a white nylon frock" (116). When she subjects the family to a traditional English hot Christmas dinner at midday on a sizzling hot summer's day, the narrator informs us that "Aunt Hester even had the weather under her heel. She had a big air conditioner working full tilt in the dining room, and the blinds were partly drawn" (123).

Through his characterization of Aunt Hester, Thiele turns his narrative exploration of the etiology of bushfire into a study in the hazards of domination. Accustomed to exercising a high level of technologically assisted control of her immediate environment, Aunt Hester disapproves of "wildness" in any form, including that which she detects in the decidedly androgynous Turps (*FD*, 90). Yet her very discomfort with other-than-human agency appears to make her more susceptible to its undesirable effects: her panicky efforts to pull Pinch off the leg that he had unobtrusively climbed, for example, interrupting one of her narratives, only cause him to dig his claws into the flesh beneath her skirt. When, on another occasion, she is nipped by one of the yabbies that Columbine had forgotten were in the bucket he had grabbed to hand around the crackers on Christmas eve, Aunt Hester exclaims, "Every time I visit the Pines something attacks me" (119). Yet, in fatally overestimating her mastery of the protean element of open flame, it is she who will trigger a far more devastating "attack" on the Pine household, human and otherwise, and on their rural-wild environs.

Aunt Hester, though, is only one of many actors and factors that are shown to be entangled in the etiology of this catastrophe. Another, once again, is the private car. Powered by the combustion of ancient biomass, abundantly and cheaply available as never before, the possession of a car makes it feasible, first, for Hester's cousin Harold and his family to drive nearly three hundred miles from Melbourne for a mere weekend visit; and, second, for both families to drive another thirty miles from Summertown on a day trip to have a "chop picnic" at Rowett's Reserve in the Big Scrub. In addition, there are the vagaries of the weather and the peculiarities of climate and vegetation: Hester's visitors have arrived in the middle of a heat wave during one of southern Australia's extended dry periods, and the pyrophitic forest is like tinder. Thiele nonetheless stresses that it is reckless human action that triggers the blaze, while indicating also that this recklessness is culturally conditioned. Thus, it is not only her obstinate and domineering character that leads Hester to insist, against her more prudent husband's softly spoken objections, that her relatives from the Big Smoke should be given a true country experience during their brief visit by being subjected to a barbeque in the bush, regardless of the weather, but also the social expectation that human intentions should not be derailed by the vagaries of the weather. Similarly, it is the cultural privilege accorded to human comfort and convenience that leads her to decree that in order to avoid the searing heat of the midday sun, the campfire should be lit, not in the designated fireplaces in the open center of the reserve, but under the patchy shade of the eucalypts lining its forested perimeter, regardless of the risk.

At this point, Thiele's tale, true to the model of classical tragedy that structures many a catastrophe narrative, becomes a study in hubris. Hester prides herself on being a model citizen, declaring "aggressively" that "nobody is more careful" than she is "when it comes to fire" (*FD*, 137). Before they leave (most of the party having surreptitiously deposited their inedible and fly-coated chops into the flames before taking the obligatory cup of billy tea), she sets her nephews to putting out the fire with a combination of sand and dirt and water from the toilet block, taking responsibility herself for dousing the long smoldering log that the boys had poked into their campfire with water from the billy. What she did not notice, however, and might not even have seen had she turned it over, was that "hidden and buried in the warm flesh of the wood," "fire still lived" (141, 140). And free-burning fire, allied with fuel, terrain, and weather, has its own tricky agency: by morning, the limb was "barred red like a snake's belly, sinuous and angry along the ground. . . . Hester had left the cage door ajar, and now the Red Dragon was sniffing at the chink" (141). What really sets the dragon on its rampage, though, is the strong north wind that builds up during the day, driving the temperature up to 107 degrees Fahrenheit. A gust sends sparks from the smoldering log into the Big Scrub "like hot shrapnel," and within five minutes, "a full scale bushfire was roaring" (149).

In the dramatic penultimate chapter, Thiele paints a vivid picture of the swift spread of the bushfire into farmland and toward the township of Gumbowie, where the children are at school, witnessing its terrifying approach in the advancing plume of smoke "as big as a mountain" propelled by a fierce wind that is now blowing "like a blast furnace" (*FD*, 150). He also takes the opportunity to give a plug for the Emergency Fire Service, who had previously impressed the children with their prowess in quenching a grassfire in what is likened to a successful military campaign (an association etched deeply into the Australian cultural imaginary by the close conjunction of Black Friday with the outbreak of the Second World War later that year). Thiele nonetheless stresses the limits of their capacity in the face of the February inferno: "Although ten E. F. S. Units and five hundred volunteers were battling their hardest they could barely make a mark" (151). While they do succeed in protecting the town, one hundred square miles of bush and farmland are "laid waste" (162). Such fires, it is made clear, cannot be controlled, and every effort must therefore be made to prevent their occurrence. In the event of an outbreak, moreover, those who are, literally, in the line of fire will have to be prepared to fend for themselves and to assist one another as best they can. In this connection, Thiele provides a model of ethical comportment in the midst of catastrophe in the figure of the Pines' gruff, penny-pinching neighbor, old Emil Eckart. Together with the children's father, Emil is among the ordinary men who risk their lives in battling the blaze. But he is singled out for having "fought with a heart like a lion; he had rescued two men from almost certain death when they had collapsed, by carrying them, one under each arm, back to the fire truck and driving them to safety" (160). Emil's identity as a German émigré, now hailed as "a V.C. winner in his way," might be read, not simply as a nod toward Thiele's own German heritage, but more importantly as an affirmation of social inclusivity at a time when anti-German (not to mention anti-Japanese) sentiment still ran high; and his heroism is made all the more poignant by virtue of the fact that he "lost everything he owned" (160).

February Dragon is one of several survival stories for children that appeared in Australia during the 1960s, including Ivan Southall's *Ash Road*, also published in 1965. Here too the conflagration is ignited from a campfire carelessly lit by townspeople: three city boys, in this case. But whereas Southall affords his rural child protagonists the opportunity to come of age by playing an active role in fighting the fire, Thiele keeps his in a position of passivity. Their school day ends early, and the farm kids are bundled into a bus to be driven home to their parents. I assume that Thiele intended this to be a negative example, as this bad decision on the part of their well-meaning teachers is shown to very nearly cost them all their lives. Reading what follows is especially chilling in the wake of the 2009 firestorm, in which several fatalities occurred in or around the incinerated vehicles of those who had left it too late to evacuate. As it turns out, Strarvy and Lemon (now Mr. and Mrs. Harvey) are driving their busload of twenty-five children right into the danger zone. They are spared only because of a combination of local knowledge and quick thinking on the part of Burp, together with a highly fortuitous mischance. With the air "thick with ash and drifting cinders," the road back into town now blocked by fire, and another "wild" wave of flame sweeping toward them from the ridge on their right, shooting out "huge masses of flame like outbursts from the sun's rim" and causing whole trees to explode "like gun powder" (*FD*, 155, 156, 157), Burp directs Strarvy to drive the bus onto the fallow field on their farm to the left. But the "crimson sea" (155) was also heading that way, so this is unlikely to have saved them were it not for one of the bus tires, which, "tormented by heat and angular gravel, suddenly burst with a bang" (157), sending the vehicle lurching off the track and, happily, into the same dam in which Woppit had previously succeeded in quenching the "fire," caused by the medicinal turps, on his "drought"-ridden back (33, 26). Only by inadvertently following the dog's wise example and plunging into the remaining two feet of water in the drying dam are the children and their teachers able to avoid being burned alive as the fire front passes over them.

By emphasizing chance, and depriving his protagonists of an active role as firefighters, Thiele militates against the risk courted by Southall of romanticizing the battle with bushfire as an exciting rite of passage for young Australian males. This is an especially prudent narrative strategy in a country where the thrill, satisfaction, and acclaim of fighting bushfire has been shown to be a key factor in at least some of the blazes lit by arsonists.[51] Moreover, in order to engage his young readers' emotions in imagining the terrible suffering and loss wrought by such eco-catastrophes, he wagers on their capacity to empathize with their nonhuman victims: it is above all through the death of the animals with whom the lives of the children have been shown to be so intimately entwined that *February Dragon* drives home its message of the tragic cost of carelessness with fire.

The first animal death that they encounter in the harrowing final chapter ("Aftermath") is that of the canary, Mr. Whistler, whom they had given to their teachers when they returned from their honeymoon and moved into the old pioneer's cottage on the edge of the Big Scrub, which they were renting from Mr. Pine, just weeks earlier. Amid the blackened rubble of their home, in the presence of the Pines, Lemon discovers the remains of Mr. Whistler's wire cage. Here, too, the Whoppit story proves significant: by contrast with the freedom of movement claimed by the old sheepdog, the canary, as Lemon realizes to her dismay, had been "locked in a cage so he couldn't escape. Locked up till he was burnt alive" (*FD*, 163). Their confinement sealed the fate of most of the animals at Bottlebrush Barn as well. Their old cat, winner of the "homeliest pet" award at the Gumbowie Show, had eluded their mother that morning when she was hurrying off to her Country Women's Association meeting and been left in the house, which the family finds burned to the ground. Mrs. Pine had also forgotten to let Ginger out of the stable, Turps having left her run for the bus too late to do it herself. Imagining her beloved horse "hurling itself against the rails in a mad frenzy as the flames roared down on it," Turps discovers her "charred and horrible corpse" in the ruined stable (165, 163). Reinforcing the message about making provision for those animals in your care when bushfire threatens—and for those you cannot take with you if you are evacuating that generally means giving them their freedom—the grieving children discover also the remains of their rabbits, Fluff and Tuft, dead in their cage, and the smoking corpses of over a hundred sheep piled up in a corner of the house paddock: "Panic-stricken, crazy with pain and fear, the flock had stampeded into the fences and died there slowly and horribly with their wool on fire" (165). Only Pinch appears to have survived, having somehow escaped from his cage and sheltered under the roof of the water tank. But while freedom of movement might increase some animals' chances of survival, the reader is reminded that much wildlife will also have perished: Pinch might be singed and shaken, but, as Mr. Pine observes, looking out "across the blackened slope," "At least he's alive. . . . I wonder how many of his mates in the Big Scrub didn't even manage that!" (169).

The salience of peoples' involvement with (other) animals in disaster situations, which Thiele brings so movingly to the fore here, has only recently started to be seriously considered in the field of disaster studies and by emergency services. The advice prepared by the Victorian state government for people living in bushfire-prone areas now contains the recommendation that you make contingency plans for pets. But this issue has much wider ramifications. The mass deaths of caged animals on burned-out factory farms, for instance, can help raise awareness of the cruelty of industrial capitalist food production.[52] Similarly, impacts on wildlife can draw attention to ongoing conservation concerns. Such is the case, for instance, with Victoria's faunal emblem, the endangered leadbeater's possum, which lost 40 percent of its remaining habitat in the 2009 Victorian firestorm. Because it nests in mountain ash hollows, which only form when the trees reach around 120 years of age, the prevention of further clear-felling and the provision of nest-boxes are critical if it is to have any chance of survival.[53] On the domestic front, animal companions are generally seen as a risk factor in disasters, as people are often reluctant to evacuate if they cannot take them with them. In addition, some have died endeavoring to rescue pets, stock, and wildlife. As Thiele shows in *February Dragon*, the grief of losing other-than-human loved ones can also contribute to the trauma experienced in the aftermath of eco-catastrophe, especially if it is compounded by guilt at having failed to protect them.[54]

As Kirrilly Thompson has argued, however, human-animal bonds could be "leveraged to motivate people to develop better emergency preparedness and response compliance."[55] Moreover, the desire to safeguard animals could also help to promote disaster mitigation. This, at any rate, is what Thiele wagers on.

February Dragon ends with an affirmation of the ethos of hospitality in the face of eco-catastrophe. The toll is relatively modest by Australian firestorm standards, but still significant for this one small community: thirty-three houses destroyed, four human fatalities, along with ten thousand sheep, hundreds of cattle, horses, pigs, poultry, and other livestock. "Wildlife too had perished" (*FD*, 173). The Gumbowie Memorial Hall, where Strarvy and Lemon had recently celebrated their wedding breakfast, is refunctionalized to provide emergency accommodation and donated supplies to those survivors who had lost their homes, while Aunt Hester insists that the Pines come and stay with her family in Summertown. The emphasis on hospitality with which the narrative concludes contrasts with the opening chapter, which introduces the children as motivated primarily by appetite, greedy for the sweets they are purchasing from Barnacle: part of the learning modeled by the story concerns the cultivation of compassion and the readiness to assist others, human and nonhuman, in times of need or danger. Even Hester is partially redeemed by proving herself to be "generous at heart" (170). However, she is not afforded the grace of *anagnorisis:* an unwitting Oedipus, she joins Stan in wishing a painful punishment on whoever is found to have started the fire. Nor does she open her suburban doors to the children's inappropriate pet, her little furry nemesis, whose miraculous survival is shown to be critical to the children's ability to come to terms with the catastrophe. Pinch is nonetheless given sanctuary in the ark of the Pine family truck, the sole possession, apart from their charred land and the clothes on their backs, to have survived the blaze.

For the children, this eco-catastrophe spells the end of their rural childhood and a traumatic coming-of-age for Resin and Turps. The rain that falls on the blackened earth following the southerly change, "as if the weather was now trying to spread salve over the ruins of Bottlebrush Farm, the grotesque carcasses of the sheep, the dead body of Ginger" (173), will quicken the regeneration of the Big Scrub. But Mr. Pine estimates he will have to work for twenty years in the city before accumulating enough capital to restock and rebuild. The children will evidently have to do the rest of their growing up in an urban environment. Ironically, Mr. Pine's projected return to the farm would have coincided with the next major bushfire catastrophe in southeastern Australia: the Ash Wednesday firestorm of February 16, 1983, which was preceded by a long dry spell so severe that thousands of tons of topsoil from western Victoria's Mallee district had blown into Melbourne, eclipsing the sun, the month before. In South Australia, this became known as Ash Wednesday II, since parts of that state had also been besieged by fire on Ash Wednesday, 1980. Several of the seventy-two people who died in the 1983 fires, many of them triggered by sparks from overhead electrical power lines, were situated in the area where *February Dragon* appears to be set. Any postscript to Thiele's narrative composed after that date would therefore be unlikely to have a positive prognosis for the restoration of Bottlebrush Barn.

Thiele was not to know that, of course, although the omnipresent threat of bushfire is acknowledged in Turps's grief-stricken outburst: "Bushfires! It's always bushfires! Every summer it's bushfires! I *hate* them, I *hate* them, I *hate* them!" (*FD*, 168). What Thiele does surely recognize, however, is that the pastoral world of Bottlebrush Barn, which he depicts so fondly in the early chapters, was already on the wane. Among the signs of change scattered throughout the narrative are references to Mr. Pine's milking machine and his interest in the new combine harvesters on display at the Gumbowie Show. Together with Stan's job with the Instant Insurance Company, these can be read as metonymic of the capitalist industrialization of Australian agriculture that was stepping up another gear during the 1960s. So too is the supermarket and shopping center foreshadowed for Gumbowie. Old Barnacle is scornful of this prospect, confident that he stocks everything that anyone could wish for in this district—not without justification, as is shown when he digs out the part for Emil's Sunshine harvester that he had been unable to find in the supermarket in Summertown. But Bill is among those who fall victim to the fire, and his death in the shop that he never leaves bears poignant witness to the end of an era.

In a further historical irony, the new order of increasingly petroleum-dependent industrial agriculture would also help to stoke the firestorms of a new regime change—one that began to show its fearsome face in southeastern Australia in the firestorms of 2003 and 2009.[56] In this context, it is important to address what now appears as a significant blind spot in Thiele's account of the etiology of his "February Dragon": namely, the exclusion of any reference to controlled burning as a bushfire mitigation measure in the management of Australia's pyrophitic forests. This is also the point at which his cautionary tale diverges from Stretton's recommendations, which had, in the meantime, led to the development of what Pyne terms the "Australian strategy" of broadcast fuel-reduction burning. This included the use of aerial incendiaries, trialed for the first time by Australian foresters in the very year that *February Dragon* appeared.[57] Thiele's exclusive focus on fire prevention and suppression is almost certainly a concomitant of his preservationist leanings, foreshadowing the hostility toward Australian forestry's enthusiastic embrace of anthropogenic fire, which intensified among environmentalists in the following decades.[58] In this connection, it is telling that the other human victims of Thiele's bushfire are a family living in the midst of the Big Scrub. The implication is that people, along with the fires they light, do not belong in Australia's remaining forested areas, which should instead be preserved as "wilderness," as Thiele recommended, for example, for the Flinders Ranges in *Range without Man*. Yet the underlying opposition of "man" and "nature" presupposed by this construction—one that runs counter to Thiele's own narrative disclosure of human-nonhuman, rural-wild entwinement—is itself part and parcel of that urban-industrial modernity, the depredations of which Thiele bemoans and which now threatens to deliver even more intense firestorms to these "wild," which is to say depeopled, places and their increasingly urban-rural surrounds.

Embedded within this blind spot is another, which is troubling from a postcolonial as well as an ecological perspective. Elsewhere, Thiele writes respectfully of Aboriginal ecological knowledge and values, as in the figure of Fingerbone Bill, who mentors the child protagonist in *Storm Boy*. There is no trace of Indigenous presence in *February Dragon*, however, and it is apparent that Thiele shared the general white Australian ignorance of his era with respect to Aboriginal peoples' highly skilled deployment of fire, not only to mitigate against firestorms but also to sustain biodiversity, while providing themselves with a good living from their carefully tended land. Aboriginal firestick farming, as Rhys Jones dubbed it in his landmark essay of 1969, was, and—where it is still practiced—remains, very different in both in its intention and effects from forestry fires. Whereas the latter are geared toward the protection of human life and fixed property, the former presupposes detailed local knowledge of the life cycles of local flora and fauna and is embedded in an ethico-religious system that imposes upon human landholders the responsibility for ensuring the flourishing of their fellow countryfolk, human and otherwise.[59] As Mak Mak elder April Bright explains in Deborah Bird Rose's *Country of the Heart*, people are bound to burn in order to "save" country: up in the Waigait floodplains area of the tropical north, April explains, "If we don't burn our country every year, we are not looking after our country."[60] If contemporary Australians, along with those living in other fire-prone regions of our warming planet, are to learn how to use controlled burning to ecological ends, a better appreciation of what Gammage terms the "monumentous achievement" of Aboriginal "land management" is, in my view, imperative.[61] The specific knowledge of what kinds of fire to light where and when may have been lost in many places, especially in the southeast, as a consequence of the depredations of colonization, and where it has been retained, such knowledge will require revision in the context of a changing climate. The underlying ethos of enlisting fire in the care of country holds good, however. And it is that ethos of "caring for country" that I will explore more deeply in the following chapter.

5

DRIVING WINDS

On February 3, 2011, a particularly powerful cyclone churned across the coast of northeastern Australia. Yasi, as this big blow was dubbed, measured category 5 on the Australian scale when it made landfall, and its force was felt along a seven-hundred-kilometer stretch of Queensland's magnificent Pacific coastline. Luckily, the eye of the storm passed midway between the two urban centers in north Queensland, Townsville and Cairns, which were only moderately affected. However, five small coastal towns were devastated as the cyclone made its way deep inland, shredding native forests, ripping up rural properties, injuring animals, devastating wildlife habitat, and wiping out most of the "banana state's" banana crop. One thousand kilometers from the sea, although downgraded to a tropical storm, Yasi was still generating winds gusting up to one hundred kilometers per hour. Remarkably, the storm made it all the way to the border between Queensland and the Northern Territory, delivering floods to Australia's usually arid heartlands, before finally blowing itself out.

Queenslanders are no strangers to cyclones, but this one was a whopper. Moreover, it came hard on the heels of unprecedented flooding, which had put two-thirds of the state underwater, covering an area roughly the size of France and Germany combined and taking twenty-two human lives. Floods such as these commonly occur in eastern Australia during La Nina phases of ENSO, such as the one that had recently set in, but the sea temperatures that were being documented in northeastern Australia that summer broke all previous records. As a consequence, there were higher than usual levels of evaporation and correspondingly greater precipitation, which brought widespread flooding to parts of New South Wales and Victoria at this time as well. It was these unusually warm sea temperatures that are likely to have ramped up the intensity of Cyclone Yasi.

While scientists are necessarily cautious about attributing any one event directly to climate change, it was notable that the same edition of Melbourne's *Age* newspaper that carried reports of "Yasi's trail of destruction" also featured an article on the first of Ross Garnaut's updates for the Australian federal government on his landmark 2008 Climate Change Review. Garnaut is quoted as saying that "Australia was seeing an intensification of extreme weather events consistent with warnings from climate scientists." According to this report, the impacts of climate change were now thought to be more severe than had been estimated only three years previously and included an increase in the number of extreme cyclones, a trend already noted with respect to hurricanes in the North Atlantic since the 1970s, along with more frequent and intense flooding. Swiss Re, one of the world's largest reinsurance companies, is reported in this same article as "warning that Australia was becoming a riskier place to do business after a string of extreme natural disasters over the past two years."[1]

A great deal of business is nonetheless still being done in this land of lengthening droughts, intensifying floods, and strengthening winds, most of it in the resource extraction industry and above all in coal mining. Australia's domestic energy consumption remains largely coal fired, but the bulk of the annual circa 470 million tons of petrified primeval forest that is being dug up twenty-four hours a day, seven days a week, is being shipped out. Most of it is destined for China, where it powers the factories that produce the cheap commodities that have contributed to the demise of much of Australia's manufacturing industry. Chinese power stations burning Australian coal are also pumping out an ever-increasing share of the carbon dioxide emissions that are currently heating the planet and spawning those nasty weather surprises to which Australia is particularly vulnerable.

In light of these interconnectivities, it was strange, and somewhat spooky, to see from the meteorological charts tracking Yasi's trajectory that this turbo-charged cyclone, which had graciously avoided the places of highest population density on the Queensland coast, was seemingly making a bee line for Mt. Isa, one of the country's largest and longest-standing coal mining centers. By the time it hit town, Yasi had weakened sufficiently to do minimal damage. However, the combined effect of the cyclone and floods, which closed railway lines and inundated several mines, served to disrupt the coal trade for several months. For all its apparent fury, Yasi is not recorded to have taken a single human life. Yet the floods alone are estimated to have reduced Queensland's coal harvest by around 30 percent, lowering annual coal production nationally to 405 million tons for 2010–11, down from 471 million for 2009–10.[2] The total cost to the Australian economy is estimated at somewhere in the region of thirty billion Australian dollars.[3]

While it might be possible to discern a certain grim irony in this outcome, to the extent that Australia's fossil-fueled economic system, and especially its coal exports, almost certainly contributed to the intensity of these extreme weather events, there was precious little justice in their impacts, which fell hardest on those who had benefited least from the resources boom: namely, those people who lacked the financial resources to readily recover from flood and cyclone damage, along with countless non-human victims, such as the cassowary colonies, whose dwindling habitat was blitzed as Yasi headed inland. Any attribution of intentionality to such wild weather phenomena in the mainstream media is only likely to appear as an "odd spot" in the guise of a quirky statement by some evangelical preacher or fundamentalist mullah, for whom "natural disasters" remain legible, literally, as "acts of God." Troubling as such reactionary reassertions of the monotheistic punishment paradigm might be, so too was the far more pervasive and consequential marginalization of scientific analyses of the anthropogenic aspect of these extreme weather events by the thundering rhetoric of Nature's violence. Even in so enlightened a publication as the *Age,* the article cited above was relegated to page 5, while the front-page headlines foregrounded human resilience in "surviving a night of hell" in the face of what is described, in a headline on page 2, as "YASI'S INVASION." In the same incipiently ecophobic vein, the front-page headline of the previous day declared, "Yasi unleashes its fury," followed on page two with a map showing which places were in the firing line of "NATURE'S RAMPAGE."

All of the historical disasters and literary narratives that I focus on in the previous chapters of this book predate the onset of anthropogenic global warming, even though my discussion of them has been situated within the hermeneutic horizon of climate change and the associated escalation of a range of risk scenarios. In this chapter, however, what has been thus far largely on the horizon moves into center stage. Because of the temporally and geographically dispersed character of its causes, along with continuing (and possibly irresolvable) difficulties in specifying its future impacts, climate change not only poses a challenge to prevalent practices of ecocritical inquiry; it also appears resistant to literary representation.[4] Speculative fiction in the burgeoning subgenre of "cli fi" offers opportunities for imagining a climate-changed future, but its capacity to come to grips with so complex and amorphous a socioecological phenomenon—what Timothy Morton terms a "hyperobject"—and to do so in ways that could helpfully reorient current practices seems uncertain.[5] As I state at the outset, however, and as the Intergovernmental Panel on Climate Change's (IPCC) 2014 report "Impacts, Adaptation, and

Vulnerability" makes clear, the time of climate change is already upon us. What I want to do in this chapter, then, is to consider how its early impacts might be encountered and their moral significance discerned as part of a wider set of vexing socioecological circumstances, pertaining in particular to the legacies of colonialism in conjunction with contemporary forms of corporate neocolonialism. In this context, I will be considering a work of literature that counters the implicit disavowals of human responsibility for stirring up the elements, which are evident, for example, in press reports on Cyclone Yasi, but from a perspective that also differs from Western versions of the monotheistic punishment paradigm: namely, the multiple-award-winning novel *Carpentaria* (2006), by one of Australia's foremost contemporary Aboriginal authors, Alexis Wright.[6]

As we have seen throughout this book, when the elements intervene in a big way in human affairs, they rarely do so singly. Coastal regions shaken by earthquakes beneath the sea floor are also susceptible to tsunamis, and when towns are affected, fire too can break out. Climatic changes can foster the spread of pathogens and render disease outbreaks more difficult to deal with. And wind patterns and atmospheric pressure play a significant role in the etiology of both floods and fires. Not unlike *The Dykemaster*, Wright's novel too culminates in a massive flood that destroys a town. But whereas the focus of Storm's novella is on man's battle with the waves, *Carpentaria* invites a consideration of human interactions with the agency of air.

For all terrestrial, oxygen-dependent creatures, air is about as close as it gets to an unconditional good. The spirit that hovers over the waters in Genesis 1, summoning a differentiated world out of the watery abyss, like the spirit that enlivens the clay in the composition of the first earthling in Genesis 2, is a thing of air: literally, a divine wind or breath in the wonderfully onomatopaeic Hebrew *ruach* (*pneuma* in Greek). This airy agency, which also came to comprise the third person of the Christian Holy Trinity, was only later stripped of its materiality in dualistic interpretations of the Latin *spiritus* and its various vernacular renderings. Powerful wind deities feature in many mythological systems, including the Egyptian Amun-Ra and the Aztec Ehecatl-Queztelcoatl, both of whom were also revered as creator gods. In addition, there are any number of more localized deities associated with specific winds that blow from one of the four directions. Not unlike YWHW when angered, these divine winds are far from universally benign, however, and some, such as the fearsome Japanese Fūjin, are positively demonic. This is hardly surprising: like the other three elements, air too constitutes a material grounding of our existence that can be withdrawn; a creative power that can also turn into a destroyer. The air that gives us life, thanks, as we now know, to the multitude of other beings on land and in the sea that oxygenate it, can become a vector of disease, whether from organic or inorganic causes. And the winds that lift our spirits as they cool our skin on hot days are also wont to rise up, from time to time, and descend upon the living with lethal force.

The most terrifying winds are those that transmogrify into moving columns of swiftly circling air, known in English as tornadoes and cyclones (or hurricanes or typhoons, as cyclones are called in North America and East Asia, respectively). While the former almost always develop over land in stormy conditions, forming a funnel with its narrow end touching the earth and the wider end reaching up into a cumulonimbus cloud, cyclones arise only above oceans and eventually dissipate after they have made landfall. Tornadoes can reach wind speeds of 480 kilometers per hour, acquiring a girth of over three kilometers and traveling up to one hundred kilometers across the ground, dismantling everything in their path. Most are considerably smaller, though, and dissipate within minutes (during which they can nonetheless wreak considerable havoc). Cyclones, by contrast, persist for days, potentially growing to hundreds of kilometers in diameter and encompassing several storm cells.[7] Cyclones can occur in polar regions, but the kind that I am concerned with here are those that form during the summer in the tropics and subtropics, generally between eight and twenty degrees of latitude north and south of the equator. These cyclones perform a valuable ecological service in mixing warm and cold water, thereby helping to prevent the tropics from getting ever hotter and the poles ever colder. But if you are a tree, say, or a cassowary, or a cow, or a woman, you definitely do not want to get caught in a cyclone's path.

"Cyclogenesis," as the meteorologists call it, is a complex phenomenon, involving the conjunction of innumerable conditioning factors, from the rotation of the planet to such minute and untraceable perturbations of the atmosphere as the flapping of a butterfly's wings (as meteorologist and chaos theorist Edward Lorenz famously hypothesized with respect to the formation of a tornado in his address to the 1972 meeting of the American Association for the Advancement of Science). The proximate causes, though, can be stated more simply: tropical cyclones arise when a low pressure system develops over sufficiently warm water (at least twenty-six degrees Celsius), causing several cumulonimbus clouds to be drawn together into an inward-spiraling gyre, turning anticlockwise in the Northern Hemisphere and clockwise in the Southern, around a still center of extreme low pressure: the so-called eye of the storm. As they wheel across the sea, cyclones grow in power and girth by sucking up the warmth from the waters below, which in turn increases their wind speeds. And it is the anthropogenic warming of the oceans that appears to be turbo-charging today's cyclonic storms, including, in all likelihood, the devastating super-typhoon ("Heiyan") that ploughed into the Philippines on the very eve of the United Nations climate change congress that was held in Warsaw in November 2013, adding affective and moral force to the Filipino delegation's plea that, in addition to concerted mitigation measures, proper financial assistance to help developing countries deal with the impacts of global warming, including such extreme weather events, be included any forthcoming agreement.[8]

Tropical Australia too has long been highly cyclone prone. From the Pilbara and Kimberley in the West, across Arnhem Land and the Top End, the Gulf of Carpentaria and the Cape York Peninsula, and down the east coast as far as Brisbane, northern Australia has experienced on average seven cyclones each summer, two of them classified as severe, throughout the relatively short period that modern scientific records have been kept. Because of the low population density of most of this region, the number of human fatalities of even the worst cyclones thus far recorded has been a tiny fraction of those that regularly afflict the Asian nations to the north. The Bathurst Bay cyclone of March 4, 1899, is still the deadliest on record in Australia, with an estimated 407 fatalities, compared, for example, with around 140,000 left dead or missing in Burma in the wake of Cyclone Nargis in 2008 and upward of 500,000 in East Pakistan (now Bangladesh) following Cyclone Bhola in 1970.[9] Statistics only tell part of the story, however, and there is one cyclone that holds a particularly prominent place in modern Australian history: named Tracy, the cyclone that struck Darwin early on Christmas Day, 1972, only took an estimated sixty-five to seventy-one human lives, several of them lost at sea; but it almost entirely razed the strategically most important city in northern Australia and is widely recognized as one of the disasters that "changed the nation."[10]

This was by no means the first major calamity to strike Australia's northernmost town. Dubbed Darwin in 1839 by Commander John Clements Wickham, who had been first officer on HMS *Beagle* when it sailed with the famous English naturalist, the port only began to grow into a town in 1869 when the South Australian government, which held responsibility for the Northern Territory at that time, established a small

Euro-Australian settlement there, called Palmerston. The following year, work began on the 3,200-kilometer-long Australian Overland Telegraph Line, which stretches from Darwin to Port Augusta and connected Australia with the rest of the world. In the construction process, gold was discovered around 200 kilometers south of Palmerston. The subsequent gold rush contributed further to the growth of the town, as did the development of a pearling industry in the 1880s, which brought divers and their families from Timor, the Philippines, and Japan. Darwin's principle raison d'être, however, was strategic, playing a vital role in Australia's communications and defense.[11] It was as a consequence of its importance as both a Royal Australian Airforce (RAAF) base and a harbor for US Navy ships during the Second World War that it was subjected to a devastating Japanese bombing raid, which struck in two waves on February 19, 1942. At least 243 people died, more than 300 were injured, and most of the public buildings were destroyed, along with the RAAF base and nine military aircraft. The explosion of a dump holding three hundred thousand rounds of ammunition added to the mayhem and alarm, and as rumors circulated of a Japanese invasion, about half the civilian population fled in panic, as did some RAAF personnel. Both the extent of the damage and the debacle that ensued were covered up by the federal government, and the royal commission report into the incident was only made available to the public in the 1960s.

For millennia, the Darwin area has been part of the traditional homeland of the Gulurmirrgin people of the Larrakia nation.[12] These "saltwater people" had long-established trading routes with southeast Asia, as well as with other Aboriginal peoples in southern and western Australia, and they had accrued a detailed knowledge of the powerful agency of sea and sky in their part of the world. Like all Indigenous Australians, however, those who had survived the depredations of colonization were only granted full citizenship rights under the constitution in 1967 and continued to suffer from many forms of disadvantage and discrimination. Among these, for much of the twentieth century, was the genocidal government policy of forcibly removing "mixed-race" (i.e., not particularly dark-skinned) children from their Aboriginal families to have them raised in orphanages or "white" (i.e., Euro-Australian) homes, the continuing trauma of which is explored by Alexis Wright in her first novel, the ironically named *Plains of Promise* (1997).[13]

Darwin, which was officially granted city status on Australia Day, 1959, and had grown rapidly since, was therefore a decidedly white-dominated city when Cyclone Tracy demolished it, and one with a highly transient non-Indigenous population. This was, and to some extent remains, a "place where people were posted: by government agencies, or large corporations, or the defence forces," retaining a quasi-colonial character as "a sort of transit lounge for nation builders from the populated southern cities."[14] Lacking a cultural memory of earlier weather-borne disasters, such as the cyclone that had previously destroyed the town in January 1896, or that which did significant damage in March 1937, and disinclined to have their festivities derailed by warnings of another on its way (not least, perhaps, because they had recently experienced a near miss from Cyclone Selma, which had veered north and west away from the city on December 3), most Darwin residents were woefully unprepared for the mighty winds that tore the town apart while they were sleeping off their pre-Christmas drinks. Despite the warnings that had been issued in the middle of the day on Christmas Eve after Cyclone Tracy had changed direction from the northeast to the southwest and begun heading straight toward the Northern Territory's capital city, revelers in Darwin's pubs that night are said to have been "laughing, and joking, and even singing how cyclones never struck Darwin."[15] To make matters worse, during the building boom of the previous years, warnings of the city's vulnerability to major cyclones had gone largely unheeded, and most housing was totally unsuited to withstand such strong winds. Only around 10 percent of homes survived, while 70 percent of all buildings throughout the city suffered structural failure. The worst damage occurred in the newer suburbs of the north, which journalists likened to Hiroshima in the wake of the atomic bomb.[16] This was partly due to the greater strength of the onshore winds on the northern side of the cyclone; but it almost certainly also had an anthropogenic aspect. As Kevin Murphy explains: "In the new suburbs there were few trees to provide a sheltering effect, and furthermore there were large amounts of building material lying around where new homes were under construction (much damage was caused by wind-borne debris). It may have been also that home building construction standards had slipped during the boom years of the early seventies."[17]

So extensive was the damage that there were even discussions as to whether the site should be abandoned and the city rebuilt elsewhere. This more radical course of action—one that might well have been more adaptive in the long run—was not followed. The new (and more rigorously applied) building codes that were introduced in the wake of Cyclone Tracy nonetheless ensured that the city that was eventually reconstructed was significantly sturdier. As Richard Evans wryly observes, however, a lot of roads, schools, and hospitals could have been built elsewhere in the territory for the cost of Darwin's reconstruction, which is estimated at somewhere between six hundred thousand and one billion Australian dollars. Cyclone Tracy did nonetheless have the effect of making the rest of the country more aware of its northern tropics, helping to forge a stronger sense of national identity, and enhancing cyclone preparedness throughout the north.[18]

As Alexis Wright recalls in an essay prompted by Cyclone Yasi entitled "Deep Weather," the destruction of Darwin also prompted Aboriginal artist Rover Thomas to create the Gurrir Gurrir (or Krill Krill) Ceremony. Inspired by a dream about his mother a few months after she died, the songs, dances, and images of this ceremony follow the journey of a woman across the Kimberley back to her home in Warmum, where she witnesses the destruction of the city through the agency of the ancestral creator figure, the Rainbow Serpent. Intended to remind Aboriginal people to keep their knowledge and culture strong,[19] in Wright's view this ceremony also "demonstrates the continuing way Indigenous people have retained knowledge through a cultural sense of what the great ancestors in the environment are telling us. This is how the stories tie us to the land as guardians and caretakers, and the land to us as the most powerful source of law."[20]

Cyclone Tracy occurred prior to the oceanic warming of recent decades, and its physical causation is highly unlikely to have had an anthropogenic component. In the view of some of the local Larrakia people, though, the destruction of Darwin was strongly associated with the "whitefellas'" refusal to grant them land rights. Things were beginning to change, however. Following decades of activism—from the petition of leaders from Victoria's Cummeragunja mission station to the British king in 1938, through the strike of Aboriginal pastoral workers in the Pilbara in 1946 and the protest of Yolngu people at Yirrkala against bauxite mining in 1966, to the establishment of a Tent Embassy outside Parliament House in 1972—a National Aboriginal Advisory Council had finally been established by the visionary, if short-lived, Whitlam Labor government in 1973. The returning conservative government under the leadership of Malcolm Fraser continued this reformist agenda in Aboriginal affairs, and in 1976, certain highly restricted land rights were awarded to Indigenous people in the Northern Territory and the Australian Capital Territory (ACT), with piecemeal legislation following in other states. The most significant changes did not take place until the 1990s, however, prompted by the High Court ruling in the Eddie Mabo case of 1992. This brought legal recognition of the existence of native title throughout Australia and the Torres Strait Islands and their offshore waters prior to colonization and, importantly, of its persistence into the present on unalienated Crown land. Overturning the convenient colonial fiction of *terra nullius,* this paved the way for many Aboriginal communities to reclaim their ancestral lands. The Native Title Act of 1993 established criteria and a process for such claims, which included the contradictory and unjust requirement that only those who could prove the continuity of their customary connections with the land, as if they had never been invaded, were entitled to regain it. In conjunction with the Wik judgment of 1996, which found that native title could continue to exist in limited form on or under pastoral lease, these statutory processes have nonetheless enabled traditional landholders to reclaim an estimated 1.7 million square kilometers (nearly 23 percent of the Australian continent).[21]

Disadvantage and discrimination nonetheless persist, as can be glimpsed by the grim figures collected by the Australian Bureau of Statistics (ABS). The average life expectancy of Aboriginal and Torres Strait Islander people, for example, is eight to nine years lower than that of non-Indigenous Australians. The ABS attributes this to higher infant mortality rates, along with higher rates of diabetes and cardiovascular and respiratory diseases. But it is surely also bound up with the psycho-physical and sociocultural legacies of oppression and dispossession. This "legacy of brokenness," as Alexis Wright frames it in *The Swan Book* (2013),[22] is at once evidenced and exacerbated by widespread alcohol and substance abuse, also contributing to suicide rates that are around twice the national average, with the greatest discrepancy being among young people: in the fifteen- to nineteen-year-old age bracket, during the first decade of the twenty-first century, Aboriginal suicides were 5.9 percent higher for girls and 4.4 percent higher for boys than in the non-Indigenous population.[23] Indigenous people are also far more likely to find themselves behind bars, currently constituting nearly a quarter of the prison population, but only around 2 percent of the nation. Over two decades after the 1991 Royal Commission into Aboriginal Deaths in Custody—most of the recommendations of which have still not been acted upon—they are also still more likely to die there, whether from suicide, from disease, or from injuries sustained before, during, or after their arrest.[24]

Meanwhile, in 2007, justified concerns over the drug- and alcohol-fueled sexual abuse of young children in some remote communities, as detailed in the "Little Children Are Sacred" report to the Northern Territory Board of Inquiry into the Protection of Aboriginal Children,[25] provided the occasion for a return to a strongly assimilationist government policy agenda in the guise of the Northern Territory National Emergency Intervention. Whereas the report had shown that a significant proportion of the offenders were white men, black-marketeering in petrol and alcohol in order to gain access to Aboriginal children, the Intervention effectively reinforced the racist tendency to criminalize black men. Instead of working with respected community leaders to address this terrible problem in ways that made sense within Aboriginal frames of reference, the Intervention, while not without some Aboriginal supporters, is widely regarded as demeaning and destructive: an "iron fist in a velvet glove," as Carole Ferrier puts it.[26] In Alexis Wright's judgment, it functions largely as a vehicle for the government to "further entrench its domination over the lives of Indigenous people."[27] Policies subsequently developed under the "Closing the Gap" scheme, moreover, tend to assume that Aboriginal culture is the primary problem and are therefore directed toward "normalizing" remote Aboriginal communities by Westernizing their education, employment, and social norms, while progressively relocating people away from their traditional homelands and into towns.[28] This has been occurring right at the time when those homelands are coming under an ever-expanding assault from the resources boom. Native Title does not extend to the mineral wealth under the soil, but it has afforded some bargaining power to Aboriginal landholders when confronted with companies that have been granted mining leases on their country. Disturbingly, Native Title has been suspended in those areas subject to the Intervention.[29] It is, then, within this nexus of concern, in which Aboriginal disadvantage, transnational mining interests, and environmental despoliation are intimately entangled, that Alexis Wright locates her complex anticolonial catastrophe narrative.

The fictitious township that is swept away by a cyclone in the denouement of *Carpentaria* is situated on the other side of Australia's Top End from Darwin, in the Gulf country, which not only gives the novel its name but is also a central player in the plot. The part of this region that Wright knows best is the ancestral land of the Waanyi people, which includes 1,730,031 hectares in northwestern Queensland, as well as part of the 40,000 hectares in the Northern Territory currently managed by the Garawa and Waanyi Rangers association. Wright's understanding of the creative agencies and traditional law of this land is informed by the stories that were told to her by her Waanyi grandmother. One of the challenges of reading this novel for those, such as myself, who are unfamiliar with this style of storytelling and the geocultural world to which it belongs is that it has been written, at least in part, "as though some old Aboriginal person was telling the story," as Wright puts it, using a vernacular tone that "belongs to the diction of the tribal nations of the Gulf."[30] Reconstructing the tale from the telling is a tricky undertaking in itself, as the narrative disavows linearity, twisting and turning, roiling and coiling like the volatile serpentine river and swirling atmospheric and oceanic currents that govern the Gulf country, switching dizzyingly between timeframes and storylines, voices and perspectives. While this narrative style and structure have invited comparisons with both European modernism and Latin American magic realism, Wright stresses the situatedness of this "spinning multi-stranded helix of stories" in the "condition of contemporary Indigenous storytelling that is a consequence of our racial diaspora in Australia."[31] Together with its vernacular diction, this nonlinearity is integral to what I have elsewhere termed Wright's "poetics of decolonisation,"[32] rendering the reading experience decidedly unsettling for non-Aboriginal and perhaps also for non-Waanyi and urban Aboriginal readers (the assumption of a homogeneous Aboriginal culture being itself a colonial fiction).[33] I was certainly made powerfully aware that I was stepping into foreign territory in reading this book and accept that there is much in it that escapes my grasp. While Wright hopes that her novel will speak strongly to Indigenous readers, I am nonetheless grateful for the generous invitation that the author also extends to "whitefellas" and other strangers to Waanyi land and culture, namely to come to "believe in the energy of the Gulf country, to stay with a story as a welcomed stranger as if the land was telling a story about itself as much as the narrator is telling stories to the land."[34]

The fictitious Gulf town that is undone by the energy of the Gulf country in *Carpentaria* is called "Desperance," a name that satirically inverts that of an actual township in northern Australia—"Esperance"—while alluding to the many other colonial place names across the continent that evince not the hopes but the disappointments that attended the advancing frontier: names such as "Dry Creek," "Foul Bay," and "Mt. Disappointment." Not unlike Darwin, this town had been established by the colonial authorities for strategic reasons, namely "as a port for the shipping trade for the hinterland of Northern Australia."[35] Unlike Darwin, however, it had been "jilted" by the tricksterish river at the mouth of which the port was originally situated: "In one moment, during a Wet season early in the last century, the town lost its harbour waters when the river simply decided to change course, to bypass it by several kilometres" (*C*, 3). Subsequently, the town's continued existence was justified largely by xenophobic paranoia: "to safeguard the northern coastline from invasion by the Yellow Peril" (3) and, in more recent years, from boatloads of asylum seekers. And, again not unlike Darwin in the 1970s (or any number of small towns in the north and center of Australia to this day), the topography of Desperance is racially inscribed, with the almost exclusively white "Uptown" sharply divided from the "Pricklebush," an Aboriginal encampment on the edge of town, at the center of which lies the local rubbish dump, or tip. Not only are the Indigenous people of this place positioned as fringe dwellers, living in Third World conditions in a First World Nation, "all choked up, piled up together in trash humpies made of tin, cloth and plastic too, salvaged from the rubbish dump" (4); they are also obliged to reside on land that had itself been trashed in the first wave of colonization.

As the pioneering environmentalist and Aboriginal rights activist, poet, and essayist Judith Wright explains in *Cry for the Dead* (1981), the cactacious prickly pear was introduced into Queensland in the 1860s to create hedges around the colonists' huts both "to deter Aboriginal attacks and to provide fresh fruit."[36] *Cry for the Dead* is a family history focusing on the devastating impact of Wright's forbears' pioneering activities on the peoples and places they sought to conquer. The hard hoofs and voracious appetites of their cattle and sheep quickly degraded the native grasslands that had long been crafted by Aboriginal seasonal burning and sustainably grazed by kangaroos and other native herbivores. The prickly pear, meanwhile, fast went feral. By the 1890s the cost of clearing it on some freehold land was more than the land itself was worth. Attempts to poison it in the early twentieth century failed, but "the empty poison drums which soon littered the country leached into waterholes and creeks and poisoned the grass, and their precious livestock died. As in the days of the strychnine campaign [against dingoes], the country was now laced with death to animals and men."[37]

In the dominant settler culture of Desperance, racial oppression and environmental degradation are also shown to be shot through with a strong measure of sexism. Here, the mutual imbrication of patriarchy and anthroparchy in what Val Plumwood terms the "logic of colonisation" is personified to perfection in the figure of Stan Bruiser, the "big, beefy, six-two, no fuss" town mayor, who "overshadowed the town with his power" (*C*, 34). Bruiser's instrumentalist guiding principle is, "If you can't use it, eat it, or fuck it, then it's no bloody use to you" (35). Bruiser is a cattle man who made a fortune in mining shares, and his exploitative attitude to animals and land is mirrored in his treatment of black women: he "bragged about how he had chased every Aboriginal woman in town at various times, until he ran them into the ground and raped them. He had branded them all, like a bunch of cattle, he gloated" (41). One of the women whom Bruiser claims to have raped is Angel Day, whose two youngest sons, Luke and Tristram Fishman—harmless, if self-harming petrol-sniffers—together with a third teenager, Aaron Ho Kum, the unacknowledged mixed-race son of the local barman, get framed by the mayor for the murder of the coast guard Gordie, in which, it is hinted, he was himself implicated. With the complicity of the local policeman, ironically named Truthful, Bruiser instigates their arrest and proceeds to beat them senseless in the police cell where they subsequently hang themselves, for fear of worse to come.

It should be stressed that this is not a social realist novel, even though it is addressed to very real socioecological issues. The figure of Bruiser is, without doubt, a caricature, but one that discloses the brutal face of a more generalized pattern of systemic violence, the brunt of which is borne by Aboriginal people, especially women and children. The conjunction of sexism and racism that Bruiser manifests to a satirical extreme is echoed, for example, in Truthful's sexual exploitation of one of Angel's daughters, Girlie Phantom: "If Girlie tried to ignore him, he just hung around the place for hours waiting until she gave in to the pressure placed on all of them" (C, 227). While Truthful is no rapist, his lust for Girlie is shown to have a marked sadistic streak: "He knew ways of making Girlie scream for being mean to him. . . . The handcuffs in his pocket pressing into his groin roused the sensation of good times to come" (226, 228).

Living amid the thorny legacy—figurative and literal, cultural and environmental, social and psychological—of the colonial cattle runs, the Pricklebush mob now face a second wave of colonization in the guise of a multinational mining company bent on maximizing its profits by extracting minerals from their land. Rob Nixon's assertion that Australia, like Canada, is resource rich but, unlike the African nations that he discusses in *Slow Violence,* not "resource cursed,"[38] does not hold good from an Aboriginal perspective. Aided and abetted by a succession of state and federal governments from both sides of politics with a shared commitment to shoring up the national economy by turning Australia into the "world's quarry,"[39] such companies have met with concerted resistance from some traditional owners in those areas governed by the Native Title Act, which requires that all commercial activities on leasehold land are negotiated with the Indigenous landowners. They are generally unable to veto such developments, however, unless their land is made an Indigenous Protected Zone or granted national or world heritage listing (as traditional owner Jeffrey Lee achieved in the case of the twelve thousand hectares of his country that was saved from uranium mining by being incorporated into Kakadu National Park in 2012).[40] Faced with the choice of opposing a new mine, which is likely to go ahead anyway, or agreeing in order to negotiate a share in the royalties and possibly some environmental safeguards and/ or compensation for damages, it is hardly surprising that some Aboriginal people have preferred the latter tack.[41] These royalties can be considerable: since it began extracting uranium at the Ranger site, which skirts Kakadu National Park, in 1981, Energy Resources Australia (a subsidiary of Rio Tinto) is said to have paid around two hundred million Australian dollars to the federal government to be distributed to Native Title holders. Some traditional landowners have nonetheless remained adamant in their opposition to uranium mining in this area for reasons that are inextricably ecological and cultural, spiritual and practical, and that extend beyond possible local impacts to concerns about the damage that this particular mineral could cause elsewhere in the world. Such fears are clearly well founded. In 2009, the Ranger mine was found to be leaking one hundred thousand liters of contaminated water every day into the ground under Kakadu, threatening resident Aboriginal communities along with the park's world-heritage-listed wetlands.[42] Meanwhile, uranium from the Ranger mine could well be contributing to the contamination that is currently leaking from the tsunami-damaged Fukushima power station in Japan. This unfolding eco-catastrophe prompted Mirrar elder Yvonne Margarula, who has led the Indigenous campaign to prevent the expansion of uranium mining to the adjacent Jabiluka site since 1998, to write to United Nations secretary-general Ban Ki-Moon, expressing her peoples' sadness and frustration that they had been unable to prevent the excavation of uranium on their land. Margarula explains that both of these mine sites are believed by her people to contain a potent agency, called *Djang*, and that "when this *Djang* is disturbed a great and dangerous power is unleashed upon the world."[43]

A similar concern was expressed by a group of Yanyuwa, Gudanji, Garawa, and Waanyi people in 2006 when they sought unsuccessfully to prevent the expansion of the British- and Swiss-owned Xstrata zinc mine in the southern Gulf of Carpentaria from an underground to an open pit mine. This involved diverting the McArthur River, and in so doing, it has "broken the back" of the Rainbow Serpent, a particularly powerful creator spirit who is believed to dwell at that site, as well as increasing the threat of toxic pollution affecting several species valued as food, such the dwindling dugongs who graze in the sea grasses at the river's mouth. As Garawa-Waanyi Rangers Jack Green and Jimmy Morrison wryly observe, this expansion was found to be in contravention to due process in a court hearing; but "the next day the Northern Territory Government changed the law to allow the expansion to go ahead," and they "felt cheated, again."[44] Despite the potential financial benefits of participating in the resources boom, along with new opportunities for training and employment, which, according to controversial Aboriginal academic Marcia Langton, is contributing to the creation of a growing Indigenous middle class,[45] many communities that have eventually condoned mining on their traditional lands have become divided in the process. This was the case with another zinc mine in the southern Gulf, this time on Waanyi land. In 1997, the Waanyi, through the Carpentaria Land Council (whose spokeperson was Murrandoo Yanner, one of the two "Waanyi heroes" to whom *Carpentaria* is dedicated), mounted a successful challenge in the High Court against the construction of the Chinese-owned Century Zinc mine, slated to be the largest of its kind in the world. The mine finally went ahead, however, following a twelve-to-eleven vote in favor in the divided community.[46]

In Wright's novel, such divisions are attributed to a number of factors. First, there are the clever machinations of the company, whose front men, in the eyes of Angel's son, Will, a leading antimine activist, "broke and won the hearts and minds of more and more of his own relatives and members of their own community" (*C*, 391). In so doing, they were able to capitalize on existing tensions in the community arising from a dispute regarding the custodianship of the prickly-pear-infested, trash-strewn wetlands, which, according to Angel's husband, Norm Phantom, were a powerful snake Dreaming site. Believing that she best "filled the shoes of Norm's grandfather, who had been the keeper of this land" (27), Angel, "Queen of the Pricklebush," lays sole claim to the largesse of the dump that now exists there and out of which she built her serpentine home. This reignites a long-standing conflict over tribal boundaries, prompting all but her immediate family to leave and create a second shantytown on the other side of the bewildered Uptown. It is the senior Law man of this Eastside mob, Joseph Midnight, whose father, Old Cyclone, claimed to be the true traditional owner of the proposed mine site, whom the company negotiators manage to get on side, bribing him with a new house (which he subsequently declines to inhabit) and one thousand dollars to be spent on eradicating feral pigs (whose young, instead, he allows the Eastside kids to adopt and breed up as kin). In addition, the company is able to garner wider support within this impoverished and marginalized community with their promise of plentiful food and good pay, an offer that the two oldest Phantom brothers, Danny and Inso, have happily embraced. Wright nonetheless stresses the risks entailed in accepting this bargain by telling how their youngest brother, Kevin, who had "inherited all the brains" (108), was "rendered an idiot" (109) by an underground explosion on the day he joined his schoolmates down the mine (since nobody was checking the age of the kids who turned up to work). Brain damaged by this industrial accident, Kevin subsequently becomes an easy target of racist thugs, whose brutal drunken assault one night nearly kills him and leaves him a paraplegic.

From Will Phantom's perspective, moreover, any material advantages that might accrue to his people through the resources boom are outweighed by what he perceives to be its poisonous effects, both on their land, through the contamination of soil and waterways, and on their relations with one another and with their "country." Here, we confront one of those hermeneutic challenges referred to earlier, in that the Aboriginal words that are commonly translated into Australian English as "country" do not correspond with the meanings that English speakers elsewhere are likely to associate with this term, for it refers neither to the nation of one's birth or adopted residence nor to the country or countryside, as opposed to the city. Rather, to speak of one's "country" in Aboriginal English is to invoke the interconnected matrix of entities, living and deceased, biotic and abiotic, human and otherwise, that sustains the life of those whose forbears dwelt in the territory to which they remain bound by ancestral kinship ties. In addition, "country" can be used to refer to particular aspects or parts of this territory that are distinguished by predominant features or species and linked with ancestral Dreaming figures, whose movements, which often cross clan boundaries, are said to have shaped the topography of the land. Thus, in the Gulf of Carpentaria there is Waanyi and Yanyuwa country; but both Waanyi and Yanyuwa country have regions that might be referred to, for instance, as Groper country or Spirit People country, each corresponding to a Dreaming "songline" that, as in the case of the Bujimala and Walalu Rainbow Serpent songlines, might traverse Waanyi and Yanyuwa country.[47] Such songlines, which are understood to arise from country and to be active in its ancestral and ongoing (re)creation, encode the Law of right relationship among fellow "countrymen," human and otherwise. Country extends into the sky, out to sea, and beneath the ground. As Deborah Bird Rose explains in her landmark book *Nourishing Terrains* (1996):

> Country in Aboriginal English is not only a common noun but also a proper noun. People talk about country in the same way they would talk about a person: they speak to country, sing to country, visit country, worry about country, feel sorry for country, and long for country. People say that country knows, hears, smells, takes notice, takes care, is sorry or happy. . . . Country is a living entity with a yesterday, today and tomorrow, with a consciousness, and a will toward life.[48]

Unlike the feminized Nature of Euro-Western patriarchal culture, then, Aboriginal country, like each of the diverse (and not infrequently conflictual) entities that collectively constitute its ongoing life, has its own agency and voice. Country is the vital source of the principles and practices that constitute what Rose has termed "Dreaming Ecology."[49] As Aboriginal philosopher Mary Graham explains: "The land, and how we treat it, is what determines our human-ness. Because land is sacred and must be looked after, the relation between people and land becomes the template for society and social relations. Therefore all meaning comes from the land."[50] Caring for country is intrinsic to Aboriginal social and emotional well-being, and, as anthropologist John Bradley observed during his thirty years of living with the Yanyuwa people and learning their language and songs, Aboriginal people "worry greatly about country and speak longingly of places they are unable to visit because it is now a part of a pastoral property, a mining lease, or just too hard to get to without transport."[51]

To redefine land and sea, in accordance with the instrumentalist logic of colonization, as a mere storehouse of "natural resources" thus constitutes an onto-epistemological assault upon country, regardless of the degree of environmental damage that might be entailed in its physical exploitation. And to bind Aboriginal people into the neocolonial economy of the resource extraction industry is potentially to undermine a core dimension of their cultural identity as custodians of their country. The aggressively anthropocentric and hypermasculinist culture of this industry is eloquently encapsulated in *Carpentaria* in the name that Wright gives her fictitious mining company: "Gurfurrit International," an appellation that brilliantly conjoins an allusion to the colonial practice of appropriating or inventing Aboriginal-sounding names with a phonetic echo of the phrase "Go for it!," alluding to the assumption that Australia's mineral wealth, like the bodies of Aboriginal women for older-style colonialists, is there for the taking by transnational businesses with insufficient appreciation of the negative impacts of their operations. Indeed, while Gurfurrit is a fictitious company, the machinations of which are again exaggerated to a satirical extreme, there is a distinct echo in this name of the original designation of the McArthur River zinc deposit when it was found in the 1950s, namely, "Here's your chance."[52]

For Will, the activities of Gurfurrit, which, it is hinted, extend to arson, kidnapping, and possibly even murder, constitute nothing less than "a new war on their country," in which there were "no rules" and "nothing was sacred" (*C*, 378). Yet this novel is no lament for a lost cause: *Carpentaria* tells of many-faceted forms of resistance to this neocolonial assault, and this is, in the end, a story of hope. In opening an imaginative pathway out of the intertwining bonds of andro-, Euro-, and anthropocentric domination, moreover, Wright's novel skillfully avoids both the Skylla of assimilation to the privileged identity of the master and the Charibdys of uncritical reversal of the ruling dualism.[53] Instead, *Carpentaria* deftly discloses the dysfunctionality of the logic of colonization, while restoring voice and agency to the colonized, both human and otherwise.

The fatal flaws in the project of colonial mastery that are hinted at in the very name of "Desperance" can be traced in the paranoid fear of the Other that legitimates the town's continued existence, once it could no longer function as a port. This same paranoia also informs Uptown's relations with the local "blacks," whose condition is a matter of constant (if largely uncomprehending) vigilance, as well as with those aspects of the nonhuman environment that cannot readily be tamed and commercially exploited. Importantly, these fears are exposed as a source of potential vulnerability. For example, in their frenzied effort to fell "the remaining few poor, poor old trees" (*C*, 462)—mangoes, cedars, and poinsettias—that attracted the fruit bats whom the townsfolk so feared as a source of disease that they were also busy shooting them, they fail to observe "the enormous clouds surging across the coast, which ought to have been enough warning to anyone on earth that a cyclone was heading their way" (465). More reliant upon technology than the evidence of their senses, and lacking cultural knowledge of how to interpret such sensory signals, Uptown's residents only respond to this rapidly approaching threat when their radios communicate a warning from the Bureau of Meteorology and almost leave it too late to evacuate safely.

Dangerously unskilled in reading the environment, the settler society is also shown to be ineffective in its surveillance of the local Aboriginal community, precisely on account of their homogenization of the racialized Other: on the run from the authorities for sabotaging the construction of the Gurfurrit mine, Will is able to pass right through a police road block in the midst of a convoy of other Aboriginal men, since, to the colonial gaze, all blacks "look the same" (*C*, 368). As Plumwood argues, homogenization is intrinsic to the logic of colonization, whereby the Other is not regarded as an individual, but as a "member of a class stereotyped as interchangeable, replaceable, all alike. . . . The colonised are stereotyped as 'all the same' in their deficiency."[54]

In her narrative subversion of this kind of homogenization, Wright creates an extremely diverse cast of characters, countering not only the racial but also the gender stereotypes of the dominant discourse. Contrary to Euro-Western constructions of women as inherently "closer to nature," Wright shows that for Indigenous Australians, understanding, living from, and caring for country is the job of men no less than women. While Angel declares herself the keeper of the trash-filled pricklebush swamp, guarding "those whose fractured spirits cried of rape, murder and the pillage of their traditional lands" (*C*, 27), it is her son, Will, and her lover, Mozzie Fishman, who lead the most active resistance to the neocolonial exploitation of their country. Parenting too necessitates the involvement of both men and women, along with country itself, and a key element of Mozzie's crusade of cultural revival is the inclusion of boys and young men in his ceaseless ceremonial traversal of thousands of kilometers of songlines in a tireless endeavor to pass on the Law. Yet for all his traditionalism, Mozzie exemplifies the cultural hybridity manifest in all of Wright's Aboriginal characters, traveling the old pathways with the assistance of a new technology appropriated from colonizers: a convoy of battered old Holdens and Fords, kept on the road against the odds by the blackfellas' genius for bush mechanics (a genius paralleled by Angel's for building a blackfella home out of whitefella trash). Ironically, however, Mozzie's unending pilgrimage absents him from Angel and their two sons, whom he fails to wrest away from the toxic environment of Uptown, where he had installed Angel after she left Norm. For the same reason, following the mine explosion, he fails to go and look for her when she disappears one night on the highway after he had sent her into hiding in a southern city in the wholly inadequate care of two young lads from his convoy. Troublingly, Angel is last seen accepting a lift from a truck driver. Although one of Mozzie's men later dreams of her improvising a new life for herself in a city where she is staying true to her Snake Dreaming by working as an eel catcher, her fate (like so much else in this slippery tale) is left in doubt. Following their sons' deaths in custody, Mozzie, accompanied by Will and the other men, does nonetheless succeed in restoring Angel's sons, together with Aaron, to their spirit country in a traditional water burial on an inland sea deep within a cavern filled with the traces of millennia of Aboriginal inhabitation and the palpable presence of the ancestors.

Here, and elsewhere, Wright takes the reader into a world in which the spirit-matter dualism that predominates within modern Western culture finds no purchase. This is a world where the spirits of the old people might manifest as a cloud of seagulls, come to take their dead descendants back into country (C, 440); where a skilled fisherman like Norm might have to fight for his life with the seductive "sea woman," set on luring him to a watery grave (261), while being assailed by the spirits of the widows of men lost at sea, wailing in the swirling winds driving the clouds that herald an approaching cyclonic storm (364–65); or where the hands of hungry hunters might be stayed by the look in the eyes of a large red kangaroo, holding her paws as if in prayer (442–45). This is a world where nothing is only ever one thing; where everything is, in some sense, alive; where anything might be, or become, "supervital," charged with an indwelling sacred power.[55] Strikingly, this nonmodern yet contemporary Waanyi world converges in some respects with the postmodern, dynamically intra-active world of "vibrant matter," as Jane Bennett puts it, in which things emerge differentially in and through their constitutive interrelations with other things and where any and all material entities are liable to take you by surprise with their lively agency.

It is this dimension of the novel that has evoked comparisons with "magic realism," but as Alison Ravenscroft has observed, this is a misleading categorization, at least insofar as "the real and the fantastic are determined by white critics as being across two cultural locations."[56] Norm, for instance, believes that his highly prized feats of fish taxidermy are assisted by the spirit that has coalesced with his work room, an eerily enchanted place where a "massed choir of crickets that sang *Glory! Glory!*" from the "the nooks and crannies of dark places inside the walls, behind jam jars full of chemicals, or under benches," and even from "deep inside the fishes' horsehair bellies" where they had taken up residence (C, 209–10). How-ever, he also prides himself on being "scientify" in whitefella terms, and his navigation of the seas in accordance with traditional knowledge of the map of the night sky is both highly skilled and entirely rational. Similarly, Will is said to be able to commune with birds and the spirits of the dead, and he "moves lightly through the bush to the beat of the muddied and cracked dancing feat of a million ancestors," as Midnight informs the puz-zled police officers who are trying in vain to track him down (161); but he also has shrewd insight into the machinations of multinational corpo-rations and a firm grasp of the use of whitefella explosives in sabotaging their endeavors.

The white inhabitants of Desperance, for their part, are clearly captive "to their own dreams and delusions."[57] Self-professed believers in "an origi-nal God who had come along with all the white people, who created every-thing for them" (C, 55–56), some seek to quell their sense of "primordial insecurity" (46) by casting "a giant net made of prayers and god-fearing devotion" over the town to protect it from cyclones at the start of the Wet (82), while others claim to have been abducted by aliens (73). One Up-towner, Lloydie, absentee father of Aaron, has fallen under the spell of the mermaid spirit woman incorporated into the timber of his bar, suggesting that even though their rationalistic onto-epistemology will not admit of their existence, whitefellas too can be affected by the supervital agencies of the land that they have colonized.[58] When confronted with the strange apparition of a dreadlocked white man walking in across the mudflats in the wake of a cyclonic storm that had wrecked his fishing boat and stolen his name and identity, the Uptowners, overcoming their initial apprehen-sion, decide that "they were witnessing the emergence of an aquatic aura, a God-sent water angel," and even "downright proper, respectable Uptown women, could not escape the spell that the mariner had cast on them" (63).

Elias Smith, as the mysterious man from the sea is dubbed by mad Cap-tain Finn, who takes him for a messiah and names him after a Christian saint, is made town coast guard following the violent death of his prede-cessor, Gordie. Elias nonetheless turns out to have a stronger affiliation with the Pricklebush mob, and especially Norm, with whom he comes to share a Groper Dreaming. Since Norm had renounced the ocean for his fishroom, it was Elias who took Will fishing as a child, "growing him up in the sea" (C, 163–64). It is also Elias whom Midnight begs to take his daughter Hope, Will's partner, and their child, Bala, to the safety of his own Dreaming place across the sea, when he fears that they will be used as bait to catch Will. These fears are evidently well founded, for when their escape is intercepted by agents of the mining company, Hope and Bala are abducted, and Elias is killed. His corpse, tied upright in a boat placed in the middle of a lagoon, is subsequently used to lure Will into a trap, from which he only narrowly escapes, once again by virtue of his talent for becoming invisible to white eyes. Ably assisted by the larger-than-life Irish priest, Father Danny, an ex–heavyweight boxer and true Christian champion of the oppressed, Will manages to smuggle Elias's body back to Desperance and into Norm's fishroom, knowing that his father will ensure that his friend is returned to his Groper kin at the sacred sea burial ground where the big fish congregate and leap, ferrying their dead kinsmen into the sky country that English speakers call the Milky Way. For Euro-Australian readers, the figure of Elias holds out the hopeful possibility of alliance with Aboriginal people and acceptance into, and by, their country; but only, it is implied, at the price of losing their own Euro-, andro-, and anthropocentric identity—and at the risk of being branded as traitors and treated accordingly.

In some of her late essays, influenced in part by the emergence of eco-criticism, Plumwood began to explore the prospects for what she called a critical green writing project that could disrupt the logic of centrism and rematerialize spirit as "speaking matter."[59] In her analysis, "the colonising framework's exclusion of the non-human from subject status and from intentionality marginalizes the non-human as narrative subject and agent, and pushes the more-than-human sphere into a background role as a mere context for human thought and life."[60] This form of backgrounding is inscribed into the Euro-Western literary form of the novel to the extent that the nonhuman generally only figures as part of the "environment" or "setting" for the main action, which sometimes includes animals in its cast of characters but is predominantly interhuman. In my reading, *Carpentaria* effects the disruption that Plumwood was calling for precisely by means of Wright's subversive decolonization of the very form of the novel. In a manner analogous to Angel's appropriation from Uptown's tip of a figurine of the Virgin Mary, which she transforms into "a brightly coloured statue of an Aboriginal woman who lived by the sea" (*C*, 38), Wright decolonizes the novel by placing the "big story" of her country—that is to say, a story that is not just told about but is actually scripted by country—center stage.

As we learn in the opening chapter, this is, first and foremost, Rainbow Serpent country, formed "from time immemorial" by "a creature larger than storm clouds [who] came down from the stars, laden with its own creative enormity. . . . When it finished creating the many rivers in its wake, it created one last river, no larger or smaller than the others, a river which offers no apologies for its discontent with people who do not know it. This is where the giant serpent continues to live deep down under the ground in a vast network of limestone aquifers. They say its being is porous; it permeates everything. It is all around in the atmosphere and is attached to the lives of the river people like skin" (C, 1–2). The capacity of this volatile country to "spurn . . . human endeavour" (3) is demonstrated not only in the jilting of Desperance by the river but repeatedly throughout the narrative, as the intra-actions of the elements, and in particular the unruly agency of air, are shown to interrupt human actions and intentions: in the dust storm, for example, that disrupts the ceremony to rename the river, Wangala, which had previously been reinscribed with a whitefella name, after Norm Phantom (much to his amusement); in the downpour that colludes with Angel's curses in deterring an Uptown delegation's inquiry into the decampment of Midnight's mob; in the pre–wet season humidity that "jiggered up" (44) all the town's watches and clocks, overriding whitefella timekeeping on the very morning that Elias mysteriously walked in from the sea; in the sudden storms that prevent Gurfurrit's hired assassins from continuing their pursuit of Will from a helicopter and, later, Truthful's investigation into the fire that Norm's daughters lit to burn Elias's body for fear that their father would be falsely accused of his murder; and, spectacularly, in the whirly wind that descends from the hills above the mine where Will is being held captive, picking up piles of rubbish, the refuse of white civilization, swirling them around with balls of native spinifex and the wishes of Mozzie's men, who had come to free Will, thereby fueling the small fire that they had lit to distract the guards and ferrying it down the petrol bowsers to ignite the underground explosion that destroys the mine: "The finale was majestical. Deoro, dearie, the explosion was holy in its glory. All of it was gone. The whole mine, pride of the banana state, ended up looking like a big panorama of burnt chop suey. On a grand scale of course because our country is a very big story. Wonderment, was the ear on the ground listening to the great murmuring ancestor, and the earth shook the bodies of those lying flat on the ground in the hills" (411).

The ancestral spirit that had apparently been stirred up by the operations of the mine, and was now "murmuring" at its demise, is manifest also in the massive cyclone that constitutes the most dramatic incursion of the other-than-human into the action of the novel, ultimately facilitating its optimistic (if open-ended) conclusion. Following his rescue by means of the felicitous intra-activity of sundry human and nonhuman agents, Will returns to Desperance in a mad attempt to get back to sea in search of Hope and Bala, despite Midnight's warning of the imminent destruction of the town and his own awareness of "what the sea ahead was doing once more": "Although he knew it was kilometres away, he heard the spirit waves being rolled in by the ancestral sea water creatures of the currents, and conspiring with the spirits of the sky and winds to crash into the land as though it was exploding. The earth murmured, the underground serpent, living in the underground river that was kilometres away, responded with hostile growls. This was the old war of the ancestors making cyclones grow to use against one another" (C, 470). Having found refuge from the wild winds and sea surge in the upper story of Lloydie's pub, Will is visited by an old mission-educated woman, whom he recognizes as the "baggitty old Queen of the Pricklebush" (478). This unnerving apparition reminds him of the tale she once told him as a child about a cyclone that came far inland, "following along the flat surface of that river so it never died out" on the track of a Law breaker hiding out in a town that was consequently "wrecked . . . into smithereens" (480). When Desperance too is obliterated by another mega-cyclone, which Will visualizes Norm, a powerful storm-maker, stirring up (481–87), it seems the elements have once again acquired a moral force. However, just as Will's attribution of the cyclone to his father's sorcery is contradicted by the previously narrated story of Norm's experience of the storm, so too is the notion of such narrowly targeted vengeance gently questioned. If, as Joseph Midnight had observed, cyclonic activity has been increasing in the Gulf (401), then, it is implied, this cannot be pinned on an errant individual, but implicates the entire resource-intensive, fossil-fueled society, the neocolonial frontier of which is emblematized in the fictional world of Desperance.

As well as obliterating the town, this cyclone also acts as a corrective in the lives of some of the Aboriginal characters, and it is with their unfinished stories that the novel ends. Will, who, as his name implies, is fired by a manly determination not only to defeat the mine but also to defy the elements in rescuing his loved ones single-handedly, "adamant in his resolve" (C, 483), gets washed out to sea and marooned on an island of rubbish. Recalling his mother's trash-built home, Will's stranding could be seen to connote a kind of return to the womb. Finding himself in a condition of enforced passivity, Will is obliged to recognize his own vulnerability and

eventually learns to cultivate patience and a kind of hope that is something other than a wish-fulfillment fantasy. His father, meanwhile, who
had finally been drawn out of his fishroom and back to sea in order to bury
Elias, gets caught in the precyclonic wind storm and conveyed by powerful ocean currents to a distant shore, the Dreaming place of his arch-rival
Midnight, where he is found by the grandson whom he had previously
disowned. When the cyclonic sea surge hits, he narrowly manages to save
both himself and Bala, with the assistance of a mob of "phantom people,"
or *yinbarras* (303). Hope, too, they discover, has landed up on this shore,
and in the course of the journey in which Norm brings them all safely back
home, skillfully reading the night sky to navigate his way across unfamiliar
sea country, he finally lets go of his bitter prejudice against her and her
kin. Left in Norm's care, Bala becomes at last what Will had hoped he
would be: "the adhesive needed to create peace between the groups" (381).
Hope herself, meanwhile, is propelled by her love of Will to overcome her
deep fear of the sea into which she had been dumped from a helicopter
by Gurfurrit's security guards after their capture of Will and is last seen
courageously setting out on a boat to find him, in the protective company
of a school of Norm and Elias's groper kin. Significantly, Hope acquires
her own agency at the end of the novel, not as the autonomous individual
valorized within Euro-Western liberalism (including liberal feminism),[61]
but rather as part of a multispecies collective.

Countering the Euro-, andro-, and anthropocentric logic of colonization, Wright's novel shows how human history could be "rolled, reshaped,
undone and mauled as the great creators of the natural world engineered
the bounty of everything man had ever done in this part of the world into
something more of their own making" (*C*, 491–92). The fiery destruction
of the mine and the oceanic engulfment of Desperance, conjoined with
the survival and reconciliation of members of three generations of the divided and downtrodden Aboriginal community, open a utopian horizon,
within which Wright imagines that the life of the country and its people,
once released from neocolonial heteronomy and restored to their own
land, might be renewed.

There is, to be sure, a mythic quality to this ending, which bears some
resemblance to the outcome of the biblical deluge. There are two crucial differences, though. First, this cleansing catastrophe is not wrought
by a punitive external deity, but rather manifests the indwelling powers
of country, enjoining people (Indigenous and otherwise) to respect its
ways. Second, whereas the biblical new covenant reiterates the message

of human dominion from Genesis 1:28 with the assurance (one that reads to me more like a curse than a promise) that "the fear and dread of you shall rest on every animal of the earth, and on every bird of the air, and on all the fish of the sea" (Gen. 9:2), *Carpentaria* concludes with an affirmation of human participation in a vibrant earthly communion of more-than-human creatures. The final image of the novel is of Norm and Bala walking "hand in hand out of town, Westside, to home," to the accompaniment of a "mass choir of frogs—green, grey, speckled, striped, big and small, dozens of species all assembled around the seafarers. . . . It was a mystery, but there was so much song wafting off the watery land, singing the country afresh" (519).

In a manner comparable to Yvonne Weekes's Caribbean catastrophe narrative *Volcano*, published in the same year as *Carpentaria*, the ending of Wright's novel also "emphasises how the destruction wrought by the disaster can be reconfigured in ways that help to 'sustain' cultural identity at the beginning of another temporal and ecological cycle"[62]—except that in this case, the eco-catastrophe in question functions, first and foremost, as a corrective, at once material and metaphoric, to the prior catastrophe of colonization. In the world beyond the page, however, the intervention of the elements rarely benefits the oppressed in quite so just a manner; and it is clear that an explosion down one mine is not going to stop new ones from being dug. Some of these mines, extracting all manner of minerals, will doubtless win the approval of some Native Title holders, to whom they might well bring tangible benefits. Some of those minerals, moreover, will be required to make the renewable power generators that will hopefully allow most of Australia's abundant coal to remain in the ground: iron ore for steel manufacturing, along with rare earths, are used, for example, in the production of wind turbines. But Australian traditional landowners do not have to hitch their fortunes exclusively to mining. An alternative path of development, one that resonates with Wright's poetics of decolonization, can be found in the "caring for country" movement, which enables Native Title holders to remain in, or return to, their ancestral lands as "rangers," tasked with tackling environmental degradation at the same time as helping to regenerate their culture and communities, and exploring sustainable forms of income generation (such as eco-cultural tourism). Not unlike the Aboriginal figures in Wright's novel, who draw selectively on Western science and technology in the pursuit of Indigenous ends, most of these rangers deploy an intercultural approach. As Jon Altman observes, this hybrid modus operandi is "essential to deal with 21st century postcolonial problems including depopulation, the orphaning of country that needs human presence for management, and broadscale and pervasive environmental threats."[63] One of the groups featured in Altman's study of this movement of Aboriginal ecological, social, and cultural renewal are the Waanyi-Garawa Rangers of the southwest Gulf, who won the 2011 Leighton Holdings Indigenous Award (part of the Northern Territory Landcare Awards) for their fire management program.[64] Earlier that year, as Cyclone Yasi was bearing down on the "banana state," Waanyi people in Queensland finally won a Native Title claim that had been running since 1999. This opened the way for the negotiation of an Indigenous Land Use Agreement with the state of Queensland, granting Waanyi people the right to hunt, fish, camp, light fires, and conduct burials and other ceremonies in an area of about 3,798 square kilometers in the Boodjamulla National Park, some 120 kilometers south of the Gulf of Carpentaria, which contains important rock art and artifact sites and holds particular eco-cultural significance as Rainbow Serpent country. Encompassing Bidunggu Aboriginal Community on the Gregory River, along with several large pastoral holdings, this area—the largest ever granted under Native Title in Queensland—also includes the MMG Century zinc mine site, and it was there that the special court hearing to decide the case was held.[65] Like most Indigenous people throughout Australia and elsewhere, the Waanyi will continue to face many challenges. This agreement nonetheless affords them new opportunities to care for country and forge a new future for themselves in alliance with their land, at a time of rapid and unpredictable socioecological change.

As Bonnie Roos and Alex Hunt observe: "Our world is locked in a dance of cultural, economic and ecological interdependence. This interdependence calls for a multiplicity of voices to address the problems we face today."[66] Among those whose voices have been suppressed by colonial and neocolonial regimes of domination are those of Indigenous peoples, who are now availing themselves of new ways to communicate with one another and the wider society, both nationally and internationally. As the planet heats up and weather gets weirder and wilder, it is essential that these voices are heard. Australian Aboriginal cultures, in particular, have proven themselves resilient and adaptive in the face of several major climatic changes in the distant past, and their lifeways have been honed by the challenge of creating a sustainable modus vivendi on a continent with the climatic characteristics of high variability, low predictability, and frequent extremes that are now going global.[67] Aboriginal people discerned long ago that annual calendars are not much use when it comes to antici-pating meteorological phenomena under these conditions and therefore look instead to the patterns of connectivity linking the activities of plants and animals to changes in the prevailing weather conditions.[68] The irregu-lar climatic rhythms that they have learned to read so well, along with the ecologies that they helped to engender, are changing. But indigenous eco-logical knowledge does not constitute a static database or toolkit, and such changes do not render it redundant. On the contrary, as a situated, dynamic, and adaptive onto-epistemology, which recognizes other-than-human agency and interests, the limits of human knowledge, and the in-terconnections between human social relations and the more-than-human environment, it has acquired a new relevance in addressing the global prob-lems of the Anthropocene.[69] This way of knowing, in conversation with both modern empirical science and the environmental humanities, has a vital contribution to make in discerning human accountability for socio-ecological ills, and responsibility for their redress, as the winds of change blow ever more violently around the planet. This is something that the IPCC too has acknowledged in its 2014 report on climate change impacts, vulnerability, and adaptation: "Indigenous, local, and traditional knowl-edge systems and practices, including indigenous peoples' holistic view of community and environment, are a major resource for adapting to climate change, but these have not been used consistently in existing adaptation efforts. Integrating such forms of knowledge with existing practices in-creases the effectiveness of adaptation."[70] For that to occur, however, the deeply entrenched inequities that continue to marginalize Indigenous voices and to blight Indigenous lives and lands would need to be redressed. Learning to "dance with disaster" in a perilously warming world, in other words, demands also an ethics and a politics of decolonization.

POSTSCRIPT

In 1799, as the coal-fired Industrial Revolution in Britain was launching the planet into the era of the Anthropocene, a young Protestant theologian in Berlin, Friedrich Schleiermacher, wrote a series of talks on religion "to its cultured despisers" (among whom he counted his close friends among the early German Romantics).[1] Having considered as many of the world's religions as he was able to research from written documents, including travelers' reports on Aboriginal culture in the British penal colony at Botany Bay, Schleiermacher came to the conclusion that these diverse texts and traditions had arisen historically from a common core human experience. This he framed as an embodied sense of the inherence of every finite entity in the infinite and, as a corollary, of the profound dependence of one's own limited existence on the boundless becoming of the universe. You do not have to believe in God or the gods to enter into this ineffable experience, Schleiermacher acknowledged, and some forms of belief might actually hinder it. But so too, he discerned, would such religious feelings be "blocked and barricaded" by the narrowly human-centered and individualistic mode of instrumental thinking that he saw taking root in contemporary "bourgeois life."[2]

In retrospect, Schleiermacher's cultural critique appears prescient. One of the salient tendencies of secular modernity has indeed been the suppression of any sense of eco-cosmic interconnectedness, or at least, its confinement to the realm of individual aesthetic experience. In the West especially, institutionalized religion has offered little to counter this trend, becoming either narrowly focused on questions of morality, whether personal or political, to the neglect of the mystical, or, worse, fostering fundamentalist fantasies of divine intervention and personal ascension into an immaterial beyond. Meanwhile, the wider society has embraced an aggressive ethos of human self-assertion, both individual and collective, which actively militates against the recognition of the unfathomable indebtedness of each of our lives and all human cultures to countless more-than-human, vitally material entities and processes, whether from the deep past or here and now, in our midst but outside our limited horizon of consciousness.

Yet the very experience identified by Schleiermacher as the essence of religion and the wellspring of ethical sensibility can now be seen to find rational support and inspiration, as he also anticipated it would,[3] in the witness of the natural sciences, themselves one of the precious fruits of Janus-faced modernity. The lithosphere, biosphere, hyrdrosphere, and atmosphere, upon which we "late-coming earthlings . . . remain utterly dependent," as Nigel Clark observes, "retain the capacity to withdraw the support and sustenance they provide."[4] The question of how we relate to this unstable ground, though, cannot be answered within the terms of science alone, because this is properly an ethical, and for some a spiritual, matter. As I see it, the question is whether, owning up to and honoring this indebtedness, we seek to act in such a way as to foster the flourishing of more-than-human life, by, among other things, becoming more adept at "dancing with disaster," or whether we continue to background Earth's multiple other-than-human agencies and communicative overtures, denying the interests of those strange strangers who are also our fellow earthlings, and thereby "squander our inheritance, fail to acknowledge our debts, forget the bodies and the materials that have made us what we are."[5]

Despite the proliferation of warnings, some spoken by scientists, others legible in the earth itself, the prevailing social system, governed in large part by the interests of a turbo-charged variant of global capitalism, remains set on the path of squandering. While continuing to dig up the dead, exhuming and consuming the remains of ancient forests and sea creatures to power our industries and light our cities, this system is now promoting new techniques of assaulting the earth through such desperate measures as the exploitation of coal-seam gas and tar sands. Our inequitable consumption of seafood having risen to such levels that ever more fisheries are facing collapse, the continued combustion of these fossil fuels by those who can afford it is also causing the world's oceans to become warmer and more acidic, placing further pressure on marine life. Similarly, while many of the terrestrial plant and animal species into whose midst humans evolved are also endangered by anthropogenic global warming, native vegetation and wildlife habitat continue to be lost to industrial monocultures, roads, megastores, and suburban sprawl, while innumerable animals remain subject to an array of largely commercially motivated forms of brutal mistreatment. And, even as the weather gets wilder, maladaptive modes of development, underpinned by the mantra of economic growth and the delusion of mastery, are escalating all manner of risks and amplifying social vulnerability to the only partially predictable, and potentially catastrophic, impacts of climate change.

Conscious of both the peril and the possibility of this *kairos* moment, I am sending *Dancing with Disaster* out into the world in the hope that the historical narratives that I have traced and the literary ones that I have discussed here might help to engender a renewed appreciation of dependence and indebtedness; a greater readiness to discern in disaster both the lineaments of human folly and wrongdoing and the bonds that bind us with others, human and nonhuman; and an enhanced capacity to prepare for, and respond to, coming calamities in ways that are resilient, compassionate, and potentially transformative. This does not mean, however, that I share the idealist illusion that all we need is a "new story" to budge the entrenched socioeconomic and power-political interests that are keeping us on the path to catastrophe. Narratives alone do not determine attitudes, let alone actions. From the material ecocritical perspective that I have brought to this study, stories arise, inter- and intra-actively, out of practices: that is to say, narratives and practices coconstitute one another. This implies that the work of fostering new bio-inclusive narratives about eco-catastrophe, in place of human-centered ones of natural disaster, will have to be undertaken, in large part, beyond the page.

Such alternative narratives are being told; some of them, such as the tangled weave of stories that Alexis Wright threads through *Carpentaria*, have ancient origins; and there are no doubt many more arising from other non-European cultures, which would repay reconsideration along the lines that I have mapped out here. But such narratives will only take root and bear fruit if they fall on fertile ground—ground that has already been prepared by multispecies practices of communication, collaboration, and care. I take heart from the evidence that some such practices persist and others are emerging, many of them in the shadow of catastrophe— whether remedial, as in the endeavors of those wildlife carers researched by Deborah Bird Rose, who are providing assistance to ill and injured flying foxes in the face of widespread habitat loss and human hostility;[6] anticipatory, such as the Transition Towns movement that is building resilient communities for a postcarbon, climate-changed future; or in the aftermath, as in the transformative initiatives that Rebecca Solnit describes as having emerged from the wreckage of Hurricane Katrina.[7]

The historical record also provides some grounds for hope, indicating that when circumstances change, a counternarrative obtaining to a previously marginal sociocultural formation can come to significantly reconfigure hitherto dominant material-discursive practices. As the German sociologist Max Weber famously demonstrated, this is what happened when the Protestant work ethic, first embraced only by an oppositional minority, early followers of Luther and Calvin, went mainstream in the developing capitalist societies of northwestern Europe from the sixteenth century.[8] By finding innovative ways of "dwelling actively within . . . crisis,"[9] as Frederick Buell puts it, honing our improvisational skills of "dancing with disaster," contemporary societies could well become more receptive to those narratives that disclose human dependence upon, and answerability to, the multispecies collectives to which they belong. As Rose has shown, "Catastrophes offer unprecedented opportunities for the formation of new transnational and transpecies communities. . . . Our challenge as scholars is to identify processes of moral friendship and to work to enhance the moral possibilities inherent in catastrophe."[10]

That brings me to one final word of qualification and clarification. Only rather late in the process of preparing this work for publication was I struck by the realization that none of the literary texts that I had selected for discussion tells the story of post-trauma reconstruction. Not unlike classical tragedy, these narratives conclude in the more-or-less immediate wake of the catastrophe, offering a moment of *anagnorisis* in the case of one or more of the central characters but leaving the story of how the wider community regrouped and recovered untold. After a few anxious hours when I wondered whether I should have chosen other works that told a fuller story of the aftermath of disaster, I decided that this lacuna was actually an advantage. For it leaves a space for the reader to consider the implications of the narrative for the actual or potential eco-catastrophes of their own time and place. In this way, such works of fiction have the potential to provoke the kind of extra-textual "epilogue" that Serenella Iovino identifies as part of the process of "narrative reinhabitation" in disrupted or injured places: "From an ethical perspective, the epilogue of a story is a task rather than an accomplished reality. By telling a story, narrations not only confer a *shape* (namely, a sense) to the events that happen in a given context, making them understandable; they also creatively enable a *project* that takes on society and its values."[11] It is to this transdisciplinary, transnational, and transpecies project of material-discursive reinhabitation, forged in the danger zone of anthropogenic climate change, that *Dancing with Disaster* is dedicated.

NOTES

INTRODUCTION

1. McCrae et al., "Australian Pyro-Tornadogenesis Event."
2. Rose and Robin, "Ecological Humanities."
3. Griffiths, "Humanities," n.p.
4. See also Carrigan, "(Eco)Catastrophe."
5. Timothy Morton coins the expression "strange strangers" as a gloss of Jacques Derrida's concept of the *arrivant* (from Derrida and Dufourmantell, *Of Hospitality*) in *Ecological Thought*, 41.
6. On the pertinence of "frame analysis" to the analysis of climate change literature, see Goodbody, "Frame Analysis."
7. As shown, e.g., by the data collected by EM-DAT (see especially the graph for disaster trends, 1975–2012, http://imgur.com/a/KdyTV#4 [accessed Nov. 1, 2013]), Munich Re Reinsurance.
8. Adorno and Horkheimer, *Dialectic of Enlightenment*, 3.
9. Ibid., 5.
10. On the pertinence of Adorno and Horkheimer's critique of modernity for postcolonial as well as eco-socialist and ecofeminist analyses, along with the importance (and hazards) of the revaluation of precolonial onto-epistemologies, see DeLoughrey and Handley, "Introduction," 16–20. German feminist theorists engaged early and fruitfully with the value and limitations of the *Dialectic of Enlightenment*: see Beinssen-Hesse and Rigby, *Out of the Shadows*, 1–17.
11. Rigby, "Dancing with Disaster."
12. Serres, *Natural Contract*, 31–32.
13. On "hybrids" see Latour, *We Have Never Been Modern*, 108.
14. Crutzen and Stoermer, "Anthropocene."
15. "Bushfires Burn across Southern Australia," ABC News, Jan. 20, 2013, http://www.abc.net.au/news/2013-01-19/saturday-bushfire-live-coverage/4472026.
16. "Cyclone Rusty Gathers Strength Off the Pilbara Coast," ABC News, Feb. 26, 2013, http://www.abc.net.au/news/2013-02-26/pilbara-residents-nervously-monitoring-cyclone-rusty/4539804.
17. "Another Record Broken in Melbourne's Heatwave," ABC News, Mar. 13, 2013, http://www.weatherzone.com.au/news/another-record-broken-in-melbournes-heatwave/23993.

18. Steffen, "Angry Summer," 1.

19. Commonwealth of Australia Bureau of Meteorology, "Australian Climate Influences," 2010, http://www.bom.gov.au/watl/about-weather-and-climate/australian-climate-influences.html. See also Sherratt, Griffiths, and Robin, *Change in the Weather*.

20. Field et al., *Climate Change 2014*.

21. Tredinnick, *Australia's Wild Weather*, 8–9.

22. Solnit, *Hope in the Dark*, 136–37.

23. Johns-Putra and Trexler, "Climate Change in Literature." See also *English Studies* 91.7 (2010), ecocritical special issue edited by Astrid Bracke and Marguérite Corporaal; Milner, Burgmann, and Sellars, *Changing the Climate*; and *The Invention of Eco-Futures*, Ecozon@ 3.12 (2012), special issue edited by Ursula Heise.

24. This is also made clear in the IPCC Working Group II's report Impacts, Adaptation, and Vulnerability (Field et al., *Climate Change 2014*).

25. Adam Vaughan and John Vidal, "Extreme Weather Is 'Silver Lining' for Climate Action: Christiana Figueres," *Guardian*, Mar. 6, 2014, http://www.theguardian.com/environment/2014/mar/05/extreme-weather-climate-change-political-christiana-figueres-un.

26. "Major Flood Crisis Hits Queensland, Australia," BBC World News, Feb. 2, 2013, http://www.bbc.co.uk/news/world-asia-21226178.

27. For a sustained critique of the concept of nature "over yonder," see Morton, *Ecological Thought*.

28. See, e.g., Plumwood, *Environmental Culture*.

29. Robin, "Battling the Land."

30. Estok, "Theorising in a Space of Ambivalent Openness."

31. "Tasmanian Fires Prompt PM's Grim Warning," *Age*, Jan. 7, 2013, http://www.theage.com.au/environment/weather/tasmanian-fires-prompt-pms-grim-climate-warning-20130107-2ccon.html.

32. Judith Ireland, "Heatwave, Climate Change Link Simplistic: Truss," *Sydney Morning Herald*, Jan. 9, 2013, http://www.smh.com.au/opinion/political-news/heatwave-climate-change-link-simplistic-truss-20130109-2cfv6.html.

33. Emma Griffiths, "Tony Abbott Accuses UN Official of 'Talking through Her Hat' on Climate Change," ABC News Online, updated Oct. 23, 2013, http://www.abc.net.au/news/2013-10-23/tony-abbott-fires-climate-change-rfs-un/5039932.

34. Clarissa Thorpe and Ben Atherton, "FOI Emails Reveal Abuse of Climate Scientists," ABC News, May 24, 2012, http://www.abc.net.au/news/2012-05-11/anu-releases-abusive-emails-sent-to-climate-scientists/4005132.

35. *2009 Victorian Bushfires Royal Commission Report*, 2010, http://www.royalcommission.vic.gov.au/Commission-Reports/Final-Report.

36. Freya Mathews, "Fires the Deadly Reality of Climate Change," *Age,* Feb. 10, 2009, http://www.theage.com.au/opinion/fires-the-deadly-inevitability-of -climate-change-20090209-8289.html#ixzz2NZQ6NvfF.
37. Griffiths, "'Unnatural Disaster'?"
38. Miranda Devine, "Green Ideas Must Take Blame for Deaths," *Sydney Morning Herald,* Feb. 12, 2009, http://www.smh.com.au/environment/green-ideas -must-take-blame-for-deaths-20090211-84mk.html.
39. Lindsay Murdoch and Ben Doherty, "Marysville's Survivors Ready to Start Journey Home," *Sydney Morning Herald,* Feb. 14, 2009, http://www.smh.com .au/national/marysvilles-survivors-ready-to-start-journey-home-20090213 -8774.html.
40. N. Clark, *Inhuman Nature,* xii.
41. McGuire, *Surviving Armageddon,* 16.
42. See, e.g., Steinberg, *Acts of God;* and, with respect to Hurricane Katrina, Hartman and Squires, *There Is No Such Thing.*
43. Oliver-Smith, "Theorizing Disasters," 28.
44. Roos and Hunt, *Postcolonial Green,* 1. See also DeLoughrey and Handley, *Postcolonial Ecologies,* 13.
45. Hoffman and Oliver-Smith, *Angry Earth,* 1.
46. Bolin and Stanford, "Constructing Vulnerability," 90.
47. On the contribution of religious studies to disaster research in the context of climate change specifically, see, e.g., the two volumes edited by Bergmann and Gerten: Bergmann and Gerten, *Religion and Dangerous Climate Change;* and Gerten and Bergmann, *Religion in Environmental and Climate Change.*
48. Hoffman and Oliver-Smith, *Angry Earth,* 12.
49. Nixon, *Slow Violence,* 58.
50. Kuhlicke and Steinführer, "Soziale Verwundbarkeit."
51. Oliver-Smith, "Theorizing Disasters," 32.
52. Plumwood, *Environmental Culture,* 97–98.
53. Oliver-Smith, "Theorizing Disasters," 31.
54. Rigby, "Dancing with Disaster," 135.
55. For an overview of the field, with a helpful clarification of key terms and approaches, see Alexander, *Natural Disasters;* Alexander, *Confronting Catastrophe.*
56. *Shorter Oxford English Dictionary,* 558. See also Morton, "Romantic Disaster Ecology."
57. Rigby, "Noah's Ark Revisited."
58. See, e.g., Greg Garrard's critique of the trope of "apocalypse" in *Ecocriticism.*
59. Buber, "Prophecy, Apocalyptic." On the "counter-apocalyptic," see Keller, *Apocalypse Now and Then.*
60. Eagleton, *After Theory,* 175.
61. Berger, *After the End,* 5.

62. Morgan, *Earth's Cry*.

63. Billingham provides a detailed postcolonial and ecological exegesis of this passage in "The Earth Mourns."

64. Northcott, *Moral Climate*, 12–15.

65. Levene, "Climate Blues," 162–63.

66. Heise, *Sense of Place*, 141.

67. Huet, *Culture of Disaster*, 3.

68. Ibid.

69. In "Dancing with Disaster" I liken it to the practice of "contact improvisation," as theorized by Gronda in her doctoral thesis, "dance with the body you have."

70. See, e.g., Scarry, *Thinking in an Emergency*.

71. See, e.g., Brunner and Lynch, *Adaptive Governance*.

72. See, e.g., Coole and Frost, *New Materialisms*; Alaimo and Hekman, *Material Feminisms*; and Iovino and Oppermann, *Material Ecocriticism*.

73. N. Clark, *Inhuman Nature*, xiv.

74. I take the concept of "intra-active becoming" from Barad, *Meeting the Universe Halfway*.

75. Oliver-Smith, "Theorizing Disasters," 45.

76. Zapf, "Ecocriticism and Literature as Cultural Ecology." See also Dürbeck, "Introduction."

77. Griffiths, "Humanities," n.p. See also Mathews, "Ecophilosophy in Australia"; Mathews, "Environmental Philosophy."

1   MOVING EARTH

1. De Boer and Sanders, *Earthquakes in Human History*, 90–98.

2. Neiman, *Evil in Modern Thought*, 241.

3. Weinrich, "Literaturgeschichte eines Weltereignisses," 65; Araujo, "Focus: The Lisbon Earthquake," 318.

4. Darwin qtd. in de Boer and Sanders, *Earthquakes in Human History*, 1.

5. N. Clark, *Inhuman Nature*, 5 (with reference to Edmund Husserl's *Origins of Geology*).

6. Dutton, *Earthquakes*, 12, 14.

7. De Boer and Sanders, *Earthquakes in Human History*, 2.

8. Araujo, "Focus: The Lisbon Earthquake."

9. Krüger, "Gedanken," 46. Unless otherwise stated, all translations are my own.

10. On the diversity of views among German Protestants, see Löffler, *Lissabons Fall*.

11. Neiman, *Evil in Modern Thought*, 244.

12. Kendrick, *Lisbon Earthquake*, 227.

13. Krüger, "Gedanken," 50.

14. Bassnett, "Faith, Doubt, Aid, and Prayer."
15. Krüger, "Gedanken," 36–37, 40–41.
16. Schmidt, *Wolken krachen, Berge zittern*, 66–71.
17. Dynes, "Dialogue between Voltaire and Rousseau."
18. Kendrick, *Lisbon Earthquake*, 78.
19. Neiman, *Evil in Modern Thought*, 249.
20. De Boer and Sanders, *Earthquakes in Human History*, 99–101.
21. Neiman, *Evil in Modern Thought*, 249.
22. Ibid., 250.
23. Immanuel Kant, "Von den Ursachen der Erderschütterungen bei Gelegenheit des Unglücks, welches die westlichen Länder von Europa gegen des Endes des vorigen Jahres betroffen hat"; Kant, "Geschichte und Naturbeschreibung der merkwürdigen Vorfälle des Erdbebens, welches an dem Ende des 1755sten Jahres einen großen Teil der Erde erschüttert hat"; Kant, "Fortgesetzte Betrachtung der seit einiger Zeit wahrgenommenen Erderschütterungen." All originally published in the *Königsbergische wöchentlichen Frag- und Anzeigungs-Nachrichten*, Jan. and Apr. 1756, in Breidert, *Die Erschütterung der vollkommenen Welt*.
24. Ibid., 97–143.
25. Huet, *Culture of Disaster*, 41.
26. De Boer and Sanders, *Earthquakes in Human History*, 95.
27. Merchant, *Death of Nature*.
28. Kant, in Breidert, *Die Erschütterung der vollkommenen Welt*, 143.
29. Pope, *Essay on Man*, 12, 15.
30. Kant, in Breidert, *Die Erschütterung der vollkommenen Welt*, 131–35.
31. Ibid., 135.
32. Voltaire, "Poème sur le désastre de Lisbonne," 341, 344, 348.
33. Rousseau, "Lettre à Voltaire."
34. Dynes, "Dialogue between Voltaire and Rousseau."
35. Voltaire, *Candide*, 34–37.
36. N. Clark, *Inhuman Nature*, 90, 89.
37. Ray, "Reading the Lisbon Earthquake," 11.
38. Kant, *Critique of Judgment*, 331.
39. Walter, *Katastrophen*, 96–129; Huet, *Culture of Disaster*, 41–42.
40. N. Clark, *Inhuman Nature*, 85.
41. Rigby, "Romanticism."
42. I take the term "vital materialism" from Bennett, *Vibrant Matter*.
43. Appelt and Grathoff, *Heinrich von Kleist*, 76–79; Kircher, "Das Erdbeben in Chili," 22–24.
44. Košenina, "Friedrich Theodor Nevermanns 'Alonzo und Elvira.'"
45. Araujo, "Focus: The Lisbon Earthquake."
46. Kleist, "Earthquake in Chile," 51 (hereafter referred to in the text as *EiC*).

47. Stephens, *Heinrich von Kleist,* 194–206.
48. The German original uses *verschüttet . . . werden* here, which can refer to being either poured out or buried. See Kleist, "Das Erdbeben in Chili," 207.
49. Kircher, *"Das Erdbeben in Chili,"* 9.
50. Girard, "Theorie der Mythologie/Anthropologie."
51. Hoffman, "Worst of Times," 137–38.
52. Serres, *Natural Contract;* N. Clark, *Inhuman Nature,* 146.
53. Walter, *Katastrophen,* 105.
54. Schneider, "Der Zusammensturz des Allgemeinen."
55. Solnit, *Paradise Built in Hell.*
56. Hoffman, "Worst of Times," 148–49.
57. Rigby, "Discoursing on Disaster."
58. Schlegel, "On Romantic Poesy," 192–93. On early German Romantic aesthetics and literary theory, see also Rigby, *Topographies of the Sacred,* 101–11.
59. Watts, *When a Billion Chinese Jump,* 57.
60. Kim, "Induced Seismicity."
61. McGuire, *Waking the Giant.*

2   SPREADING PESTILENCE

1. Alexander, *Natural Disasters,* 9.
2. N. Clark, *Inhuman Nature,* 28.
3. Pfueller, "Nature of Health."
4. Alcabes, *Dread,* 10–13.
5. Ibid., 18.
6. Crawford cites the case of a middle-aged couple from New Mexico, who were diagnosed with bubonic plague in 2002, probably contracted from a wood rat in their backyard, whose plight was not reported to the public until they were well on the road to recovery (*Deadly Companions,* 215).
7. Ibid., 99–103.
8. N. Clark, *Inhuman Nature,* 40–45.
9. Margulis and Sagan, *Acquiring Genomes.*
10. Crawford, *Deadly Companions,* 211.
11. Haraway, *When Species Meet,* 3–4.
12. Crawford, *Deadly Companions,* 25.
13. Ibid., 19.
14. Diamond, *Guns, Germs and Steel,* 195–214.
15. Alcabes, *Dread,* 24.
16. Ibid., 26.
17. Crawford, *Deadly Companions,* 88.
18. Tuchman, *Distant Mirror,* 93.
19. Crawford, *Deadly Companions,* 97.
20. Alcabes, *Dread,* 23.

21. Derrida and Dufourmantelle, *On Hospitality,* 25,

22. Bulst, "Die Pest verstehen," 154.

23. "Plague: Ecology and Transmission," Centers for Disease Control and Prevention, Bacterial Diseases Branch, Foothills Campus, Fort Collins, CO, last modified June 13, 2012, http://www.cdc.gov/plague/transmission/.

24. Jenner, "Great Dog Massacre."

25. N. Clark, *Inhuman Nature,* 59.

26. Ibid., 60.

27. Boccaccio, *Decameron,* 9.

28. Alcabes, *Dread,* 35, 36.

29. Ibid., 36. See also Bulst, "Die Pest verstehen," 158.

30. Tuchman, *Distant Mirror,* 116.

31. Alcabes, *Dread,* 34.

32. Bulst, "Die Pest verstehen," 152.

33. Ibid., 160.

34. This term was coined by Andrew Milner in "On the Beach."

35. Alcabes, *Dread,* 27.

36. Crawford, *Deadly Companions,* 83.

37. Bulst, "Die Pest verstehen," 150.

38. Alcabes, *Dread,* 42.

39. Adorno and Horkheimer, *Dialectic of Enlightenment,* 4.

40. I take the term "anthroparchal," referring to the human domination of nonhuman nature, from Cudworth, *Developing Ecofeminist Theory,* 8.

41. See Cudworth, *Developing Ecofeminist Theory,* for an excellent analysis and refutation of this common misconstruction of critical ecofeminism.

42. See, e.g., Plumwood, *Feminism and the Mastery of Nature;* White, "Historical Roots."

43. L. Williams, "Reflections on Modernity."

44. Sitter, "Eighteenth-Century Ecological Poetry."

45. Morton, *Shelley and the Revolution,* 221.

46. P. B. Shelley, "Queen Mab," 127.

47. M. Shelley, *Journals,* 476–77.

48. Paley, "Mary Shelley's *The Last Man,*" 1.

49. Ibid., 2.

50. Kant, *Opus postumum,* 66–7.

51. Bate, "Living with the Weather." See also Wood, *Tambora.*

52. Paley, "Mary Shelley's *The Last Man,*" 3.

53. Following Hugh J. Luke's University of Nebraska Press edition of 1965, which was reprinted with an introduction by Anne K. Mellor in 1993, other major editions of *The Last Man* include those of Brian Aldiss (Hogarth Press, 1985), Anne McWhirr (Broadview, 1996), Morton Paley (Oxford Paperbacks, 1998), and Pamela Bickley (Wordsworth Classics, 2004).

54. Johnson, "Last Man," 261.
55. M. Shelley, *Last Man*, 2–4 (hereafter cited in the text as *LM*).
56. Goldsmith, *Unbuilding Jerusalem*, 276.
57. Plumwood, *Feminism and the Mastery of Nature*.
58. Goldsmith, *Unbuilding Jerusalem*, 268. See also Hutchings, "'Dark Image,'" 228–29.
59. Aaron, "Return of the Repressed."
60. Berger, *After the End*, 5.
61. Hutchings, "'Dark Image,'" 238. On *The Last Man* and colonialism see also Cantor, "Apocalypse of Empire"; Lew, "Plague of Imperial Desire"; and Bewell, *Romanticism and Colonial Disease*. I take the term "trans-corporeal" from Alaimo, "Trans-Corporeal Feminisms."
62. Mellor, "Introduction," xxiv.
63. In referring to smallpox as extinct, Shelley implicitly recalls Edward Jenner's development of a successful vaccine against this disease from the related bovine infection cowpox. See Fulford, Lee, and Kitson, "Beast Within."
64. Alcabes, *Dread*, 56.
65. Bewell, *Romanticism and Colonial Disease*, 298.
66. This part of the narrative is evidently informed by contemporary reports of atrocities committed by the Greek army in the city of Tripolitza in 1821, where thousands of resident Turkish women and children were massacred, and the town's Jews tortured. See Adams, "Revolt of Nature," 155.
67. "Abduction" is a term coined by C. S. Pierce to refer to intuitive insights that arise from biosemiotic processes that generally transpire below the level of consciousness. See Wheeler, "Biosemiotic Turn."
68. My reading of the imaginary ecocultural space that opens toward the end of this narrative as "queer" is informed by Sandilands, "Queering Ecocultural Studies."
69. Adams, "Revolt of Nature," 94, 110.
70. Melville, *Romantic Hospitality*, 140.
71. Thomas Malthus's essay *On Population*, which argues that human population is kept in check by disease, war, and famine, was published in 1798. Adams discusses *The Last Man* as, among other things, a response to Godwin's counterarguments to Malthus. See also Strang, "Common Life"; Fulford, "Apocalyptic Economics."
72. C. S. Williams, "Mary Shelley's Bestiary," 140.
73. Wood, *Tambora*, 72–96.
74. Wood, *Tambora*, 95–96. See also McWhirr, "Mary Shelley's Anti-Contagionism."
75. McKusick, *Green Writing*, 109.
76. Ryan, *Virus X*, 337–38.
77. Rose, "Flying Foxes." See also Quammen, *Spillover*.

78. Ryan, *Virus X,* 322.
79. Huet, *Culture of Disaster,* 7.
80. Da Costa et al., "Transfer of Multidrug-Resistant Bacteria."
81. Ryan, *Virus X,* 381.
82. Ibid., 380.
83. Camus, *Plague,* 34.

3   BREAKING WAVES

1. Goethe, *Faust. Part Two,* 104 (hereafter cited in the text by act, scene, and line number).
2. Darwin, *Temple of Nature,* Canto 1, "The Production of Life," lines 295–302.
3. Leeming and Leeming, *Dictionary of Creation Myths,* 79–80.
4. This narrative subsequently gave rise to the theological postulate of *creation ex nihilo,* creation out of nothing, which, as Catherine Keller (an ecotheologian in the process tradition) has demonstrated, is actually unbiblical. See Keller, *Face of the Deep.*
5. Eisenberg, *Ecology of Eden,* 121.
6. Pritchard, *Ancient Near Eastern Texts,* 104–6.
7. Tuana, "Viscous Porosity," 196–97.
8. Pickering, "New Ontologies," xx.
9. Ibid., xx.
10. Franklin, "Choreography of Fire," 44.
11. P. Murphy, *Ecocritical Explorations,* 173–84.
12. Storm, *Dykemaster* (hereafter cited in the text as *D*).
13. Holander, *Theodor Storm,* 73.
14. Blackbourn, *Conquest of Nature,* 122.
15. D. Meier, "Man and Environment"; Blackbourn, *Conquest of Nature,* 123.
16. D. Meier, "Sturmfluten." Blackbourn cites somewhat lower figures: nine thousand and sixty thousand respectively (*Conquest of Nature,* 124), whereas Jakubowski-Tiessen also refers to eleven thousand human fatalities ("Gotteszorn und Meereswüten," 101).
17. "Sturmflut," in Gesellschaft für Schleswig-Holsteinische Geschichte, "Schleswig-Holstein von A bis Z," http://www.geschichte-s-h.de/vonabisz/sturmflut.htm (accessed Feb. 25, 2013).
18. Blackbourn, *Conquest of Nature,* 3.
19. D. Meier, "Sturmfluten"; Niemeyer, Eiben, and Rohde, "History and Heritage of German Coastal Engineering," 7.
20. Holander, *Theodor Storm,* 75–80.
21. Blackbourn, *Conquest of Nature,* 124.
22. Other estimates vary between 4.62 and 5.23. See D. Meier, "Sturmfluten."
23. Jakubowski-Tiessen, "Gotteszorn und Meeresflüthen," 115–18.
24. Blackbourn, *Conquest of Nature,* 3.

25. Holander, *Theodor Storm*, 21.

26. Goethe, *Scientific Studies*, 147.

27. Luke, "Introduction," liv.

28. Goethe, *Faust. Part One*, 52.

29. See Berman's interpretation of *Faust* as a "tragedy of development" in *"All That Is Solid Melts into Air."*

30. Rigby, *Topographies of the Sacred*, 213.

31. Sullivan, "Affinity Studies and Open Systems." See also Rigby, "Freeing the Phenomena"; Rigby, "Prometheus Redeemed?"

32. Sullivan, "Affinity Studies and Open Systems," 241.

33. Ibid., 245; Taylor, "Distributed Agency."

34. Sullivan, "Affinity Studies," 241.

35. Ibid., 246.

36. See, e.g., Moritz Necker, review of *Der Schimmelreiter* in *Die Grenzboten* (no. 48, 1889), in Storm, *Werke*, 3: 1086–88; Silz, "Theodor Storm's *Schimmelreiter*"; Loeb, "Faust ohne Transzendenz"; Demandt, *Religion und Religionskritik*, 185–248.

37. Thus, e.g., Ernst Loeb (echoing Walter Silz): "In Wahrheit wird er [Hauke] nicht eigentlich zwei Feinde haben, sondern nur *einen*: Ist doch der irrationale, stumpf-kreatürliche Unverstand nur die in die menschliche Sphäre übertragene Kehrseite der elementaren, widervernünftigen Dämonie der Naturgewalten." (In truth, he does not really end up with two enemies, but only *one*: the irrational, dumbly-creaturely irrationality is simply the flip-side of the elemental, arational daemonism of the powers of nature, transposed into the human sphere.) See "Faust ohne Transzendenz," 125.

38. In his unpublished preface for the 1881 publication of his collected works, Storm describes the novella as the "sister of [tragic] drama." See Fasold, *Theodor Storm*, 121. For a detailed analysis of the tragic dramatic structure of *The Dykemaster*, see Demandt, *Religion und Religionskritik*, 185–248.

39. This interpretation follows from my discussion of Storm and ecological modernity in Rigby, "(K)ein Klang der aufgeregten Zeit?"

40. Bollenbeck, *Theodor Storm*, 69.

41. Ibid., 107.

42. Laage, editorial commentary on *Der Schimmelreiter*, in Storm, *Werke*, 3: 1088.

43. Blackbourn, *Conquest of Nature*, 121.

44. Holander, *Theodor Storm*, 11.

45. Hermand, "Hauke Haien."

46. See, e.g., Segeberg, *Literarische Technik-Bilder*, 55–106; Fasold, *Theodor Storm*, 152–67; Demandt, *Religion und Religionskritik*, 185–248.

47. Jackson, "Afterword," 149, 155.

48. See, e.g., Plumwood, *Feminism and the Mastery of Nature*, for a critique of the

"logic of colonisation" that integrates socialist, feminist, and postcolonial perspectives. See also DeLoughrey and Handley, "Introduction."

49. Plumwood reads this metaphor as exemplary of the reason/nature hierarchical dualism that structures the prevailing "logic of colonisation" within Western culture (*Feminism and the Mastery of Nature*, 87–90).

50. A. Meier, " 'Wie kommt ein Pferd auf Jevershallig?' "

51. As Demandt has demonstrated, this view is probably a closer approximation of Storm's own perspective than that of either the rationalistic schoolmaster or the postmodern ironist. Storm, e.g., considered the possibility that there was an as yet unidentified material basis for the phenomenon of ghosts. See Demandt, *Religion und Religionskritik*, 203–5.

52. In the German original, this sympathy is articulated in a somewhat more qualified way: "ich verdachte es nicht den Krähen und Möwen, die sich fortwährend krächzend und gackernd vom Sturm ins Land hineintreiben ließen" (Storm, *Werke*, 3: 635).

53. Mathews, "Anguish of Wildlife Ethics."

54. The classic critique of the interpretation of this passage as licensing human domination over nature, which emerged within Western Christianity in the Middle Ages and came to prominence through the scientific revolution, is Lynn White Jr.'s brief article "The Historical Roots of Our Ecologic Crisis."

55. Adorno and Horkheimer, *Dialectic of Enlightenment*, 9–10.

56. Giblett, *Postmodern Wetlands.*

57. Blackbourn, *Conquest of Nature*, 7.

58. Plumwood, *Environmental Culture*, 162.

59. Adorno and Horkheimer, *Dialectic of Enlightenment*, 55 and 57.

60. Frühwald, "Hauke Haien, der Rechner," 442.

61. Tang, "Two German Deaths," 112, 113.

62. Ibid., 110, 113.

63. This line of interpretation is informed not only by recent material feminist analyses but also by earlier German feminist correctives to Adorno and Horkheimer's pessimistic diagnosis of the "dialectic of enlightenment." See Beinssen-Hesse and Rigby, *Out of the Shadows*, 1–17.

64. Knottnerus, "Malaria in den Nordseemarschen."

65. Frühwald, "Hauke Haien," 445.

66. See, e.g., Böhme, "Aesthetic Theory of Nature"; Rigby, "Gernot Böhme's Ecological Aesthetics."

67. Goethe, *Scientific Studies*, 147.

68. Withington, *Flood.*

4   PROLIFERATING FIRE

1. Pyne, "Consumed by Fire or Fire," 80.

2. Ibid.

3. Ibid., 83.
4. Pyne, *World Fire*, 3.
5. Pyne, "Consumed by Fire or Fire," 78.
6. Ibid., 83.
7. Sandilands, "Queer Life?"
8. Pyne, "Consumed by Fire or Fire," 82.
9. Ibid., 91.
10. Schama, *Landscape and Memory*, 76–84.
11. Rigby, *Topographies of the Sacred*, 217–23.
12. Griffiths, *Forests of Ash*, 5.
13. Paterson, "Enduring Contact," 4–5.
14. Jones, "Fire-Stick Farming."
15. Gammage, *Biggest Estate on Earth*.
16. N. Clark, *Inhuman Nature*, 169–70.
17. T. L. Mitchell, *Journal of an Expedition into the Interior of Tropical Australia* (1848), cited in Pyne, "Consumed by Fire or Fire," 87–88.
18. Mary Gilmore, *Old Days: Old Ways—A Book of Recollections* (1934), cited in N. Clark, *Inhuman Nature*, 166.
19. On culture and climate in Australia, see Sheratt, Griffiths, and Robin, *Change in the Weather*.
20. Pyne, *Still-Burning Bush*, 32, 33.
21. "Place Names and Their Meanings," Casey-Cardinia Library Corporation, http://www.cclc.vic.gov.au/placenames#D (accessed Apr. 23, 2014).
22. Daryl Taylor and Lucy Filor, personal communication, Nov. 4, 2012. The fullest official account of these fires is the *2009 Victorian Bushfires Royal Commission Report*, http://www.royalcommission.vic.gov.au/commission-reports/final-report (accessed May 25, 2013).
23. Evans, *Disasters That Changed Australia*, 106.
24. Pyne, *World Fire*, 38.
25. Griffiths, *Forests of Ash*, 134.
26. Lawson, *Poems*, 40.
27. Joseph Kelly, "The Drought," in Gillespie, *Early Verse of the Canberra Region*, 106.
28. Griffiths, *Forests of Ash*, 141.
29. Stretton, *Report*, 5.
30. Ibid.
31. Ibid., 10.
32. Hansen and Griffiths, *Living with Fire*, 36.
33. Stretton, *Report*, 20, 23.
34. Ibid., 32.
35. Ibid., 7.
36. Ibid., 25.

37. Hansen and Griffith, *Living with Fire,* 166.
38. Pollak and MacNabb, *Hearts and Minds,* esp. 52–55, 327–33.
39. Dobrin and Kidd, *Wild Things.*
40. Kelly, *Did You Know?* 42.
41. "Bushfire History," South Australian Country Fire Service, http://www.cfs .sa.gov.au/site/bushfire_history.jsp (accessed May 15, 2012).
42. Niall, *Australia through the Looking Glass,* 5.
43. R. Williams, *Country and the City;* Bate, *Romantic Ecology.*
44. Niall, *Australia through the Looking Glass,* 228.
45. Thiele, *February Dragon,* 14 (hereafter cited in the text as *FD*).
46. Plumwood, *Environmental Culture,* 165.
47. A. W. Larkins in the *Lilydale Express,* Jan. 12, 1962, cited in Hansen and Griffiths, *Living with Fire,* 87.
48. Hansen and Griffiths, *Living with Fire,* 82.
49. Ibid., 87.
50. Niall, *Australia through the Looking Glass,* 236.
51. Franklin, "Choreography of Fire," 34–36.
52. Irvine, "Animals in Disasters." See also Irvine, *Filling the Ark.*
53. Lindenmayer et al., "After the Fire."
54. Lowe et al., "Impact of Pet Loss."
55. Thompson, "Save Me, Save My Dog," 129.
56. Hughes and Steffen, *Be Prepared.*
57. Pyne, *World Fire,* 41.
58. Pyne, *Still-Burning Bush,* 99–106. See also Adams and Attiwill, *Burning Issues;* and Altangerel and Kull, "Prescribed Burning Debate in Australia."
59. Gammage, *Biggest Estate on Earth,* 4.
60. Rose, *Country of the Heart,* 25.
61. Ibid., 165.

5   DRIVING WINDS

1. Lenore Taylor, "Future Cyclones Could Be More Extreme: Garnaut," *Age,* Feb. 4, 2011, http://www.theage.com.au/environment/weather/future -cyclones-could-be-more-extreme-garnaut-20110203-1afj9.html. On anthropogenic oceanic warming, see also Gleckler et al., "Human-Induced Global Oceanic Warming."
2. "Coal Production," Australian Coal Association, http://www.australiancoal .com.au/coal-production.html (accessed Feb. 15, 2013).
3. "Flood Costs Tipped to Top $30 Billion," ABC News Online, updated Jan. 18, 2011, http://www.abc.net.au/news/2011-01-18/flood-costs-tipped-to -top-30b/1909700.
4. T. Clark, *Cambridge Introduction to Literature,* 10–11. Clark is (appropriately enough) less sweepingly condemnatory of ecocriticism's alleged neglect of

climate change here than he is in his earlier article "Some Climate Change Ironies," but as I point out in "Confronting Catastrophe," he still overlooks a significant amount of important ecocritical work on this subject.

5. See nonetheless Johns-Putra, "Ecocriticism, Genre, and Climate Change"; Johns-Putra and Trexler, "Climate Change in Literature"; Maxwell, "Postcolonial Criticism"; Milner, Burgmann, and Sellars, *Changing the Climate;* and Milner, "Sea and Eternal Summer."

6. *Carpentaria* has won five national literary awards, including Australia's most prestigious, the Miles Franklin Award (2007).

7. Australian Bureau of Meteorology, "About Tropical Cyclones: Frequently Asked Questions," http://www.bom.gov.au/cyclone/faq/ (accessed Oct. 8, 2013).

8. John Vidal and Adam Vaughan, "Philippines Urges Action to Resolve Climate Talks Deadlock after Typhoon Haiyan," *Guardian,* Nov. 11, 2013, http://www.theguardian.com/environment/2013/nov/11/typhoon-haiyan -philippines-climate-talks. As reported in the *Guardian* (Australia), the gains made in this respect, as well as with regard to mitigation, were limited. See "How Rich Countries Dodged the Climate Change Blame Game in Warsaw," *Guardian,* Nov. 25, 2013, http://www.theguardian.com/ environment/planet-oz/2013/nov/25/climate-change-warsaw-rich-countries -blame-paris-deal.

9. "Asia: Top 10 Deadliest Cyclones," *IRIN Humanitarian News and Analysis,* UN Office for the Coordination of Humanitarian Affairs, Sept. 23, 2010, http:// www.irinnews.org/report/90556/asia-top-10-deadliest-cyclones.

10. Evans, *Disasters That Changed Australia,* 1–20. Evans cites the figure of sixty-five fatalities, which accords with initial assessments, but Richard Whitaker's article of 2007 ("Tropical Cyclone Tracy") indicates that this figure was revised to seventy-one.

11. Evans, *Disasters That Changed Australia,* 2.

12. Larrakia Nation Aboriginal Corporation, "Welcome to Country," http://www .larrakia.com/#/welcome (accessed Oct. 10, 2013).

13. The damning report of the National Inquiry into the forced separation of Aboriginal and Torres Strait Islander children from their families, "Bringing Them Home" (1997), can be found online at http://www.humanrights.gov. au/publications/bringing-them-home-report-1997 (accessed Oct. 10, 2013).

14. Evans, *Disasters That Changed Australia,* 2–3.

15. Eyewitness account by subeditor of the *Northern Territory Times,* in Alan Stetton, *The Furious Days,* qtd. in Whitaker, "Tropical Cyclone Tracy," 21.

16. K. Murphy, *Big Blow Up North,* 58.

17. Ibid.

18. Evans, *Disasters That Changed Australia,* 17–18.

19. Rose, "Rhythms, Patterns, Connectivities," 33.
20. A. Wright, "Deep Weather," 72–73.
21. Altman and Kerins, *People on Country,* 8–9.
22. A. Wright, *Swan Book,* 86.
23. "Life Expectancy of Aboriginal and Torres Strait Islander Peoples," Australian Bureau of Statistics, updated Aug. 20, 2012, http://www.abs.gov .au/ausstats/abs@.nsf/Lookup/by+Subject/4125.0~Jan+2012~Main+ Features~Life+expectancy~3110; "Aboriginal and Torres Strait Islander Suicide Deaths," Australian Bureau of Statistics, updated Jan. 21, 2013, http://www.abs.gov.au/ausstats/abs@.nsf/Products/3309.0~2010~Chapter~ Aboriginal+and+Torres+Strait+Islander+suicide+deaths?OpenDocument.
24. Martin Cudihy, "Aboriginal Deaths in Custody Rise Sharply over Past Five Years," ABC News Online, May 24, 2013, http://www.abc.net.au/news/2013 -05-24/sharp-rise-in-number-of-aboriginal-deaths-in-custody/4711764.
25. Mackerle, "Little Children Are Sacred."
26. Ferrier, "'Disappearing Memory,'" 37–38.
27. A. Wright, "Talking about an Indigenous Tomorrow."
28. Altman and Kerins, *People on Country,* 19.
29. This aspect of the Intervention is highlighted in the documentary film *Our Generation: Land, Culture, Freedom* (2010), made in collaboration with the Yolngu people of Northeast Arnhem Land, by Damien Curtis and Sinem Saban, and available online at www.ourgeneration.org.au.
30. A. Wright, "On Writing *Carpentaria,*" 89, 88.
31. Ibid., 84.
32. Rigby, "Poetics of Decolonisation." The following discussion of the novel is drawn, in part, from this essay.
33. In the context of criticizing Wright's white readers, who are in her view insufficiently unsettled by the work's hermeneutic challenges, Alison Ravenscroft, in her article "Dreaming of Others," also emphasizes the risk of subsuming a Waanyi perspective to an Aboriginality falsely presumed to be homogenous.
34. A. Wright, "On Writing *Carpentaria,*" 87.
35. A. Wright, *Carpentaria* (hereafter cited in the text as *C*).
36. J. Wright, *Cry for the Dead,* 257.
37. Ibid., 256. Dingoes, the Australian wild dog, have long been highly valued companions of Aboriginal people and are viewed as kin by those for whom the dingo is an ancestral Dreaming figure. On the anguish caused to Indigenous Australians by the ruthless eradication campaign against their canine companions and kin, see Rose, *Wild Dog Dreaming.*
38. Nixon, *Slow Violence,* 70.
39. Lines, *Taming the Great South Land,* 196–231.

40. Emma Masters, "Kakadu Victory and Uranium Battle Ends," ABC News on-line, June 2, 2012, http://www.abc.net.au/news/2012-06-01/jeffrey-lee-land -uranium-kakadu/4047458.

41. Altman and Kerins, *People on Country,* 20.

42. Lindsay Murdoch, "Polluted Water Leading into Kakadu," *Age,* Mar. 13, 2009, http://www.theage.com.au/national/polluted-water-leaking-into -kakadu-from-uranium-mine-20090312-8whw.html. In December 2013 there was a further spill of around one million liters of radioactive slurry of uranium and industrial acid, which escaped from a decades-old contain-ment tank at Ranger Uranium Mine in Kakadu, a few kilometers upstream from the Mirrar community of Mudginberri. See Luke Batersby and Peter Ker, "Investigation as Radioactive Leak Leaves Ranger Uranium Mine under a Cloud," *Sydney Morning Herald,* Dec. 9, 2013, http://www.smh.com .au/federal-politics/political-news/investigation-as-radioactive-leak-leaves -ranger-uranium-mine-under-a-cloud-20131208-2yzeo.html.

43. Yvonne Margarula to Ban ki-Moon, Apr. 6, 2011, http://www.mirarr.net/ media/Yvonne_ki-Moon_6Apr2011.pdf.

44. Green and Morrison, "No More Yardin' Us Up," 199. See also Green's beauti-ful visual essay accompanying his paintings charting changes in land use in the Gulf in "Flow of Voices."

45. Langton, *Boyer Lectures 2012.* Critics of Langton's rosy representation of the resources sector observe that her research has received a considerable amount of funding from several mining companies. See Gina McColl, "Langton Failed to Disclose Mining Company Funding," *Sydney Morning Herald,* Mar. 3, 2013, http://www.smh.com.au/national/langton-failed-to -disclose-mining-company-funding-20130301-2fbtx.html.

46. Devlin-Glass, "Politics of the Dreamtime," 398.

47. Ibid., 394–95.

48. Rose, *Nourishing Terrains,* 7.

49. Ibid., 47–51.

50. Graham, "Some Thoughts."

51. Bradley, *Singing Saltwater Country,* 228. On the importance of caring for country to Aboriginal health and well-being, see also Grieves, *Aboriginal Spirituality.*

52. "McArthur River Mine," Glencore: McArthur River Mining, 2014, http:// www.mcarthurrivermine.com.au/EN/ABOUTUS/Pages/McArthurRiver Mine.aspx. On the appropriation of Aboriginal place names, see Plumwood, "Decolonizing Relationships with Nature."

53. Plumwood, *Feminism and the Mastery of Nature,* 27–34.

54. Plumwood, *Environmental Culture,* 102.

55. Devlin-Glass, "Politics of the Dreamtime," 395.

56. Ravenscroft, "Dreaming of Others," 202.

57. Ibid., 204.
58. According to Devlin-Glass, Lloydie is "a European reincarnation of the voyeur Yurrunju, a powerful Dreaming figure associated with fire and the rituals of circumcision" ("Politics of the Dreamtime," 401–2).
59. Plumwood, "Journey to the Heart of Stone," 18.
60. Plumwood, "Decolonizing Relationships with Nature," 66.
61. The liberal feminist politics of assimilation to the Euro-Western "master model" of the human is profoundly problematic from an Aboriginal perspective. On the mismatch between Indigenous women's experiences and aspirations and the assumptions of white Australian middle-class liberal feminists, see Moreton-Robinson, *Talkin' Up to the White Woman*.
62. Carrigan, "(Eco)Catastrophe," 120.
63. Altman and Kerins, *People on Country*, 221.
64. Green and Morrison, "No More Yardin' Us Up," 194.
65. "Landmark Decision for the Waanyi People," announcement on Chalk & Fitzgerald Lawyers & Consultants Web site, http://chalkfitzgerald.com.au/News/13 (accessed Oct. 31, 2013); "Waanyi People Boodjamulla National Park Indigenous Land Use Agreement (ILUA)," Agreements, Treaties and Negotiated Settlements Project, updated Nov. 19, 2011, http://www.atns.net.au/agreement.asp?EntityID=5499.
66. Roos and Hunt, *Postcolonial Green*, 3.
67. Griffiths, "Humanist on Thin Ice."
68. Rose, "Rhythms, Patterns, Connectivities."
69. Muir, Rose, and Sullivan, "From the Other Side of the Knowledge Frontier."
70. Field et al., *Climate Change 2014*, 26.

POSTSCRIPT

1. Schleiermacher, *On Religion*. See also Rigby, "Another Talk on Religion."
2. Schleiermacher, *On Religion*, 146.
3. Ibid., 118–19.
4. N. Clark, *Inhuman Nature*, 52.
5. Ibid.
6. Rose, "Flying Foxes."
7. Solnit, *Paradise Built in Hell*, 299–303.
8. Weber, *Protestant Ethic*.
9. Buell, *From Apocalypse to Way of Life*, 206.
10. Rose, "'Moral Friends,'" 94.
11. Iovino, "Restoring the Imagination of Place," 106.

BIBLIOGRAPHY

Aaron, Jane. "The Return of the Repressed: Reading Mary Shelley's *The Last Man*." In *Feminist Criticism: Theory and Practice*, ed. Susan Sellers, Linda Hutcheon, and Paul Perron, 9–21. Toronto: University of Toronto Press, 1991.

Adams, M., and P. Attiwill. *Burning Issues: Sustainability and Management of Australia's Southern Forests*. Melbourne: CSIRO Publishing Victoria, 2011.

Adams, Vicky Lynn. "The Revolt of Nature: Mary Shelley's 'The Last Man' in an Ecofeminist Critical Perspective." PhD diss., University of Alabama, 2003.

Adorno, Theodor, and Max Horkheimer. *Dialectic of Enlightenment*. Trans. John Cumming. London: Verso, 1979.

Alaimo, Stacy. *Bodily Natures: Science, Environment, and the Material Self*. Bloomington: Indian University Press, 2010.

———. "Trans-Corporeal Feminisms and the Ethical Space of Nature." In Alaimo and Hekman, *Material Feminisms*, 237–64.

Alaimo, Stacy, and Susan Hekman, eds. *Material Feminisms*. Bloomington: Indiana University Press, 2008.

Alcabes, Philip. *Dread: How Fear and Fantasy Have Fuelled Epidemics from the Black Death to Avian Flu*. New York: Public Affairs, 2009.

Alexander, David. *Confronting Catastrophe*. Oxford: Oxford University Press, 2000.

———. *Natural Disasters*. London: Routledge, 2001.

Altangerel, K., and C. A. Kull. "The Prescribed Burning Debate in Australia: Conflicts and Compatibilities." *Journal of Environmental Planning and Management* 56, no. 1 (2012): 103–20.

Altman, Jon, and Seán Kerins, eds. *People on Country: Vital Landscapes, Indigenous Futures*. Sydney: Federation Press, 2012.

Appelt, Hedwig, and Dirk Grathoff. *Heinrich von Kleist: Das Erdbeben von Chili. Erläuterungen und Dokumente*. Stuttgart: Reclam, 1986.

Araujo, Ana Christina. "Focus: The Lisbon Earthquake: Part Two. European Public Opinion and the Lisbon Earthquake." *European Review* 14, no. 3 (2006): 313–19.

Barad, Karen. *Meeting the Universe Halfway*. Durham, NC: Duke University Press, 2007.

———. "Posthumanist Performativity: Toward an Understanding of How Matter Comes to Matter." In Alaimo and Hekman, *Material Feminisms*, 120–54.

Bassnett, Susan. "Faith, Doubt, Aid, and Prayer: The Lisbon Earthquake of 1755 Revisited." *European Review* 14, no. 3 (2006): 321–28.

Bate, Jonathan. "Living with the Weather." *Studies in Romanticism* 55, no. 3 (1996): 431–48.

———. *Romantic Ecology: Wordsworth and the Environmental Tradition*. London and New York: Routledge, 1991.

Beck, Ulrich. *Ecological Enlightenment: Essays on the Politics of the Risk Society*. Trans. M. A. Ritter. Atlantic Highlands, NJ: Humanities Press, 1995.

Beinssen-Hesse, Silke, and Kate Rigby. *Out of the Shadows: Contemporary German Feminism*. Carlton: Melbourne University Press, 1996.

Bennett, Jane. *Vibrant Matter: A Political Ecology of Things*. Durham, NC: Duke University Press, 2010.

Berger, James. *After the End: Representations of Post-Apocalypse*. Minneapolis: University of Minnesota Press, 1999.

Bergmann, Sigurd, and Dieter Gerten, eds. *Religion in Environmental and Climate Change: Suffering, Values, Lifestyle*. London: Continuum, 2012.

Berman, Marshall. *"All That Is Solid Melts into Air": The Experience of Modernity*. London: Verso, 1988.

Bewell, Alan. *Romanticism and Colonial Disease*. Baltimore, MD: Johns Hopkins Press, 1999.

Billingham, Valerie. "The Earth Mourns/Dries Up in Jeremiah 4: 23–28: A Literary Analysis Viewed through the Heuristic Lens of an Ecologically Oriented Symbiotic Relationship." PhD thesis, Melbourne College of Divinity, 2010.

Biro, Andrew, ed. *Critical Ecologies: The Frankfurt School and Contemporary Environmental Crises*. Toronto: University of Toronto Press, 2011.

Blackbourn, David. *The Conquest of Nature: Water, Landscape and the Making of Modern Germany*. London: Random House, 2007.

Blanchot, Maurice. *The Writing of the Disaster*. Trans. Ann Smock. Lincoln: University of Nebraska Press, 1995.

Boccaccio, Giovanni. *The Decameron*. Trans., intro., and notes, G. H. McWilliam. London: Penguin, 1995.

Böhme, Gernot. "An Aesthetic Theory of Nature: An Interim Report." *Thesis Eleven* 32 (1992): 90–102.

———. *Die Natur vor uns. Naturphilosophie in pragmatischer Hinsicht*. Kusterdingen: Die Graue Edition, 2002.

Bolin, Robert, and Lois Stanford. "Constructing Vulnerability in the First World: The Northridge Earthquake in Southern California, 1994." In Hoffman and Oliver-Smith, *Angry Earth*, 89–112.

Bollenbeck, Georg. *Theodor Storm. Eine Biographie*. Frankfurt: Insel, 1988.

Botkin, Daniel. *Discordant Harmonies: A New Ecology for the Twenty-First Century*. Oxford: Oxford University Press, 1992.

Bradley, John, with Yanyuwa families. *Singing Saltwater Country: Journey to the Songlines of Carpentaria*. Crows Nest: Allen and Unwin, 2010.

Breidert, Wolfgang, ed. *Die Erschütterung der vollkommenen Welt. Die Wirkung des Erdbebens von Lissabon im Spiegel europäischer Zeitgenossen*. Darmstadt: Wissenschaftlicher Buchgesellschaft, 1994.

Brunner, Ronald D., and Amanda H. Lynch. *Adaptive Governance and Climate Change*. Chicago: University of Chicago Press, 2010.

Buber, Martin. "Prophecy, Apocalyptic, and the Historical Hour." In *Pointing the Way: Collected Essays*, trans. Maurice Friedman, 192–208. London: Routledge and Kegan Paul, 1957.

Buell, Frederick. *From Apocalypse to Way of Life: Environmental Crisis in the American Century*. London: Routledge, 2003.

Bulst, Neithard. "Die Pest verstehen: Wahrnehmungen, Deutungen und Reaktionen im Mittelalter und die frühe Neuzeit." In Groh, Kempe, and Mauelshagen, *Naturkatastrophen*, 145–64.

Camus, Albert. *The Plague*. 1947. Trans. Stuart Gilbert. Harmondsworth: Penguin, 1960.

Cantor, Paul A. "The Apocalypse of Empire: Mary Shelley's *The Last Man*." In *Iconoclastic Departures: Mary Shelley after Frankenstein: Essays in Honor of the Bicentenary of Mary Shelley's Birth*, ed. Syndy M. Conger, Frederick S. Frank, Gregory O'Dea, and Jennifer Yocum, 193–211. Madison, NJ: Fairleigh Dickinson University Press, 1997.

Carrigan, Anthony. "(Eco)Catastrophe, Reconstruction, and Representation: Montserrat and the Limits of Sustainability." *New Literatures Review* 47–48 (2011): 111–28.

Carson, Rachel. *Silent Spring*. 1962. London: Penguin, 1999.

Clark, Nigel. *Inhuman Nature: Sociable Life on a Dynamic Planet*. London: Sage, 2011.

Clark, Timothy. *The Cambridge Introduction to Literature and the Environment*. Cambridge: Cambridge University Press, 2011.

———. "Some Climate Change Ironies: Deconstruction, Environmental Politics, and the Closure of Ecocriticism." *Oxford Literary Review* 32, no. 1 (2010): 131–49.

Coogan, Michael D., ed. *The New Oxford Annotated Bible* Augmented 3rd ed. Oxford: Oxford University Press, 2007.

Coole, Diana, and Samantha Frost, eds. *New Materialisms: Ontology, Agency, and Politics*. Durham, NC: Duke University Press, 2010.

Crawford, Dorothy H. *Deadly Companions: How Microbes Shaped Our History*. Oxford: Oxford University Press, 2007.

Crossthwaite, Paul, ed. *Criticism, Crisis, and Contemporary Narrative: Textual Horizons in an Age of Global Risk*. London: Routledge, 2011.

Crutzen, Paul, and Eugene Stoermer. "The Anthropocene." *Global Change Newsletter* 41 (2000): 14–17. Reprinted, with a commentary by Will Steffen, in *The Future of Nature,* ed. Libby Robin, Sverker Sörlin, and Paul Warde, 483–90. New Haven, CT: Yale University Press, 2013.

Cudworth, Erica. *Developing Ecofeminist Theory. The Complexity of Difference.* Houndmills and New York: Palgrave Macmillan, 2005.

Da Costa, Paulo Martins, Luis Loureiro, and Augusto J. F. Matos. "Transfer of Multidrug-Resistant Bacteria Between Intermingled Ecological Niches: The Interface between Humans, Animals and the Environment." *International Journal of Environmental Research and Public Health* 10 (2013): 278–94.

Darwin, Erasmus. *The Temple of Nature; or, The Origin of Society.* London: T. Bentley, 1803. Produced for Project Gutenberg by Stephen Gibbs and Christine P. Travers, October 9, 2008. http://www.gutenberg.org/files/26861/26861-h/26861-h.htm.

De Boer, Jelle Zeilinga, and Donald Theodore Sanders. *Earthquakes in Human History: The Far-Reaching Effects of Seismic Disruptions.* Princeton, NJ: Princeton University Press, 2005.

DeLoughrey, Elizabeth, and George B. Handley. "Introduction: Toward an Aesthetics of the Earth." In DeLoughrey and Handley, *Postcolonial Ecologies,* 3–51.

———, eds. *Postcolonial Ecologies: Literatures of the Environment.* Oxford: Oxford University Press, 2011.

Demandt, Christian. *Religion und Religionskritik bei Theodor Storm.* Berlin: Erich Schmidt, 2010.

Derrida, Jacques, and Anne Dufourmantelle. *Of Hospitality: Anne Dufourmantelle Invites Jacques Derrida to Respond.* Trans. Rachel Bowlby. Stanford: Stanford University Press, 2000.

Devlin-Glass, Frances. "An Atlas of the Sacred: Hybridity, Representability and the Myths of Yanyuwa Country." *Antipodes* 19, no. 2 (2005): 127–40.

———. "A Politics of the Dreamtime: Destructive and Regenerative Rainbows in Alexis Wright's *Carpentaria.*" *Australian Literary Studies* 24, no. 4 (2008): 392–407.

Diamond, Jared M. *Guns, Germs and Steel: The Fates of Human Societies.* London: Jonathan Cape, 1997.

Diaz, Junot. "Apocalypse: What Disasters Reveal." *Boston Review* 36, no. 3 (May–June 2011). http://www.bostonreview.net/BR36.3/junot_diaz_apocalypse_haiti_earthquake.php.

Dobrin, Sidney I., and Kenneth B. Kidd. *Wild Things: Children's Literature and Ecocriticism.* Detroit, MI: Wayne State University Press, 2004.

Dürbeck, Gabriele. "Introduction." *Ecozon@* 3, no. 1, special issue, *Writing Catastrophes: Interdisciplinary Perspectives on the Semantics of Natural and Anthropogenic Disasters,* ed. G. Dürbeck (2012): 1–9.

Dutton, Clarence Edward. *Earthquakes: In the Light of the New Seismology.* New York: G. P. Putnam's Sons, 1904.

Dynes, Russell R. "The Dialogue between Voltaire and Rousseau on the Lisbon Earthquake: The Emergence of a Social Science View." *International Journal of Mass Emergencies and Disasters* 18, no. 1 (2000): 97–115.

Eagleton, Terry. *After Theory.* London: Penguin, 2004.

Eisenberg, Evan. *The Ecology of Eden: Humans, Nature and Human Nature.* London: Picador, 1998.

EM-DAT. *Disasters in Numbers.* OFDA/CRED International Disaster Database, Universite catholiqué de Louvain in Brussels, Belgium, 2005. www.em-dat .net.

Estok, Simon C. "Theorising in a Space of Ambivalent Openness: Ecocriticism and Ecophobia." *ISLE* 15, no. 2 (2009): 203–25.

Evans, Richard. *Disasters That Changed Australia.* Carlton: Melbourne University Press, 2009.

Fasold, Regina. *Theodor Storm.* Stuttgart: Metzler, 1997.

Ferrier, Carole. "'Disappearing Memory' and the Colonial Present in Recent Indigenous Women's Writing." *Journal of the Association for the Study of Australian Literature,* special issue, *The Colonial Present* (2008): 37–55.

Field, C. B., et al, eds. *Climate Change 2014: Impacts, Adaptation, and Vulnerability. Part A: Global and Sectoral Aspects. Contribution of Working Group II to the Fifth Assessment Report of the Intergovernmental Panel on Climate Change.* Cambridge: Cambridge University Press, 2014.

Fischer, J., et al. "Mind the Sustainability Gap." *Trends in Ecology and Evolution* 22, no. 12 (2007): 621–24.

Foucault, Michel. *The History of Sexuality.* Trans. Robert Hurley. London: Allen Lane, 1979.

Franklin, Adrian. "A Choreography of Fire: A Posthumanist Account of Australians and Eucalypts." In Pickering and Guzik, *Mangle in Practice,* 7–43.

Frühwald, Wolfgang. "Hauke Haien, der Rechner: Mythos und Technikglaube in Theodor Storm's Novelle 'Der Schimmelreiter.'" In *Literaturwissenschaft und Geistesgeschichte: Festschrift für Richard Brinkmann,* ed. J. Brumack et al., 438–57. Tübingen: Niemeyer, 1981.

Fulford, Timothy. "Apocalyptic Economics and Prophetic Politics: Radical and Romantic Responses to Malthus and Burke." *Studies in Romanticism* 40 (Fall 2001): 345–68.

Fulford, Timothy, and Peter J. Kitson, eds. *Romanticism and Colonialism: Writing and Empire, 1780–1830.* Cambridge: Cambridge University Press, 1998.

Fulford, Timothy, Debbie Lee, and Peter J. Kitson. "The Beast Within: Romanticism and the Jenneration of Disease." In Fulford and Kitson, *Romanticism and Colonialism,* 209–27.

Gammage, Bill. *The Biggest Estate on Earth: How Aborigines Made Australia*. Sydney: Allen and Unwin, 2011.

Garrard, Greg. *Ecocriticism*. Rev. ed. London, Routledge, 2011.

———, ed. *The Oxford Handbook of Ecocriticism*. Oxford: Oxford University Press, 2014.

Gerten, Dieter, and Sigurd Bergmann, eds. *Religion and Dangerous Climate Change: Transdisciplinary Perspectives on the Ethics of Climate and Sustainability*. Münster: LIT, 2010.

Giblett, Rod. *Postmodern Wetlands: Culture, History, Ecology*. Edinburgh: Edinburgh University Press, 1996.

Gillespie, Lyall L., ed. *Early Verse of the Canberra Region*. Campbell, ACT: Lyall L. Gillespie, 1994.

Girard, René. "Theorie der Mythologie/Anthropologie. " In Wellbery, *Positionen der Literaturwissenschaft*, 130–48.

Gleckler, P. J., et al. "Human-Induced Global Oceanic Warming on Multi-Decadal Timescales." *Nature Climate Change* 2 (2012): 524–29.

Goethe, Johann Wolfgang von. *Faust. Part One*. Trans. and intro. T. Luke. Oxford: Oxford University Press, 1987.

———. *Faust. Part Two*. Trans. and intro. T. Luke. Oxford: Oxford University Press, 1994.

———. *Scientific Studies*. Ed. and trans. D. Miller. Princeton, NJ: Princeton University Press, 1988.

Goldsmith, Stephen. *Unbuilding Jerusalem: Apocalypse and Romantic Representation*. Ithaca, NY: Cornell University Press, 1993.

Goodbody, Axel. "Frame Analysis and the Literature of Climate Change." In *Literature, Ecology, Ethics: Recent Trends in Ecocriticism*, ed. Timo Müller and Michael Sauter, 15–34. Heidelberg: Winter, 2012.

Goodbody, Axel, and Kate Rigby, eds. *Ecocritical Theory: New European Approaches*. Charlottesville: University Press of Virginia, 2011.

Graham, Mary. "Some Thoughts about the Philosophical Underpinnings of Aboriginal Worldviews." Ecological Humanities: Classic Essay. *Australian Humanities Review* 45 (2008). http://www.australianhumanitiesreview.org/archive/Issue-November-2008/graham.html#_edn1.

Green, Jacky. "Flow of Voices." *Arena Magazine* 124 (2013): 29–32.

Green, Jacky, and Jimmy Morrison. "No More Yardin' Us Up Like Cattle." In Altman and Kerins, *People on Country*, 190–201.

Grieves, Vicki. *Aboriginal Spirituality: Aboriginal Philosophy, the Basis of Aboriginal Social and Emotional Wellbeing*. Casuarina, NT: Cooperative Research Centre for Aboriginal Health, 2009.

Griffiths, Tom. *Forests of Ash: An Environmental History*. Cambridge: Cambridge University Press, 2001.

———. "A Humanist on Thin Ice." *Griffith Review* 29 (2010). http://www
.griffithreview.com/edition-29-prosper-or-perish/a-humanist-on-thin-ice.

———. "The Humanities and an Environmentally Sustainable Australia." 2003.
Ecological Humanities: Classic Essay. *Australian Humanities Review* 43 (2007).
http://australianhumanitiesreview.org/archive/Issue-December-2007/Eco
Humanities/EcoGriffiths.html.

———. "'An Unnatural Disaster'? Remembering and Forgetting Bushfire." *History Australia* 6, no. 2 (2009): 35.1–7.

Groh, Dieter, Michael Kampe, and Franz Mauelshagen, eds. *Natukatastrophen.
Beiträge zu ihrer Deutung, Wahrnehmung und Darstellung in Text und Bild von
der Antike bis ins 20. Jahrhundert.* Tübingen: Gunter Narr, 2003.

Gronda, Hellene. "dance with the body you have. body awareness practices and/
as deconstruction." Phd thesis, Monash University, 2005.

Gutscher, Marc-André. "What Caused the Great Lisbon Earthquake." *Science* 305
(2004): 1247–48.

Hansen, Christine, and Tom Griffiths. *Living with Fire: People, Nature and History
in Steels Creek.* Collingwood: CSIRO Publishing, 2012.

Haraway, Donna. *When Species Meet.* Minneapolis: University of Minnesota
Press, 2008.

Hartman, Chester, and Gregory D. Squires, eds. *There Is No Such Thing as a Natural Disaster.* London: Routledge, 2006.

Heise, Ursula K., ed. *Ecozon@* 3, no. 12, special issue, *The Invention of Eco-Futures*
(2012).

———. *Sense of Place, Sense of Planet: The Environmental Imagination of the Global.*
Oxford: Oxford University Press, 2008.

Hermand, Jost. "Hauke Haien. Kritik oder Ideal des gründerzeitlichen Übermenschen?" *Wirkendes Wort* 15 (1965): 40–50.

Heyd, Thomas. *Encountering Nature: Toward an Environmental Culture.* Aldershot:
Ashgate, 2007.

Heyd, Thomas, and Nick Brooks. "Exploring Cultural Dimensions of Climate
Change." In *Adapting to Climate Change: Thresholds, Values, Governance*, ed.
W. N. Adger, I. L. Lorenzoni, and K. L. O'Brian, 269–82. Cambridge: Cambridge University Press, 2009.

Hird, Myra. *The Origins of Sociable Life: Evolution after Science Studies.* London:
Palgrave Macmillan, 2009.

Hoffman, Susanna M. "The Worst of Times, the Best of Times: Toward a Model
of Cultural Response to Disaster." In Hoffman and Oliver-Smith, *Angry Earth*,
134–55.

Hoffman, Susanna M., and Anthony Oliver-Smith, eds. *The Angry Earth: Disaster
in Anthropological Perspective.* London and New York: Routledge, 1999.

———. *Catastrophe and Culture: The Anthropology of Disaster.* Santa Fe, NM:
School of American Research Press, 2002.

Holander, Reimar K. *Theodor Storm "Der Schimmelreiter." Kommentar und Dokumentation.* Frankfurt: Ullstein, 1976.

Huet, Marie-Hélène. *The Culture of Disaster.* Chicago: University of Chicago Press, 2012.

Hughes, Leslie, and Will Steffen. *Be Prepared: Climate Change and the Australian Bushfire Threat.* Climate Council of Australia, 2013. http://www.climate council.org.au/be-prepared.

Hutchings, Kevin. "'A Dark Image in a Phantasmagoria': Pastoral Idealism, Prophecy, and Materiality in Mary Shelley's *The Last Man.*" *Romanticism: The Journal of Romantic Culture and Criticism* 10, no. 2 (2004): 228–44.

Iovino, Serenella. "Restoring the Imagination of Place: Narrative Reinhabitation and the Po Valley." In *The Bioregional Imagination: Literature, Ecology, and Place,* ed. Tom Lynch, Cheryll Glotfelty, and Karla Armbruster, 100–117. Athens: University of Georgia Press, 2012.

Iovino, Serenella, and Serpil Oppermann, eds. *Material Ecocriticism.* Bloomington: Indiana University Press, 2014.

Irvine, Leslie. "Animals in Disasters: Issues for Animal Liberation." *Animal Liberation Philosophy and Policy Journal* 4 (2006): 2–16.

———. *Filling the Ark: Animal Welfare in Disasters.* Philadelphia, PA: Temple University Press, 2009.

Jackson, David A. "Afterword." In Storm, *Dykemaster,* 139–56.

Jakubowski-Tiessen, Manfred. "Gotteszorn und Meereswüten: Deutungen von Sturmfluten vom 16. bis 19. Jahrhundert." In Groh, Kempe, and Mauelshagen, *Naturkatastrophenn,* 101–18.

Jakubowski-Tiessen, Manfred, and Klaus-J. Lorenzen-Schmidt, eds. *Dünger und Dynamit: Beiträge zur Umweltgeschichte Schleswig-Holsteins und Dänemarks.* Neumünster: Wachholtz, 1999.

Janku, Andrea, Gerrit J. Schenk, and Franz Mauelshagen, eds. *Historical Disasters in Context: Science, Religion and Politics.* London: Routledge, 2012.

Jenner, Mark S. R. "The Great Dog Massacre." In *Fear in Early Modern Society,* ed. William G. Naphy and Penny Roberts, 44–61. Manchester: Manchester University Press, 1997.

Johnson, Barbara. "The Last Man." In *The Other Mary Shelley: Beyond Frankenstein,* ed. Audrey A. Fisch, Anne K. Mellor, and Esther H. Schor, 258–66. Oxford: Oxford University Press, 1993.

Johns-Putra, Adeline. "Ecocriticism, Genre, and Climate Change: Reading the Utopian Vision of Kim Stanley Robinson's Science in the City Trilogy." *English Studies* 91, no. 7, special issue, ed. Astrid Bracke and Marguérite Corporaal (2010): 744–60.

Johns-Putra, Adeline, and Adam Trexler. "Climate Change in Literature and Literary Criticism." *Wiley Interdisciplinary Reviews: Climate Change* 2, no. 2 (2011): 185–200.

Jones, Rhys. "Fire-Stick Farming." *Australian Natural History* (September 1969): 224–28.

Kant, Immanuel. *Critique of Judgment.* Trans. S. Pluhar. Indianapolis: Indiana University Press, 1987.

———. *Opus postumum.* Ed. Eckart Forster. Cambridge: Cambridge University Press, 1993.

Keller, Catherine. *Apocalypse Now and Then: A Feminist Guide to the End of the World.* Minneapolis, MN: Fortress Press, 1997.

———. *Face of the Deep: A Theology of Becoming.* London: Routledge, 2003.

Kelly, Frances. *Did You Know? Colin Thiele and His Books.* Adelaide: Auslib Press, 2001.

Kendrick, T. D. *The Lisbon Earthquake.* London: Methuen, 1956.

Killingworth, Jimmie M., and Jacqueline S. Palmer. "Millenial Ecology: The Apocalyptic Narrative from *Silent Spring* to Global Warming." In *Green Culture: Environmental Rhetoric in Contemporary America,* ed. Carl G. Herndl and Stuart C. Brown, 21–45. Madison: University of Wisconsin Press, 1996.

Kim, Won-Young. "Induced Seismicity Associated with Fluid Injection into a Deep Well in Youngstown, Ohio." *Journal of Geophysical Research: Solid Earth* 118, no. 7 (2013): 3506–18.

Kircher, Hartmut. *"Das Erdbeben in Chili/Die Marquise von O." Interpretation von Hartmut Kircher.* Munich: Oldenbourg, 1992.

Kleist, Heinrich von. "Das Erdbeben in Chili." In *Sämtliche Werke und Briefe in vier Bänden,* vol. 3, ed. Marie Barth et al. Frankfurt: Deutscher Klassiker Verlag, 1990.

———. "The Earthquake in Chile." In *The Marquise of O & other Stories,* trans. David Luke and Nigel Reeves, 51–67. London: Penguin, 1978.

Knottnerus, Otto Samuel. "Malaria in den Nordseemarschen. Gedanken über Menschen und Umwelt." In Jakubowski-Tiessen and Lorenzen-Schmidt, *Dünger und Dynamit,* 25–40.

Košenina, Alexander. "Friedrich Theodor Nevermanns 'Alonzo und Elvira,' eine Quelle für Kleists ‚Erdbeben in Chili' (mit Textanhängen)." *Heilbronner Kleist-Blätter* 22 (2010): 19–48.

Kozak, Jan T. "Historical Depiction of the 1755 Lisbon Earthquake." National Information Service for Earthquake Engineering, University of California, Berkeley. November 12, 1998 (updated). http://nisee.berkeley.edu/lisbon/.

Krüger, Johann Gottlob. "Gedanken von den Ursachen des Erdbebens, nebst einer moralischen Betrachtung." In *Die Erschütterung der vollkommenen Welt. Die Wirkung des Erdbebens von Lissabon im Spiegel europäischer Zeitgenossen,* ed. Wolfgang Breidert, 23–50. Darmstadt: Wissenschaftlicher Buchgesellschaft, 1994.

Kuhlicke, Christian, and Annette Steinführer. "Soziale Verwundbarkeit gegenüber Hochwasser: Lehren aus der Elbeflut." *GAIA—Ecological Perspectives for Science and Society* 21, no. 3 (2012): 202–9.

Langton, Marcia. *Boyer Lectures 2012: The Quiet Revolution and the Resources Boom.* Sydney: HarperCollins, 2013.

Latour, Bruno. *We Have Never Been Modern.* Trans. C. Porter. Hemel Hempstead: Harvester Wheatsheaf, 1993.

Lawson, Henry. *Poems.* Preface and Chronology by Colin Roderick. Sydney: John Ferguson, 1979.

Leeming, David Adams, and Margaret Adams Leeming. *A Dictionary of Creation Myths.* Oxford: Oxford University Press, 1995.

LeMenager, Stephanie, Teresa Shewry, and Ken Hiltner, eds. *Environmental Criticism for the Twenty-First Century.* London: Routledge, 2011.

Levene, Mark. "Climate Blues." *Environmental Humanities* 2 (2013): 147–67.

Lew, Joseph W. "The Plague of Imperial Desire: Montesquieu, Gibbon, Brougham, and Mary Shelley's *The Last Man.*" In Fulford and Kitson, *Romanticism and Colonialism,* 261–78.

Lindenmayer, David, et al. "After the Fire: Leadbeater's Long Journey." *Ecos* 157 (2010): 1–5.

Lines, William J. *Taming the Great South Land.* Sydney: Allen and Unwin, 1991.

Loeb, Ernst. "Faust ohne Transzendenz: Theodor Storms *Schimmelreiter.*" In *Studies in Germanic Languages and Literatures (in Memory of Fred O. Nolte),* ed. Erich Hofacher and Liselotte Dieckmann, 121–32. St. Louis, MO: Washington University Press, 1963.

Löffler, Ulrich. *Lissabons Fall—Europas Schrecken. Die Deutung des Erdbebens von Lissabon im deutschsprachigen Protestantismus des 18. Jahrhunderts.* Berlin: De Gruyter, 1999.

Lorenz, Edward. "Predictability: Does the Flap of a Butterfly's Wings in Brazil Set Off a Tornado in Texas?" Paper presented at the 139th meeting of the American Association for the Advancement of Science, 1972. http://eaps4 .mit.edu/research/Lorenz/Butterfly_1972.pdf.

Lowe, S. R., et al. "The Impact of Pet Loss on the Perceived Social Support and Psychological Distress of Hurricane Survivors." *Journal of Traumatic Stress* 22, no. 3 (2009): 244–47.

Luke, Timothy. "Introduction." In Goethe, *Faust. Part Two,* xii–lxxx.

Mackerle, Ampe Akelyernemane Meke. "Little Children Are Sacred." Report of the Northern Territory Board of Inquiry into the Protection of Aboriginal Children from Sexual Abuse. 2007. http://www.inquirysaac.nt.gov.au/pdf/ bipacsa_final_report.pdf.

Margulis, Lynn, and Dorion Sagan. *Acquiring Genomes: A Theory of the Origins of Species.* New York: Basic Books, 2002.

Mathews, Freya. "The Anguish of Wildlife Ethics." *New Formations* 75, special issue, ed. Wendy Wheeler and Linda Williams (2012): 114–33.

———. "Ecophilosophy in Australia." *Worldviews* 3, no 2, special issue, *Australian Perspectives*, ed. F. Mathews (1999): 95–96.

———. "Environmental Philosophy." In *A Companion to Australian and New Zealand Philosophy*, ed. Graham Oppy and Nick Trakakis, n.p. Clayton: Monash ePress, 2010.

Mauch, Christoff, and Christian Pfister, eds. *Natural Disasters, Cultural Responses: Case Studies Towards a Global Environmental History*. Plymouth: Lexington Books, 2009.

Mauelshagen, Franz. "Disaster and Political Culture in Germany since 1500." In Mauch and Pfister, *Natural Disasters, Cultural Responses*, 41–75.

Maxwell, Anne. "Postcolonial Criticism, Ecocriticism and Climate Change: A Tale of Melbourne under Water in 2035." *Journal of Postcolonial Writing* 45, no. 1 (2009): 15–26.

McCrae, Richard H., Jason Sharples, Stephen Wilkes, and Alan Walker. "An Australian Pyro-Tornadogenesis Event." *Natural Hazards* 65, no. 3 (2013): 1801–11.

McGuire, Bill. *Surviving Armageddon: Solutions for a Threatened Planet*. Oxford: Oxford University Press, 2005.

———. *Waking the Giant: How a Changing Climate Triggers Earthquakes, Tsunamis and Volcanoes*. Oxford: Oxford University Press, 2013.

McKibben, Bill. *The End of Nature*. New York: Random House, 1989.

McKusick, James. *Green Writing: Romanticism and Ecology*. New York: St. Martin's Press, 2000.

McWhirr, Anne. "Mary Shelley's Anti-Contagionism: *The Last Man* as 'Fatal Narrative.'" *Mosaic: A Journal for the Interdisciplinary Study of Literature* 35, no. 2 (2002): 23–38.

Meier, A. "'Wie kommt ein Pferd auf Jevershallig?' Die Subversion des Realismus in Theodor Storms, 'Der Schimmelreiter.'" In Hans Krah and Claus-Michael Ort, eds., *Weltentwürfe in Literatur und Medien: Phantastische Wirklichkeiten—Realistische Imaginationen*, 167–79. Kiel: Ludwig, 2002.

Meier, Dirk. "Man and Environment in the Marsh Area of Schleswig-Holstein from Roman to Late Mediaeval Times." *Quaternary International* 112 (2004): 65–66.

———. "Sturmfluten an der Nord- und Ostseeküste Schleswig-Holsteins zwischen 1634 und 1872." Paper presented to the state authority for coastal protection, national parks and ocean protection for Schleswig-Holstein, May 19, 2011. http://www.schleswig-holstein.de/LLUR/DE/Service/Vortraege/Hydrologisches_Gespraech_2011/PDF/01_Meier__blob=publicationFile.pdf.

Mellor, Anne K. "Introduction." In *The Last Man*, by Mary Shelley, ed. H. J. Luke, xii–xxvi. Lincoln: University of Nebraska Press, 1993.

Melville, Peter. *Romantic Hospitality and the Resistance to Accommodation*. Waterloo: Wilfrid Laurier, 2007.

Merchant, Carolyn. *The Death of Nature*. London: Wildwood, 1980.

———. *Earthcare: Women and the Environment*. London: Routledge, 1995.

Milner, Andrew. "On the Beach: Apocalyptic Hedonism and the Origins of Post-modernism." *Australian Studies* 7 (1993): 190–204.

———. "The Sea and Eternal Summer: Science Fiction, Futurology and Climate Change." *Australasian Journal of Ecocriticism and Cultural Ecology* 3, special issue, ed. Kate Rigby and Linda Williams (2013): 125–31.

Milner, Andrew, Verity Burgmann, and Simon Sellars, eds. *Changing the Climate: Utopia, Dystopia and Catastrophe*. Arena Journal 35–36, special issue (2010).

Moreton-Robinson, Eileen. *Talkin' Up to the White Woman: Indigenous Women and Feminism*. St. Lucia: Queensland University Press, 2000.

Morgan, Janet. *Earth's Cry: Prophetic Ministry in a More-Than-Human World*. Melbourne: Uniting Academic Press, 2013.

Morton, Timothy. *The Ecological Thought*. Cambridge, MA: Harvard University Press, 2010.

———. *Hyperobjects: Philosophy and Ecology after the End of the World*. Minneapolis: University of Minnesota Press, 2013.

———. "Romantic Disaster Ecology: Blake, Shelley and Wordsworth." *Romantic Circles Praxis Series* (2012). http://www.rc.umd.edu/praxis/disaster/HTML/praxis.2012.morton.html.

———. *Shelley and the Revolution in Taste*. Cambridge: Cambridge University Press, 1994.

Muecke, Stephen. "Hurricane Katrina and the Rhetoric of Natural Disasters." In *Fresh Water. New Perspectives on Water in Australia*, ed. Emily Potter, Alison Mackinnon, Stephen McKenzie, and Jennifer McKay, 259–71. Carlton: Melbourne University Press, 2007.

Muir, Cameron, Deborah Rose, and Phillip Sullivan. "From the Other Side of the Knowledge Frontier: Indigenous Knowledge, Social-Ecological Relationships and New Perspectives." *Rangeland Journal* 32 (2010): 259–65.

Munich Re Group. *Topics 2000: Natural Catastrophes—the Current Position*. Special Millenium Issue. Munich: Corporate Communications, 1999. http://www.inpe.br/crs/geodesastres/conteudo/livros/MunichRe_2000_Natural_catastrophes_the_current_position.pdf.

Murphy, Kevin. *Big Blow Up North (A History of Tropical Cyclones in Australia's Northern Territory)*. Darwin: University Planning Authority, 1984.

Murphy, Patrick. *Ecocritical Explorations in Literary and Cultural Studies*. Lanham, MD: Lexington Books, 2009.

Neiman, Susan. *Evil in Modern Thought: An Alternative History of Philosophy*. Carlton North: Scribe Publications, 2003.

Niall, Brenda, assisted by Frances O'Niell. *Australia through the Looking-Glass: Children's Fiction 1830–1980*. Carlton: Melbourne University Press, 1984.

Niemeyer, H. D., H. Eiben, and H. Rohde. "History and Heritage of German Coastal Engineering." In *History and Heritage of Coastal Engineering*, ed. Nicholas C. Kraus, 169–213. New York: American Society of Engineers, 1996.

Nixon, Rob. *Slow Violence and the Environmentalism of the Poor.* Cambridge, MA: Harvard University Press, 2011.

Northcott, Michael. *A Moral Climate: The Ethics of Global Warming.* New York: Orbis Books, 2007.

Oliver-Smith, Anthony. "Theorizing Disasters: Nature, Power, and Culture." In Hoffman and Oliver-Smith, *Catastrophe and Culture*, 23–47.

Paley, Morton. "Mary Shelley's *The Last Man*: Apocalypse without Millenium." *Keats-Shelley Review* 4 (1989): 1–25.

Paterson, Alistair. "Enduring Contact: Australian Perspectives in Environmental and Social Change." *Occasion: Interdisciplinary Studies in the Humanities* 5 (2013): 1–17.

Pfister, Christian. "Learning from Nature-Induced Disasters: Theoretical Considerations and Case Studies for Western Europe." In Mauch and Pfister, *Natural Disasters, Cultural Responses*, 17–40.

Pfueller, Sharron. "The Nature of Health: Embodying Mythology," *Philosophy Activism Nature* 1 (2000): 35–41.

Phillips, Dana. *The Truth of Ecology: Nature, Culture and Literature in America.* Oxford: Oxford University Press, 2003.

Pickering, Andrew. "New Ontologies." In Pickering and Guzik, *Mangle in Practice*, 1–14.

Pickering, Andrew, and Keith Guzik, eds. *The Mangle in Practice: Science, Society and Becoming.* Durham, NC: Duke University Press, 2008.

Plumwood, Val. "Decolonizing Relationships with Nature." In *Decolonizing Nature: Strategies for Conservation in a Postcolonial Era*, ed. William M. Adams and Martin Mulligan, 51–78. London: Earthscan, 2003.

———. *Environmental Culture: The Ecological Crisis of Reason.* London: Routledge, 2002.

———. *Feminism and the Mastery of Nature.* Routledge: London, 1993.

———. "Journey to the Heart of Stone." In *Culture, Creativity and Environment: New Environmentalist Criticism*, ed. Fiona Becket and Terry Gifford, 17–36. Amsterdam: Rodopi, 2007.

Pollak, Michael, and Margaret MacNabb. *Hearts and Minds: Creative Australians and the Environment.* Alexandria, NSW: Hale and Iremonger, 2000.

Pope, Alexander. *An Essay on Man.* Ed. Frank Brady. New York: Bobbs-Merrill, 1965.

Pritchard, James Bennett, ed. *Ancient Near Eastern Texts Relating to the Old Testament.* Princeton, NJ: Princeton University Press, 1969.

Pyne, Stephen J. "Consumed by Fire or Fire: A Prolegomenon to Anthropogenic

Fire." In *Earth, Air, Fire, Water: Humanistic Studies of the Environment*, ed. Jill Kerr Conway, Kenneth Keniston, and Leo Marx, 78–101. Amherst: University of Massachusetts Press, 1999.

———. *The Still-Burning Bush*. Melbourne: Scribe, 2006.

———. *World Fire: The Culture of Fire on Earth*. New York: Henry Hall and Company, 1995.

Quammen, David. *Spillover: Animal Infections and the Next Human Pandemic*. New York: Norton and Co., 2012.

Ravenscroft, Alison. "Dreaming of Others: *Carpentaria* and Its Critics." *Cultural Studies Review* 16, no. 2 (2010): 194–224.

Ray, Gene. "Reading the Lisbon Earthquake: Adorno, Lyotard, and the Contemporary Sublime." *Yale Journal of Criticism* 17, no. 1 (2004): 1–18.

Rigby, Kate. "Another Talk on Religion to Its Cultured Despisers." *Green Letters: A Journal of Ecocriticism* 13, special issue, ed. Patrick Curry and Wendy Wheeler (2010): 55–73.

———. "Confronting Catastrophe: Ecocriticism in a Warming World." In *The Cambridge Companion to Literature and Environment*, ed. Louise Westling, 212–25. Cambridge: Cambridge University Press, 2014.

———. "Dancing with Disaster." *Australian Humanities Review* (Ecological Humanities Corner) 46 (2009). http://www.australianhumanitiesreview.org/archive/Issue-May-2009/rigby.html.

———. "Discoursing on Disaster: The Hermeneutics of Environmental Catastrophe." *Tamkang Review* 39, no. 1 (2008): 19–40.

———. "Freeing the Phenomena: Goethean Science and the Blindness of Faust." *ISLE* 7, no. 2 (2000): 25–42.

———. "Gernot Böhme's Ecological Aesthetics of Atmosphere." In Goodbody and Rigby, *Ecocritical Theory*, 139–52.

———. "(K)ein Klang der aufgeregten Zeit? Enlightenment, Romanticism and Ecological Modernity." In *Moderne Begreifen. Zur Paradoxie eines sozioästhetischen Deutungsmusters*, ed. C. Magerski, R. Savage, and C. Weller, 145–56. Wiesbaden: Deutscher Universitätsverlag, 2007.

———. "Noah's Ark Revisited: (Counter-)Utopianism and (Eco-)Catastrophe." In *Demanding the Impossible: Utopia and Dystopia*, ed. Andrew Milner, Matthew Ryan, and Simon Sellars, 163–78. Carlton: Arena Publications, 2008.

———. "The Poetics of Decolonisation: Reading *Carpentaria* in a Feminist Ecocritical Frame." In *International Perspectives in Feminist Ecocriticism*, ed. Simon Estok, Greta Gaard, and Serpil Oppermann, 120–36. London: Routledge, 2013.

———. "Prometheus Redeemed? From Autoconstruction to Ecopoetics." In *Eco-Spirit: Religions and Philosophies for the Earth*, ed. Catherine Keller and Laurel Kearns, 270–94. New York: Fordham University Press, 2007.

———. "Romanticism." In Garrard, *Handbook of Ecocriticism*, 60–79.

———. *Topographies of the Sacred: The Poetics of Place in European Romanticism.* Charlottesville: University Press of Virginia, 2004.

Robin, Libby. "Battling the Land and Global Anxiety: Science, Environment and Identity in Settler Australia." *Philosophy Activism Nature* 7 (2010): 3–9.

———. *How a Continent Created a Nation.* Sydney: University of New South Wales Press, 2007.

Roos, Bonnie, and Alex Hunt. *Postcolonial Green: Environmental Politics and World Narratives.* Charlottesville: University of Virginia Press, 2010.

Rose, Deborah Bird. "Flying Foxes: Kin, Keystone, Kontaminant." In *Unloved Others: Death of the Disregarded in the Time of Extinctions,* ed. Deborah Bird Rose and Thom van Dooren, 119–36. Canberra: ANU E-press, 2011.

———. "'Moral Friends' in the Zone of Disaster." *Tamkang Review,* 37, no. 1 (2006): 77–97.

———. *Nourishing Terrains: Australian Aboriginal Views of Landscape and Wilderness.* Canberra: Australian Heritage Commission, 1996. http://www.environment .gov.au/heritage/ahc/publications/commission/books/pubs/nourishing -terrains.pdf.

———. "Rhythms, Patterns, Connectivities: Indigenous Concepts of Seasons and Change." In *A Change in the Weather: Climate and Culture in Australia,* ed. Tim Sherratt, Tom Griffiths, and Libby Robin, 32–41. Canberra: National Museum of Australia Press, 2005.

———. *Wild Dog Dreaming: Love and Extinction.* Charlottesville: University of Virginia Press, 2011.

Rose, Deborah Bird, with Sharon D'Amico, Nancy Daiyi, Kathy Deveraux, Margaret Daiyi, Linda Ford, and April Bright. *Country of the Heart: An Indigenous Australian Homeland.* Canberra: Aboriginal Studies Press, 2002.

Rose, Deborah Bird, and Libby Robin. "The Ecological Humanities in Action: An Invitation." *Australian Humanities Review* 31–32 (2004). http://www .australianhumanitiesreview.org/archive/Issue-April-2004/rose.html.

Rousseau, Jean Jacques. "Lettre à Voltaire sur la Providence." In *Correspondence complète de Jean Jacques Rousseau,* ed. J. A. Leigh, 4: 37–50. Geneva: Institut et Musée Voltaire, 1967.

Ryan, Frank. *Virus X: Tracking the New Killer Plagues out of the Past and into the Future.* Boston: Little, Brown and Co., 1997.

Sandilands, Catriona. *The Good-Natured Feminist: Ecofeminism and the Quest for Democracy.* Minneapolis: University of Minnesota Press, 1999.

———. "Queering Ecocultural Studies." *Cultural Studies* 22, nos. 3–4 (2008): 255–76.

———. "Queer Life? Ecocriticism after the Fire." In Garrard, *Handbook of Ecocriticism,* 305–19.

Scarry, Elaine. *Thinking in an Emergency.* New York: Norton, 2012.

Schama, Simon. *Landscape and Memory.* London: Harper Collins, 1995.

Schlegel, Friedrich. "On Romantic Poesie." In *The Origins of Modern Critical Thought: German Aesthetic and Literary Theory from Lessing to Hegel,* ed. David Simpson, 192–93. Cambridge: Cambridge University Press, 1988.

Schleiermacher, Friedrich. *On Religion: Speeches to Its Cultured Despisers.* Ed. and trans. Richard Crouter. Cambridge: Cambridge University Press, 1988.

Schmidt, Andreas. *Wolken krachen, Berge zittern, und die ganze Erde weint . . . Zur kulturellen Vermittlung von Naturkatastrophen in Deutschland 1755–1855.* Münster: Waxmann, 1999.

Schneider, Helmut J. "Der Zusammensturz des Allgemeinen." In Wellbery, *Positionen der Literaturwissenschaft,* 110–29.

Segeberg, Harro. *Literarische Technik-Bilder. Studien zum Verhältnis von Technik und Literaturgeschichte in 19. und frühen 20. Jahrhundert.* Stuttgart: Metzler, 1987.

Serres, Michel. *The Natural Contract.* Trans. Elizabeth MacArthur and William Paulson. Ann Arbor: University of Michigan Press, 1995.

Shelley, Mary. *The Journals of Mary Shelley 1814–1844.* Ed. Paula R. Feldman and Dina Scott-Kilvert. London and Baltimore, MD: Johns Hopkins Press, 1995.

———. *The Last Man.* Intro. and notes Pamela Bickley. Ware: Wordsworth Editions Ltd., 2004.

Shelley, Percy Bysshe. "Queen Mab." In *The Complete Works of Shelley,* ed. Roger Ingpen and Walter E. Peck, 1: 67–134. New York: Gordion, 1965.

Sherratt, Tim, Tom Griffiths, and Libby Robin, eds. *A Change in the Weather: Climate and Culture in Australia.* Canberra: National Museum of Australia Press, 2005.

Silz, Walter. "Theodor Storm's *Schimmelreiter.*" *PMLA* 61, no. 3 (1946): 762–83.

Simpson, David, ed. *The Origins of Modern Critical Thought: German Aesthetic and Literary Theory from Lessing to Hegel.* Cambridge: Cambridge University Press, 1988.

Sitter, John. "Eighteenth-Century Ecological Poetry and Ecotheology." *Religion and Literature* 40, no. 1, special issue, ed. Kate Rigby (2008): 11–38.

Solnit, Rebecca. *Hope in the Dark: Untold Histories, Wild Possibilities.* New York: Nation Books, 2004.

———. *A Paradise Built in Hell: The Extraordinary Communities That Arise in Disaster.* New York: Viking, 2009.

Steffen, Will. "The Angry Summer." Australian Climate Commission Report, February 2013. http://climatecommission.gov.au/report/the-angry-summer/.

Steinberg, Ted. *Acts of God: The Unnatural History of Disaster in America.* Oxford: Oxford University Press, 2000.

Stephens, Anthony. *Heinrich von Kleist: The Dramas and Stories.* Oxford: Berg, 1994.

Storm, Theodor. *The Dykemaster.* Trans. and notes Denis Jackson. London: Angel Book, 1996.

———. *Werke in vier Bänden.* Ed. Karl Ernst Laage. 4 vols. Frankfurt: Deutscher Klassiker Verlag, 1988.

Strang, Hilary. "Common Life, Animal Life, Equality: The Last Man." *English Literary History* 78, no. 2 (2011): 409–31.

Stretton, Leonard. *Report of the High Commission to Inquire into the Causes of and Measures taken to Prevent the Bush Fires of January, 1939, and to Protect Life and Property and the Measures to be Taken to Prevent Bush Fires in Victoria and to Protect Life and Property in the Event of Future Bush Fires.* Melbourne: T. Rider, Acting Government Printer, 1939.

Sullivan, Heather. "Affinity Studies and Open Systems: A Non-Equilibrium, Ecocritical Reading of Goethe's *Faust.*" In Goodbody and Rigby, *Ecocritical Theory,* 243–55.

Tang, Chenxi. "Two German Deaths: Nature, Body and Text in Goethe's *Werther* and Theodor Storm's *Der Schimmelreiter.*" *Orbis Litterarum* 53 (1998): 105–16.

Taylor, Peter. "Distributed Agency within Intersecting Ecological, Social, and Scientific Processes." In *Cycles of Contingency: Developmental Systems and Evolution,* ed. Susan Oyama, Paul E. Griffiths, and Russell D. Gray, 313–32. Cambridge, MA: MIT Press, 2001.

Thiele, Colin. *February Dragon.* Adelaide: Rigby, 1965.

Thompson, Kirrilly. "Save Me, Save My Dog." *Australian Journal of Communication* 40, no. 1 (2013): 123–36.

Tredinnick, Mark. *Australia's Wild Weather.* Canberra: National Library of Australia, 2011.

Tuana, Nancy. "Viscous Porosity: Witnessing Katrina." In Alaimo and Hekman, *Material Feminisms,* 188–215.

Tuchman, Barbara W. *A Distant Mirror: The Calamitous 14th Century.* New York: Knopf, 1978.

Voltaire, J. F. M. A. *Candide; or, Optimism.* Trans. John Butt. New York: Penguin, 1947.

———. "Poème sur le désastre de Lisbonne." In *Les oevres complètes de Voltaire,* ed. David Adams and Haydn T. Mason, vol. 45A. Oxford: Voltaire Foundation, 2009.

Walter, François. *Katastrophen. Eine Kulturgeschichte vom 16. bis ins 21. Jahrhundert.* Trans. Doris Butz-Striebel and Trésy Lejoly. Stuttgart: Philipp Reclam, 2010.

Watts, Jonathan. *When a Billion Chinese Jump: How China Will Save Mankind—Or Destroy It.* London: Faber and Faber, 2010.

Weber, Max. *The Protestant Ethic and the Spirit of Capitalism.* London: Unwin, 1930.

Weinrich, Harald. "Literaturgeschichte eines Weltereignisses: Das Erdbeben in Lissabon." In *Literatur für Leser. Essays und Aufsätze zur Literaturwissenschaft,* 64–76. Stuttgart: Kohlhammer, 1971.

Wellbery, David E., ed. *Positionen der Literaturwissenschaft. Acht Modellanalysen am Beispiel von Kleists "Das Erdbeben in Chili."* Munich: C. H. Beck, 1985.

Wheeler, Wendy. "The Biosemiotic Turn: Abduction, or, The Nature of Creative Reason in Nature and Culture." In Goodbody and Rigby, *Ecocritical Theory,* 270–82.

Whitaker, Richard. "Tropical Cyclone Tracy." *Issues* 78 (2007): 20–22.

White, Lynn, Jr. "The Historical Roots of our Ecologic Crisis." In *The Ecocriticism Reader: Landmarks in Literary Ecology,* ed. Cheryl Glotfelty and Harold Fromm, 3–14. Athens: University of Georgia Press, 1996.

Williams, Cynthia Schoolar. "Mary Shelley's Bestiary: The Last Man and the Discourse of Species." *Literature Compass* 3, no. 2 (2006): 138–48.

Williams, Linda. "Reflections on Modernity, Monkeys and Men: Edward Tyson and the Revelations of Enlightenment Science." *Philosophy Activism Nature* 5 (2008): 3–11.

Williams, Raymond. *The Country and the City.* London: Hogarth Press, 1985.

Withington, John. *Flood.* London: Reaktion, 2013.

Wood, Gillen D'Arcy. *Tambora: The Eruption That Changed the World.* Princeton, NJ: Princeton University Press, 2014.

Wright, Alexis. *Carpentaria.* Sydney: Giramondo, 2006.

———. "Deep Weather." *Meanjin Quarterly* 70, no. 2 (2011): 70–82.

———. "On Writing *Carpentaria.*" *Heat* 13 (2007): 79–95.

———. *Plains of Promise.* St. Lucia: University of Queensland Press, 1997.

———. *The Swan Book.* Sydney: Giramondo, 2013.

———. "Talking about an Indigenous Tomorrow." Open letter to Senators Bob Brown and Rachel Siewert. *The Drum—Opinion,* Australian Broadcasting Corporation, March 30, 2011. http://www.abc.net.au/unleashed/45734.html.

Wright, Judith. *The Cry for the Dead.* Oxford: Oxford University Press, 1981.

Zapf, Hubert. "Ecocriticism and Literature as Cultural Ecology." In *Nature in Literary and Cultural Studies: Transatlantic Conversations on Ecocriticism,* ed. Catrin Gersdorf and Sylvia Meyer, 49–70. Amsterdam: Rodopi, 2006.

INDEX